Basic Baking

Basic

Basic Baking

Everything You Need to
Know to Get You Started
Plus 101 Luscious Desserts
That You Can Make

LORA BRODY

William Morrow
An Imprint of HarperCollins*Publishers*

OTHER BOOKS BY LORA BRODY

The Kitchen Survival Guide
The Entertaining Survival Guide
Bread Machine Baking: Perfect Every Time
Desserts from Your Bread Machine: Perfect Every Time
Pizza, Focaccia, Flat, and Filled Breads from Your Bread Machine, Perfect Every Time
Lora Brody Plugged In
STUFF IT (with Max Brody)
Broccoli By Brody
Growing Up on the Chocolate Diet
Indulgences
Cooking with Memories
Chocolate Williams-Sonoma Kitchen Library
Fruit Desserts Williams-Sonoma Kitchen Library
Stews Williams-Sonoma Kitchen Library

Snow White Layer Cake, page 147, excerpted with permission from "All-Purpose Birthday Cake," by Stephan Schmidt, *Cook's Illustrated*, May/June 1995. For a trial issue of *Cook's Illustrated,* call 800-526-8442. Selected articles and recipes, as well as subscription information, are available online at *www.cooksillustrated.com.*

Glossary items, pages 50–53, from *Webster's New World Dictionary of Culinary Arts* by Sarah Labensky, © 1997. Reprinted by permission of Prentice-Hall, Inc., Upper Saddle River, NJ.

FIRST EDITION

Designed by Lee Fukui

Printed on acid-free paper

Library of Congress Cataloging-in-Publication Data

Brody, Lora, 1945–
    Basic Baking : everything you need to know to get you started plus 101
luscious desserts that you can make / by Lora Brody.—1st ed.
        p.   cm.
    ISBN 0-688-16724-1
    1. Baking.   2. Desserts.   I. Title.

TX765.B8295 2000
641.8'15—dc21   00-038025

00 01 02 03 04 / QW 10 9 8 7 6 5 4 3 2 1

To P. J. Hamel

Just about the smartest woman I know.
Your friendship is sweeter than any dessert.

Contents

Acknowledgments

. . . .

The first fifteen cookbooks I wrote required that I be able to cook and write at the same time. Before computers this meant that I had notebooks full of unintelligible pages, usually smeared and stuck together with whatever ingredients were used the day that recipe was written. When I moved on to computers I knew enough from what happened to the notebooks not to keep the computer in the kitchen. So I would cook, wash my hands, run upstairs to input information, run downstairs to cook, wash, run upstairs . . . you get the picture. It was aerobic. It was nuts.

All that craziness changed with this book because the cooking deity heard my cries of distress and send me a kitchen angel named Emmy Clausing. Emmy sat with her computer close enough to hear and see, far enough away to protect her laptop from flying butter, eggs, and chocolate. I baked and "talked the recipe," and Emmy wrote.

It was a match made in heaven on many levels. Emmy is organized (I operate on six playing fields at once). Emmy is a talented editor (I can't spell to save my life). Emmy settles for nothing less than perfection (I tend to throw in the towel when the first four tries don't work). Many times she went home and retested more recipes than I can count more times that I like to think about—just to get them absolutely right. She became the patron saint of the Northampton, Massachusetts, homeless shelters. Patient to a fault, possessing a rare high standard of professionalism, Emmy's unfailing enthusiasm for this project made it a joy for me. Now that I'm completely spoiled and know that thanks to Emmy I've found a better way, I can't wait for the next project. I just hope she feels the same.

I would also like to thank the Joshua Hyde Public Library in Sturbridge, Massachusetts, for giving us room to spread out and work on this manuscript.

Introduction

Introduction

• •

Hello and welcome to this book.

As far as most people are concerned that's about as long an introduction as any cookbook should have. After all, who wants to wade through a bunch of words that don't directly result in a plate of brownies or an apple pie? I have to say, as someone who isn't willing to sit down and read the manual before I plug in the VCR, I'm not in complete disagreement. Of course, living with that annoying blinking is about to drive me nuts.

There are a few important things I'd like to say, so if you don't mind taking a few minutes to read this, I'll make it worth your while. Let me know that you have gotten this far by e-mailing me at *Blanche007@aol.com* and I'll send you a very special chocolate recipe that will make you look around for more introductions to read.

This is not a book of shortcuts for "instant" desserts. It's not cooking for dimwits. I assume that you are at the point in your life where the idea of home-baked desserts is more appealing than something store-bought; that you'd like to have some control over the quality of ingredients that you put in your mouth (and the mouths of friends and family you are feeding); and that you'd rather not spend three dollars on a cookie that you can make for twenty-five cents. I assume that by picking up this book you are ready and willing to take a stab at doing some home baking. Trust me, you'll do great—and you'll have fun!

This book is more than a collection of recipes geared for the beginning baker. I wrote it as a teaching tool so that as you go along you will acquire information and learn techniques that you can then apply to any recipe in any book. You're going to find certain things that I repeat over and over—do I sound like your mother? They are essential things that can make the difference between success and failure in the kitchen. I figure that by drumming them into your head they will eventually become part of your kitchen wisdom and you will do them automatically. Time and ingredients are commodities that are too valuable to waste. Every success makes you want to succeed again; every failure makes the effort seem overwhelming. In writing this book I have dedicated myself to your success in the kitchen. I am available by e-mail and regular mail to answer your questions, solve your baking problems, and join in celebrating your successes.

How to Use This Book

There are dozens of things that make the difference between a successful foray into the kitchen to bake and one that leaves you inclined to run to the store for your next dessert. I've tried to make the lists succinct, while including as much vital information as possible. You'll also find a relevant tip or two connected to each recipe to reinforce the information here. I urge you to sit down and read these next few pages before you dive into the recipes. This will prepare you to have success, save time, and have more fun.

"How Do I . . ." explains the very basic steps of baking from getting organized and pre-heating the oven to preparing pans and storing the things you've baked. Next comes a section called "Techniques" that covers sifting, separating eggs, melting chocolate—things a little more involved than the basics in the first part.

The section called "Food Chemistry" explains the way in which ingredients interact with each other and are then affected by heat in order to create the desserts you are about to make. This is followed by the Equipment section, which contains a comprehensive list of things you'll need in order to make the recipes in this book.

The Pantry section details the most commonly used ingredients that go into these recipes. There are specialty items that appear in the book that are not listed here because they are not considered staples.

The Glossary gives definitions of cooking terms. Finally, there is a Baking Resources page where you can go to find most of the hard-to-find ingredients and equipment.

Using These Recipes

Besides telling you how to bake a specific item, each recipe gives you all the information you'll need to decide if it is something you want to make (headnote), how many people it will serve (serving/yield), and what kind of equipment you'll be using (what you'll need). Please bear in mind that the equipment list assumes, and therefore does not mention, that you'll also need measuring cups, measuring spoons, mixing bowls, and rubber spatulas.

How Do I . . .

Get organized?

- Start by creating a block of time, which you will devote to making one recipe. Turn off the phone if you can't ignore its ring. Find someone to watch the kids (or bribe them with the promise of something good to eat as a result of their cooperation). Forget, for a little while, about all the other stuff you have to do and really concentrate on what you are about to do. Remember, the more focused you are, the better your chances for success and the more you'll want to try this again.

- If this is your first time baking, do it alone—you don't need the distraction of company or someone telling you "how to do it."

- Clear a work space for yourself: Get rid of the dishes in the sink, put away the stuff in the drying rack. Clutter is distracting.

- Use a pencil or pen to write notes to yourself in the margins of this book: reaction to the final product as well as the amount of time it took you and how challenging you thought it was—my estimates are fairly arbitrary, and yours may differ significantly. I always make notes about when would be a good occasion to serve a dish, such as "a great birthday cake," or "Grandma would love this."

- Read the passage on pages 8–9 about safe cooking.

- Try to relax. Remember, this is easier than many things you've mastered . . . many, many things.

Follow a recipe?

- Read the entire recipe first before you do anything else.

- Make sure that you have all the ingredients on hand.

- Make sure that you have the right pan for the recipe you've selected.

- Take all the ingredients you need and line them up on the work space in the order in which you'll use them in the recipe.

- Pull out any equipment that you'll need—including a timer.

- Note the oven temperature and set the oven, checking the placement of the racks (the recipe will tell you where they belong).

- Prepare the pan according to the recipe directions.

- Perform each step of the recipe in the order it is given, including the part about cooling and storing.

Decide what to make first?

- If you are an absolute novice, I'd suggest you start with one of the recipes in the Bars and Squares chapter. These are the most forgiving recipes, as they won't suffer much as a result of overmixing, underrising, undercooking, or even overcooking—crispy edges are nice! If you like chocolate, try one of the brownie recipes. Another very basic recipe is the Chocolate Miracle Cake on page 135.

- Pick a recipe that requires the amount of time you have to spend on it—baking can sometimes be done in stages, such as baking, then frosting. Bear in mind that the first stage, on average, will take at least 45 minutes to an hour (including baking).

- Make something you know you'd like to eat; don't just pick a recipe because it's easy—you deserve a reward for your effort.

- Make something that's the right size for the number of people you're going to feed, unless you plan to freeze part of the yield. It's a good idea for rank beginners to taste what they've made *before* serving it to someone else.

Know if the recipe will make enough?

- There is a yield indication at the top of each recipe. Sometimes it will be specific (makes 12 cupcakes), and sometimes it will give a range: 10 to 12 servings. If you are feeding big, active, dessert-loving football players, then I'd figure the lower end of that estimate is safer than the higher one. Most of this stuff is pretty rich; don't be tempted to cut oversized pieces—it's better to have folks ask for seconds than have them leave food on their plates.

Preheat the oven?

- This is the very first thing the recipe tells you to do and you should do it first, making sure before you turn the oven on that the racks are in the position required for the recipe. I'm going to assume that you have looked at, or will look at, the Equipment section on page 36 and know how important a clean oven is. What's also important is being able to know that the number on the knob accurately represents the internal temperature of the oven. If there is any doubt, buy an oven thermometer and attach it to the middle rack. The average oven will take 12 to 15 minutes to preheat to 350°F. It's better to have the oven waiting for you than to have you waiting for the oven. If you are relying on an oven thermometer rather than the indicator light on the panel, allow the oven to preheat for at least 12 to 15 minutes before opening the door to check the thermometer reading. Try not to open the oven any more often than necessary, as each opening makes the temperature fluctuate.

- If for some reason you forgot to preheat the oven, check your recipe to see if it contains baking soda. If it doesn't contain any baking soda, or if it does but rising is not important (as in cookies, pies, and tarts), then refrigerate the filled baking pans until the oven reaches the temperature called for in the recipe. If baking soda is responsible for making your baked goods rise (cakes, quick breads, coffee cakes, bars, and squares), you should place the filled baking pan in the oven and immediately turn it on to the proper temperature.

Prepare a pan?

- Preparing the pan means coating it with fat and flour, and perhaps also lining it with a sheet of parchment paper or aluminum foil, so that the finished dessert can be unmolded successfully without falling apart. Use a piece of wax paper or paper towel—or just-washed fingers—to apply a coating of fat (lightly or generously as the recipe requires) over the entire inside surface—bottom and sides—paying careful attention to the area where the two meet. This is especially important for tube pans and decorative bundt-style pans which each have a central hollow core. Any area left ungreased is a place where a cake can stick. To dust with flour, hold the baking pan over the sink or over the flour canister, if it's large enough. Dip a small measuring cup into the flour and put 2 or 3 tablespoons of flour in the bottom of the pan. Use both hands to rotate the pan so the flour moves around and adheres to the entire surface. Invert the pan over the sink or canister and tap out the excess flour. If the recipe calls for the pan to be lined with a piece of parchment paper, lay the parchment paper in the bottom of the pan *after* the fat is applied, but *before* the flour. Coat the parchment paper with fat, then dust the whole interior with flour.

- Baking sheets can be lined with aluminum foil, parchment paper, or a sheet of reusable silicone-treated flexible matting called Silpat™ or Exopat™ (see page 315 for sources of parchment paper and silicone liners). The aluminum foil and parchment paper sheets can be secured to the pan by applying a small dot of butter to each corner of the baking sheet before placing the paper or foil on it. The butter will act as dissolving "glue."

- Sometimes a recipe instructs you to wrap the bottom and sides of a springform pan with aluminum foil. This is usually done when the pan is baked in a water bath, to prevent the water from seeping into the pan. It is also done to prevent butter in a recipe from leaking out of the pan as it cooks and spilling onto the bottom of your oven, where it will smoke. It's best to use heavy-duty aluminum foil not just for its strength, but because the roll is wider, so you only have to use one piece of aluminum foil instead of patching two together. To wrap a 9-inch or 10-inch springform pan, tear off an 18-inch square of aluminum foil, center the pan on it, then gather up the edges, molding the aluminum foil tight to the pan and tucking any overlap back down the outside.

- If you want to avoid storing or freezing a cake on the base of the springform pan (so that you have an intact pan to use again), or you want to take the cake to a party and you don't want to lose the pan base, here's what you can do: When you prepare the pan, remove the metal pan base. Wrap a 9-inch cardboard cake round completely in heavy-duty aluminum foil and use it to replace the pan base. Prepare the pan and bake the cake as directed. After it has baked and cooled, remove the sides of the pan and use the covered cardboard base for serving or freezing.

- Even if you own the new generation of heavy-duty nonstick bakeware, it's a good idea and good practice to prepare the pan the traditional way.

- Nonstick vegetable spray is an option if you wish to use it. My complaint is that it's not as foolproof as the techniques described above, and it always leaves a brown, tacky, hard-to-clean residue on the pan. If this residue isn't scrubbed off each time, it builds up, making the baking surface uneven and sticky. There is one brand, however, that does not seem to leave a film. It's called Simple Professional Baking Spray and is available from the King Arthur Flour Baker's Catalogue (see page 316).

Position the oven racks?

- Along with the oven temperature, each recipe instructs you where to position the oven rack. Normally this is the center of the oven, where the heat is evenly concentrated. Since hot air rises, the upper part of the oven will be hotter and is reserved for some cookies that need an extra burst of heat. The very lowest racks are good for baking soufflés that need bottom heat and room to rise in the oven. Some recipes have you position two racks as close to the center as possible, in order to accommodate two cake pans that won't fit side by side on one rack allowing for 3 inches between pans and 3 inches between each pan and the nearest oven wall. Since you must bake cake layers at the same time, this positioning is important. A second pan of prepared cookie dough, however, can wait, refrigerated, while the first pan bakes on the center rack alone. Most of the recipes in this book instruct you to bake cookies this way.

- If you are using the rack in the center of the oven, it's a good idea to either remove the upper rack or place it below the rack you are using so you don't have to worry about having enough headroom.

Figure out the capacity/size of a pan?

- Use a ruler to measure the diameter and height of a round baking pan, and the length, width, and height of a square or rectangular baking pan. The diameter, length, and width are all measured from inside edge to inside edge, and the height is measured on the outside of the pan.

- Measure pie pans the same way.

- Loaf pans can be measured with a ruler (length, width, depth), or by capacity (see below).

- If the pan size is designated by volume and you don't know the capacity, fill a large (4-cup) liquid measure with water and put the water in the pan to the very top, refilling the measure as necessary and keeping track of how much water you've added. The total amount needed to fill the pan will be the capacity of the pan.

Cook safely?

This is one of the first things I teach in cooking classes. It's astonishingly easy to hurt yourself in the kitchen, and almost as astonishingly easy to prevent kitchen injuries.

- Wash your hands with hot water and soap before you start cooking. This is the easiest way to prevent food contamination and spread of germs. Those signs in restaurant bathrooms reminding the staff to wash their hands should apply to you in your kitchen.

- Keep your kitchen clean. I have a house full of pets, but they know the cooking area of the kitchen is off-limits.

- Keep hot foods hot and cold foods cold to avoid spoilage.

- Always tie up long hair, keeping it away from your face and out of reach of hot burners. Not only is hair flammable, but finding a stray one in food will shut down the hungriest person's appetite. Keep your hands out of your hair while you're around food.

- Roll up your sleeves so you don't have cuffs or billowing material near burners or hot ovens. Remove dangling jewelry.

- Wear shoes while you're cooking—they prevent slips on wet floors and protect your feet.

- Keep knives sharp—a dull knife is an accident waiting to happen, as the impulse is to apply more pressure to make up for the lack of cutting edge, and the chance that the knife will eventually slip and cut you is all but certain.

- Never handle a knife with greasy or wet hands. The handle can easily slip and the risk of injury is great.

- Use the right tool for the right job. I have a little scar in the palm of my hand from the time I used a paring knife instead of a grapefruit spoon to core an apple.

- Use a kitchen timer that clips onto your apron. When you discover your two-year-old painting the VCR with grape jelly even the most focused cook can forget there's a pie in the oven.

- Keep a fire extinguisher near the kitchen as well as a large box of baking soda and make sure your smoke alarm works.

- Both stovetop and oven fires can be doused with baking soda. After throwing in the baking soda, close the oven door to deprive the fire of oxygen.

- If you are cooking with young children, make sure their hair and clothing do not come near an open flame or hot oven, and always stand right next to them during the entire process.

Wash up?

- I find that it's easier to wash up as I go along, either rinsing out equipment and putting it on the drainboard to dry, or sticking it into the dishwasher if I don't plan to use it again. I keep several sets of measuring spoons and cups so I'm not constantly washing and drying them. Always wash equipment from one job before starting another; nothing is as annoying as needing the beaters for the mixer and finding them at the bottom of a mixing bowl, covered with soap and chocolate batter.

- I try not to put my good baking pans in the dishwasher, since they eventually get scratched and dented there. The more scratched the surfaces become, the harder it becomes to unmold whatever you've baked. For that reason I never use steel wool or any other abrasive to clean my pans.

- Always make sure to remove every food stain on your pans. Leftover stains bake on harder and harder with each use, the sticky surface attracts more food, and pretty soon you have a . . . well, use your imagination—and hot water and soap.

- Measuring cups that have been used for flour should be rinsed in cold water before washing, to prevent the flour from turning into a gummy paste that's almost impossible to wash off.

Measure?

When it comes to measuring, ingredients are divided into two categories: wet and dry.

Wet is anything pourable (milk, eggs, juice, vodka, honey). Wet ingredients are measured in either measuring spoons or clear glass or plastic cups, usually with spouts. These cups have lines on the sides indicating ounces and volume. The most accurate way to measure is to start by placing the cup flat on the work surface. Pour the liquid into the cup to as near the correct line as possible, then, leaving the cup in place, bend down so that your eye is level with the line; if you look down at the cup, you will get an inaccurate reading. Add or pour off what is necessary to give you the right measurement.

- If you have a recipe that calls for both oil and honey or molasses, measure the oil first, then, after you add the oil to the recipe, use the same cup, without washing it, to measure the molasses or honey—it will slip right out.

Dry ingredients are things that can be scooped or scraped into measuring spoons or calibrated cups that are typically made of metal or dishwasher-safe plastic. These cups come in sets usually containing ¼-cup, ⅓-cup, ½-cup, and 1-cup measures. Tupperware™ makes a terrific set that also includes ⅛-cup, ⅔-cup, and ¾-cup measures. Dry ingredients include flour, sugar, salt, baking powder, baking soda, butter and solid vegetable shortening, nuts, seeds, and spices.

- When measuring flour, dip the measuring cup into the bag or canister, lift it out, and hold it over the open bag or canister. Hold a spatula parallel to the top of the cup and run it across the top to remove excess flour. This is called "leveling" and should also be done with measuring spoons and with other dry ingredients as well. Don't bang or tap the cup to make room for the excess flour—this will pack the flour down and result in an incorrect measurement. It's especially important to get rid of lumps in dry ingredients before you measure them, as this will affect the accuracy of the measurement.

- Never pour an ingredient (either liquid or dry) into a measuring spoon or cup that you are holding above the mixing bowl containing other ingredients. It's too easy to slip and add unwanted amounts which are then impossible to remove.

- When measuring brown sugar, it's easiest to dip the measuring cup directly into the bag (boxed sugar is enclosed in a removable inner bag; larger amounts of sugar are sold in just a plastic bag). With your hand on the outside of the bag, push the sugar into the cup, pressing it firmly until the cup is full. If you can't fit the measuring cup into the bag, simply spoon the sugar into the cup and press it firmly with the spoon or your fingers until the cup is full.

Create a water bath?

- Some kinds of cheesecakes and puddings that need to bake in moist, even heat to keep from drying out are placed in a *bain-marie* (French for water bath), which is simply a larger pan of hot water. A roasting pan or sturdy baking sheet, such as a jelly roll pan, is great for this use. Place the baking pan inside the roasting pan or jelly roll pan to make sure there are at least 2 inches of space around the sides. The outer pan does not have to be taller than the inner pan. Place both pans in the oven before adding hot (from the tap) water from a pitcher or cup with a spout into the outer pan. When the baking is done, remove the inner pan, leaving the water bath in the turned-off oven to cool before removing it as well.

Keep the oven clean?

- Prevent overflows from fruit-filled pies and tarts from reaching the oven floor and burning by placing the pie plate on an aluminum foil–lined baking sheet. The aluminum foil liner eliminates the necessity of scrubbing the baking sheet after use.

Tell if it's done?

- Always use a timer: It will let you know that you are within the range the recipe suggests.

- Use your nose: Aroma is a good sign that something is nearing completion.

- Take a look: When you see that golden-brown color (a result of the sugar cooking) you'll know you're almost there.

- Touch: Gently press the pads of your fingers on the top to see if the surface springs back. Gently wiggle the pan to see if the batter has set up.

Keep things from getting too brown during baking?

- If the top is looking like it might burn, but the inside isn't done, measure a square of heavy-duty aluminum foil that is slightly larger than the top of the pan. Crease the foil, dull side up, to form a tent, and place the tent over the pan. Don't tuck in the sides—you don't want to trap warm air, which will steam the food.

Sift dry ingredients?

- I find that the easiest way to combine dry ingredients and get rid of any lumps at the same time is to place a mesh sieve over a mixing bowl, add the ingredients, then gently shake the sieve or tap the side so the ingredients fall into the bowl. Use your fingers to get rid of any stubborn lumps before you pass them through the sieve. I have a sieve I use only for this purpose; when I'm through with it I rap it over the sink to remove any lingering ingredients, then store it in a large plastic bag. This way I avoid washing it and risking clogging up the mesh with flour/water paste.

Separate eggs?

- More than anything, the key to success here is practice. While there are little gadgets that purport to do the job, you can learn how to do it yourself. The larger the egg, the easier it is to handle, and the older it is, the more intact and firm the yolk will be. Have two cups ready. One should have a fairly sharp lip, which makes it easier to crack the egg cleanly. Rap the side of the egg (midway between the two ends) sharply against the lip of the cup. Immediately turn the egg over so the cracked part is facing you. Working directly over one cup, use your thumbs to separate the two halves of the shell, allowing the white to flow into the cup and the yolk to move into one of the empty shell halves. Tip the shell containing the yolk to allow any remaining white to flow into the cup. Empty the yolk into the other cup. If you accidentally get some yolk in the white, use one of the shells to scoop it out.

- Leftover egg whites can be frozen. Make sure that the freezer container is clean and grease-free. Defrosted egg whites actually whip up better than fresh, so when you make custard or bread pudding, freeze the whites for another use.

- By the way, if you drop an egg on the floor (and all of us do), the easiest way to clean it up is to cover it with a liberal sprinkling of salt, wait a few moments, and pick it up with a paper towel.

Whip egg whites?

There are several tricks to getting egg whites to behave so they'll hold the air bubbles you beat into them.

- The first is to make sure that both your mixing bowl and beaters are scrupulously clean. Any grease left behind will coat the egg whites and inhibit the bubbles of air. This is why it's also important not to allow any egg yolks in the whites when you separate eggs.

- Adding a pinch of both salt and cream of tartar (tartaric acid, which is a natural substance and a by-product of winemaking) stabilizes the egg whites and helps the air bubbles to form.

- The egg white's cell structure is more relaxed when the egg is at room temperature or when the egg is a few weeks old, so these whites will whip up faster than cold whites or those from newly laid eggs. The meringue made with these egg whites, however, won't hold up as well. Keep this in mind if you are reaching under the hen for the makings of a soufflé for dinner that night. You can warm the whites by briefly dipping the bottom of the mixing bowl containing the whites into a pan or second bowl of hot (not boiling) water, or you can submerge whole, uncracked eggs in warm water for a few minutes. Dry the shells well before separating the eggs.

Mix?

- Mixing is a gentle action that should involve a spoon (wooden or metal) or a rubber spatula. You want to stir the ingredients around in the bowl until you can no longer tell one from another, or until all the dry ingredients have been moistened by the wet ingredients and the mixture has a uniform consistency. The danger of overmixing is that the protein in the flour will become activated, making the end product tough, or that the air bubbles that are created will make the batter rise high during baking, then fall during cooling. So when you mix, remember: Less is best. To prevent that mixing bowl from slipping on the counter, dampen a double layer of paper towels and place it under the bowl.

Beat?

- This is a much more vigorous, energetic action than mixing and involves manipulating the batter in a circular motion with the goal of making it homogeneous while incorporating air into it and/or making it completely smooth. While you can beat with a spoon, it's easier to use a whisk or electric mixer. I prefer a hand-held electric mixer, so that you are in direct contact with the batter at all times.

Whip?

- Whipping is the very fast circular mixing motion that incorporates the maximum amount of air into a batter or ingredient (such as heavy cream, egg whites, or a chocolate frappe). This is done at high speed with either a whisk (if you have the endurance), an eggbeater, an electric mixer, or (my latest fun toy) an immersion blender, which is a miniprocessor on a shaft. Batters and ingredients that depend on whipping need to be treated gently (see folding on page 14) and used right away before they begin to deflate.

Fold?

- This is a motion used to combine two mixtures, one of which is much lighter than the other. Incorporating whipped egg whites into a batter is a good example of folding. A large mixing bowl and a rubber spatula are what you'll use. Typically the heavier mixture is at the bottom of the bowl and the lighter mixture is gently placed on top. Sometimes when the batter is very, very thick, it's wise to mix a spoonful of beaten egg whites into it to "lighten" the mixture before you begin to fold. Holding the rubber spatula edges perpendicular to the mixture, cut through the center to the bottom of the bowl. Swivel the spatula so the flat side is parallel to the bottom of the bowl and swivel again as you bring it up the side of the bowl. "Scooping" is the motion you are looking for. Rotate the bowl a quarter turn and repeat the action. The goal is to mix the ingredients just enough to combine them, but not so much that the lighter mixture is deflated.

Tell how high to make the heat of the burner?

- Low: On a gas burner you should barely see the flame. On an electric burner the setting is 1. The mixture should barely simmer.

- Medium: On a gas burner the flame covers two-thirds of the bottom of the pan. On an electric burner the setting is 5. The mixture should simmer gently.

- High: Both gas and electric burners are on the highest setting; the mixture should boil vigorously. If you have a small pot set on a large gas burner, take care that the flames aren't licking the sides of the pan. This will result in food burning along the sides of the pan and uneven heating.

Select chocolate?

- Unsweetened baking chocolate is available in 1- or 2-ounce squares or, occasionally, in 3-ounce bars (Ghirardelli makes some). You can find these kinds of chocolate in most supermarkets in the baking aisle. You can also buy high-quality unsweetened baking chocolate in gourmet shops as well as by mail from Dairy Fresh Candies (page 316). If you are really stuck and don't have unsweetened baking chocolate, it is possible to substitute sweet dark chocolate; the flavor impact, however, will not be as strong.

- If the chocolate isn't good enough to eat, it certainly isn't good enough to bake with. Choose the kind you like to eat, then use it when you bake. Bittersweet and semisweet chocolates are interchangeable in all recipes calling for dark chocolate. The only difference will be the taste; the sweeter the chocolate, the less intense the chocolate taste. Milk and white chocolates cannot be used in place of dark chocolate or in place of each other, except as baking chips that remain intact in the baked good.

- All these chocolates can be purchased in bars and blocks. While bars cost more, they are easier to measure, since they are scored and need only to be broken into 1-ounce sections. If you decide to use block chocolate, you need a scale to measure accurately.

- Unsweetened cocoa powder is the ground-up nib (inside) of the roasted cocoa bean. Most or all of the cocoa butter (the vegetable fat in chocolate) has been pressed out. The powder is available in two types: Dutch-processed and regular. Dutch-processed means that the cocoa has been treated with an alkali (such as potassium carbonate), which makes it darker in color and less acidic than regular cocoa. It's my experience that Dutch-processed cocoa burns faster than regular cocoa, and that's why I call for the latter in some recipes. You cannot substitute sweetened cocoa powder (the kind you turn into a drink by adding hot water or milk) for baking cocoa.

Store chocolate?

- Chocolate is sensitive to light, heat, and strong odors. Store it in a tightly covered container in a cool, dry place—not the refrigerator or freezer. (If stored in the refrigerator or freezer, moisture will collect on the surface when it is taken out, so that when it is melted it will "seize," or harden, and it will not melt smoothly.) Dark chocolate (unsweetened, bittersweet, and semisweet) will be good for up to three years. Milk or white chocolate will keep for four to six months because of the added milk solids. If you find your chocolate has "bloomed" (the white cocoa butter has separated and risen to the top), it's still fine to use for melting, but not for making chocolate decorations.

Measure chocolate?

- With bulk chocolate it's essential to use a kitchen scale to weigh amounts for recipes.

- If you use bars of chocolate, refer to the package for the weight.

- Chocolate chips are measured in volume (dry measures).

Chop chocolate?

- Thin bars of chocolate can be broken up with your fingers. Do this before you remove the wrapper—it saves cleanup and keeps the chocolate from melting.

- Cutting chunks: This is easiest done by hand using a large, heavy chef's knife in a gently rocking motion. Since chocolate picks up the taste of anything near it, make sure to use a very clean cutting board and knife. If you have a very large block of chocolate, you might want to use an ice pick and a hammer to cut it up. I don't like to use the food processor to chop chocolate—it jams, the chocolate near the drive shaft melts, and it takes too long to clean up.

- Make sure that the cutting board and knife are completely dry; any moisture that comes in contact with the chocolate can make it seize, or harden to an unusable state during melting.

Melt chocolate?

The most important things to know about melting chocolate are: Chocolate melts better and faster when chopped first; water and chocolate are a fatal combination because chocolate will seize if water touches it as it melts; and chocolate burns very easily and cannot be salvaged once it has burned.

- Chocolate is traditionally melted in a double boiler, which is two stacked pots that fit together with some water in the lower one and the chocolate in the upper one, which remains uncovered. As the water heats to a low boil, it gently heats the ingredients in the upper pot. If you don't have a double boiler, you can simulate one by placing a larger metal bowl over a pan of simmering water. The bowl should not be touching the water, and the water should not be boiling rapidly, because you don't want any steam or drips getting into the chocolate. You must not cover the pan or bowl containing the chocolate for the same reason—water droplets forming inside the lid will doom the melting process. You can control the amount of heat and steam by lowering the heat. Use a rubber spatula to stir the chocolate every few minutes until it is smooth and completely melted.

- My favorite way to melt chocolate is in the microwave oven. Using no more than 8 ounces at a time, place the chopped chocolate in a microwave-safe bowl that is several times larger than you think you'll need, so that you have room to stir. A 4-cup glass measure is good for this. Microwave on high for 40 seconds, stir, then microwave again on high for another 40 seconds. Stir again. Continue microwaving for 20-second intervals, stirring after each one, until the chocolate is almost melted, with some lumps left. Remove it from the microwave and stir until the chocolate is melted and completely smooth. Don't be tempted to rush the process or the chocolate will burn.

- Large amounts of chocolate can be melted in a large pan, uncovered, in an oven set at 200°F.

Select butter?

- The variety in the store is dazzling; no wonder you're confused. When I bake I always use sweet (unsalted) butter. It has a fresher taste, has a lower water content, and is generally superior to its salted companions. There are organic butters and imported butters that are fabulous and fabulously expensive. But I go right for the unsalted Land O' Lakes butter—I like the consistency, the price, and the way the company rewards its customers with lots of very good recipes.

Store butter?

- Butter, like chocolate, will pick up the aromas of foods stored near it. Keep your butter wrapped, in the butter compartment, separate from other foods. When it goes on sale, I stock up and store it in the freezer until I need it. Frozen butter can be defrosted in the refrigerator overnight; at room temperature (it takes an hour or so); or in the microwave: melt it partially, then allow the warm part to soften the rest at room temperature.

Melt and soften butter?

- The microwave oven is the perfect place to melt butter if you remember three important things: Use a much larger (deeper) container than you think you need, cover the container, and remember to remove the butter before the water content explodes and makes a mess of your microwave.

- A small pan set over medium heat is the other place to melt butter. Cutting it into several pieces expedites the process.

- The white foam on top of melted butter is the milk solids. For the recipes in this book, you can go ahead and use it along with the butter. It burns easily, so when you are cooking things over high heat or for an extended time you'll want to skim this off: this is called "clarifying."

- Many of the recipes call for softened or room-temperature butter; these terms mean the same thing, basically. Leaving the butter at room temperature for about an hour (unless it's January and your house isn't heated) will accomplish that. If the butter is very hard or frozen, you can partially melt it either in the microwave or in a pan on the stove, then allow it to sit for several minutes. For fastest results, cut it in several pieces before softening it. Note that melted butter and softened butter are *not* the same thing.

Measure butter?

- Even though butter, margarine, and solid vegetable shortening aren't dry ingredients, in their solid form (as opposed to melted) they are measured in the same cups as are flour and sugar. Use a flexible rubber spatula to scoop the softened fat into the cup, packing it down so there are no air bubbles. Level the top with the edge of the spatula. When you scrape the measured ingredients into the recipe, take care to empty the whole cup, scraping carefully around the bottom and sides. One stick of butter equals ½ cup or 4 ounces or 8 tablespoons. You can use the line measures on the wrapper to cut it into tablespoons if the wrapper was put on straight. If not, unwrap the stick of butter and, using a ruler if you don't trust your eye, cut it in half, then cut each portion in half, and then cut each of those four pieces in half. Cut until you reach the measurement you need. When in doubt, use a tablespoon measure.

Toast nuts?

- To toast walnuts, pecans, almonds, macadamia nuts, and hazelnuts, preheat the oven to 350°F with the rack in the center of the oven. Spread the nuts in a single layer on a baking sheet and bake for 10 to 12 minutes, shaking the baking sheet back and forth occasionally to "stir" them. If necessary, bake for another 5 to 8 minutes until the nuts are light golden brown and fragrant, but watch them carefully. Macadamia nuts will brown faster than the others. Because of the high fat content and size of pine nuts, it is easier to "toast" them in a heavy skillet over medium-high heat. Watch the nuts carefully, and shake the pan or stir with a wooden spoon frequently as they toast. Nuts toasted over surface heat will not brown as evenly as those that are toasted in the oven. Cool all nuts in the pan before proceeding with the recipe.
- It's easier to deal with hazelnuts that are skinned. You can order them from Dairy Fresh Candies (page 316) or the King Arthur Flour Baker's Catalogue (page 316).

- You can buy already ground almonds from the King Arthur Flour Baker's Catalogue. To toast these ground almonds, place them in a large, heavy-duty skillet or frying pan set over medium-high heat. Stir them continuously with a spoon or metal spatula until they are golden brown. Pour the nuts out onto a baking sheet to cool completely before using them in a recipe.

- If you can only find a salted variety of nuts for a recipe, but you want them unsalted, the easiest way to remove some of the excess salt is to place the nuts in a strainer or sieve, stand over the sink, and toss the nuts around vigorously. If you want to go a step further, rub them with very slightly damp paper towels.

Chop nuts?

- The tools you need are a cutting board and a large, heavy chef's knife with a sharp edge. If the cutting board has a lip on it, this will make your job a bit easier. Start with about ½ cup nuts, and place them in one layer on the cutting board. Hold the handle of the knife firmly in one hand and poise the blade over the nuts so that it touches the nuts below it. Push down gently on the blade of the knife with the palm of your other hand. Lift the knife just to clear the nuts and move it ¼ inch and repeat the action. Continue this action, pausing every few chops to use the blade to scrape the nuts together into a pile. Avoid smashing the blade down from any higher than 1 inch above the cutting board, to prevent the nuts from flying all over the kitchen. Once this small pile is chopped to the size you require, use the blade of the knife to scrape the nuts into a bowl, then continue with another ½ cup or so of nuts. Chopping a lot of nuts at once doesn't save you time—it makes it harder to get consistent sizes and you usually end up with more nuts on the floor than on the board.

- By the way, it's easier to toast nuts before chopping them than after.

Grind almonds?

- Even though you can buy ground almonds, if you have a food processor it's pretty easy to do your own, although they will not be as finely ground as those you buy. The key to grinding almonds in the food processor is to do about a cup at a time, and not to grind to the point where the oil starts separating from the nuts and you end up with almond butter. You will have more success if you start with slivered, rather than whole, almonds, and add a tablespoon of granulated sugar for each cup of nuts. The sugar won't drastically affect the recipe. Use the pulse button on the processor for more control; it flings the nuts upward with each pulse, which aerates the mass and prevents overgrinding.

- You can grind several pounds of almonds at a session. For maximum flavor, toast and cool them before grinding, then freeze the ground nuts in a freezer-strength recloseable plastic bag. There is no need to defrost the ground almonds before using them.

Toast coconut?

Place a medium-size heavy skillet over medium heat. When it is hot, put in unsweetened shreds of coconut and turn the heat to low. Cook the coconut, shaking the skillet occasionally, until it has turned a light golden brown, about 2 minutes. It can also be toasted in the microwave. Place the coconut in a shallow layer on a microwave-safe plate and microwave on high for 1 minute. Stir the coconut and microwave on high for another minute. If the coconut is not toasted by the end of the second minute, toss again and return to the microwave for another 30 seconds.

Crush seeds?

Freshly crushed seeds, such as anise seeds, lend a lot more flavor to baked goods than seeds that are left whole. There are several ways to crush seeds. The important thing to remember is that you do not have to pulverize the seeds into a powder. You simply want to break them up so that they release their flavor. Start with a larger measure of seeds than called for in the recipe; you can store extra seeds in a tightly sealed jar and keep it in a cool, dark place for up to two months. That way you won't have to crush the seeds every time you make a recipe.

- Use a small food processor with the steel blade. With the motor running, drop the seeds in through the feed tube.

- Grind the seeds with a mortar and pestle.

- Lay the seeds on a cutting board and roll a heavy rolling pin over them.

- Place the seeds in a small heavy-duty recloseable plastic bag on a sturdy work surface and hit them with the bottom of a heavy frying pan.

Whip cream?

- Use *heavy* cream, which has the right butterfat content to whip. The colder the cream, the more solid the butterfat will be. It's the cold butterfat that holds the air bubbles created by the whipping action. The more air bubbles the cream holds, the thicker and more stable it will be. Choose a large, deep metal bowl for whipping cream (metal both gets and stays colder; the size and depth will keep the cream from splattering you and the kitchen).

- Thirty minutes ahead of time, place the bowl in the refrigerator or freezer, along with the beaters of your electric mixer (or the metal whisk or the eggbeater). If you have forgotten to do this or not planned ahead, you can whip the cream in a mixing bowl placed in a large bowl or roasting pan filled with ice water. It's important that the cream be very cold. Beat on high speed, turning the bowl and/or moving the beaters around in the cream until the cream is thick and no longer flows. If you are adding sugar and/or a flavoring like vanilla extract, do so after the cream begins to thicken.

- It's important not to overwhip the cream, as the buttermilk and butterfat will separate and you'll end up with butter. Stop beating at the point where the cream begins to look a little like mashed potatoes.

- Ideally cream should be whipped at the last minute, as it will deflate with time. If you have no choice but to whip it ahead of time, whip it until it is firm, then scrape it into a fine-mesh sieve set over a bowl and refrigerate it until ready to serve. The cream will stay thick and usable, even though it will deflate a bit.

Keep spices fresh?

- Spices such as cinnamon, nutmeg, ginger, cloves, allspice begin to loose potency as soon as they are ground. Keeping them in a tightly lidded dark container (colored glass or tin), in a cool, dry place will help preserve the freshness. Any spice kept longer than one year probably needs to be replaced, which is why, unless you are baking every day, it makes sense to buy small quantities.

Frost a layer cake?

- The most important key to success in frosting a cake is to make sure that your frosting is completely cool; otherwise it will melt and slide off the top or squish out from the sides. The next important thing is to use the right amount of frosting to cover the surface, but not so much that it's overloaded. It's also important to use your finger, a pastry brush, or a dry paper towel before you frost, to brush off any crumbs that might be clinging to the sides and top of the cake or whatever you are frosting.

  Place one of the cake layers upside down on a flat serving plate. To avoid frosting smudges on the serving plate, cut four 3-inch-wide lengths of wax paper and slip them lengthwise under the bottom edges of the cake. Leave half of each strip exposed to cover the cake plate. Allow the ends of the wax paper to overlap each other.

  Use a rubber spatula or an icing spatula to spread one-third of the frosting over the top of the first layer. Place the second layer right side up on top and use half the remaining frosting to cover the sides of the cake. Cover the top of the cake with the remaining frosting, making swirls out from the center to the edges. Remove the wax paper.

Leave out ingredients I can't/won't eat?

- My son Sam hates nuts, so while I'm waiting for him to change his mind (it happened with mushrooms, so there is hope . . .), I can sympathize. Sometimes I just leave the nuts out. With bar cookies, I scatter half the amount of nuts over half of the batter in the pan. With other cookies, before mixing in the nuts I shape half the batter into cookies, then add the nuts, and form the rest. If you don't like something (coconut, for example) and it's a minor ingredient, then leave it out. However, if the recipe calls for more than ¼ to ½ cup of an ingredient, look for another recipe.

Double or halve a recipe?

- This is tricky for even an experienced baker. The chemistry of baking depends on ingredients in certain proportions interacting under certain conditions (mixing, heating, pan size). Changing any of those elements can cause problems.

- If you want to double a cake or quick-bread recipe, the safest way to do it is to make a double batch of batter, then bake the cake in two pans. Make sure there is room in your oven to do this—you don't want to leave one pan full of batter sitting on the counter while the other one is baking. If you're looking at a recipe that has a large volume of batter (more than 6 cups of ingredients), then I'd repeat the recipe instead of doing it all at once, since you probably won't have a bowl big enough to accommo-date all the batter. Cookie amounts can be doubled, if you have a big enough bowl to contain all the ingredients. You might want to use a heavy-duty mixer to make the dough. Until you are experienced in making piecrust dough, I suggest that you not double a recipe for a double-crust recipe, as there is simply too much dough to work with all at once. Bars that are to be baked in 9-inch-square pans can be doubled and made in an 11 by 15-inch pan, or in one with a different length and width but which holds the same volume. The cooking time will have to be increased slightly—proba-bly no more than 5 to 7 minutes. Follow the visual rules for doneness in the recipe.

- I rarely make half a recipe, since I believe that there's no such thing as too much dessert. I prefer instead to make the whole thing and freeze half after baking. With cookies, in most cases you can make the full recipe and freeze half the dough to bake another time (see below). A recipe for bars or squares made in 9-inch square pans isn't conducive to halving—there simply won't be enough batter. Quick breads can be made in two small pans, but the baking time needs to be shortened by probably one-fourth to one-third. Set the timer accordingly and keep checking (see How Do I Tell If It's Done?, page 11).

Prepare foods for freezing?

- Many of the recipes here can be frozen either after completion or at a midpoint and then finished after defrosting, as when you bake a cake and freeze it, then defrost it at a later date for icing. The recipes will indicate whether or not freezing is an option. A rule of thumb is: Do not freeze foods containing gelatin, beaten egg whites, uncooked baking soda, or fresh fruit that needs to look like fresh fruit when the dessert is served. Whipped cream can be frozen if it's used as a filling and meant to be served in a frozen state. I never met a custard dish that survived freezing.

- There are several keys to freezing baked goods successfully. One is making sure that the food is completely cooled before you wrap it for freezing; this prevents moisture from accumulating on the food and turning it soggy when it defrosts. Another is wrapping the food properly to keep it from drying out and from absorbing odors of other food in the freezer. I'm a huge fan of recloseable heavy-duty (freezer strength) plastic bags. If I'm freezing something short-term—less than a week—I stick it in a bag and push out as much air as possible before sealing it. For longer periods, I wrap the item airtight in several layers of plastic wrap before placing it in the bag.

- Always take care to label and date the bag with a permanent marker; everything looks the same after it's been frozen. If you really want to be organized, tape a list of stuff you've frozen to the outside of the freezer and cross off each item as you remove it.

- Sometimes it makes sense to freeze such items as delicate cookies, muffins, and cupcakes on baking sheets, then place them in plastic bags after they are frozen.

- You might want to consider baking cakes and quick breads destined for gifts or picnics in disposable aluminum pans so you don't have to worry about getting your pan back.

- If you have used a springform pan and you want to freeze the finished cake but you're worried about getting it off the bottom of the pan, here's what you can do: When you prepare the pan before baking, remove the bottom and replace it with a cardboard cake round, of the same size as the pan bottom, that you have wrapped securely, top and bottom, in heavy-duty aluminum foil.

Defrost?

- Baked goods defrost quickly at room temperature. If you're in a big hurry, you can use the defrost cycle on the microwave. Remove any aluminum foil wrapping, but leave the plastic wrap intact until the defrosting is complete; otherwise moisture will condense on top and your baked goods will be soggy.

- Refreezing baked goods after defrosting isn't such a good idea; each freezing, no matter how carefully you wrap, robs the frozen item of moisture and flavor.

Make stuff look pretty?

Don't confuse yourself with a bakery. A homemade dessert isn't supposed to look perfect; it should, however, look appetizing. Here are some really easy ways to make food look attractive and appealing:

- Don't serve the dessert from the pan unless you're at a picnic.

- Use a sharp, serrated knife and a ruler, if necessary, to make even, clean cuts.

- Trim off hard, crusty edges.

- Choose a plate that's suitable for what you're serving: Don't put brownies in a bowl, or a layer cake on a plate on which it barely fits.

- Use a damp paper towel to wipe crumbs, smudges, and fingerprints off the edges of serving plates and platters.

- Things that haven't survived the unmolding process (they have fallen apart or are uneven) should be cut in the kitchen and served on individual plates.

- Invest in a package of paper doilies in assorted sizes and use them to line plates for cookies, bars, and squares, or place them under cakes before serving.

- It's nice to garnish a cake with flowers—just make sure to avoid the ones that will poison your guests. These include lily of the valley and poinsettia, among others.

- Sift cocoa or confectioners' sugar over the tops of plain-looking bars, squares, and cakes.

- Sprinkle toasted shredded coconut over the tops of cakes with less than cosmetically perfect tops.

- A scoop of ice cream or dab of whipped cream can transform the homeliest dessert into a work of art.

Figure out what went wrong?

- I am absolutely committed to your success. If you make something from this book that you think falls short of the description in the headnote, or looks like the "before" photo of a makeover, then I want to know about it and hopefully try to figure out what went wrong. Of course, I'd also like to hear about your successes. You can write to me at Lora Brody Products, Inc PMB 205, 831 Beacon Street, Newton Centre, MA 02459, or e-mail me at *Blanche007@aol.com*. I have a website, *www.lorabrody.com,* and I invite you to check it out. It has recipes, baking tips, and my schedule of teaching classes.

Food Chemistry, Win a Free Trip to Jamaica

Now that I have your attention . . . With visions of everyone running off to tear open a box of brownie mix, I hesitated to label this section "Food Chemistry." Who wants to think about something like that when all you want is a fast, fudgy brownie? Because I know from experience that no one is going to sit down and wade through dense paragraphs of facts that don't appear to get you one inch closer to that dessert, I'm just going to hit the very basics here so you'll have practical applications of the things I'm talking about. If you're the type that likes to sit down and read the manual before you assemble the VCR, then this is the place to start.

Chemistry is actually the "magic" that takes place when ingredients are added together, mixed, then subjected to heat. Each of the basic things that goes into baked desserts—flour, sugar, eggs, butter (or another kind of fat), milk, baking powder, salt, and chocolate—has its own unique function and has to be treated right in order for it to work.

You don't need to be a rocket scientist (believe me, I'm not) to learn how these various ingredients work. The more you know, the more you'll be able to troubleshoot. If you spend enough time baking, using the information here, eventually you can even come up with your own recipes.

About Fat

Let me say right up front that this is *not* a diet book. Ninety-nine percent of these recipes not only contain fat in some form, but depend on butter, oil, cream, egg yolks, or milk to make the recipe work. Cutting back on the amount of fat in a recipe will save you calories only by resulting in something that you wouldn't be able to eat (unless you are truly desperate). The good news about making something that tastes great is that in most cases a smaller portion should be enough to satisfy your dessert craving. Try to resist licking the bowl; that batter or frosting belongs in the pan or on the cake, anyway.

Fat is what makes delicate cakes and tender cookies. Fat surrounds and cradles the air bubbles that are created as you beat batter. This not only makes your cakes rise, but gives them the light, ethereal texture that is the hallmark of a great dessert. Fat prevents the long strands of gluten (that's what the protein in flour is called) from forming, which is why cookies and piecrust have a "short," or crumbly, texture rather than being ultrachewy like a loaf of rye bread.

Fat makes things moist, which keeps foods fresh longer and, most important, it makes desserts taste rich and gives you a satisfying feeling with every bite. Fat also keeps things from sticking to the pan, which is why you apply a coating of butter or solid vegetable shortening to the inside of a cake pan or cookie sheet before you add the batter or dough.

Some fat such as solid vegetable shortening (Crisco, for example) can be kept tightly covered at room temperature for a time without turning rancid. Because of the convenience of having solid vegetable shortening already chilled for recipes such as piecrusts, I recommend that this be stored in the refrigerator where it will keep for many months. Even chilled it can still be used to grease baking pans. Vegetable oils left open and in direct sunlight or in a hot place will turn rancid—you can tell by the unpleasant smell. The longer oil is in contact with air and light, the more apt it is to deteriorate. Store vegetable oils with their caps on tightly in a cool, dark place but not in the refrigerator, since they may turn cloudy and will require extra time to come to room temperature before you can use them in baking. Don't place the oils over the refrigerator or stove, either. (Put your hand up there and you'll see how hot it is!) Think of the nasty taste of a stale cracker or chip and you'll get the idea of what rancid means.

The term "shortening" can mean both solid vegetable fat and butter. Butter has a sweet, light, natural flavor—it melts in your mouth, which solid vegetable shortening and margarine do not do. It is, however, more expensive than other forms of shortening, and it's a little more of a challenge to work with because of its low melting point. All the recipes in this book call for sweet (unsalted) butter. Sweet butter is typically a better grade, tends to be fresher, has a lower water content than salted butter, and generally tastes better. If you have any doubt, taste the two side by side. All butter, and especially sweet butter, needs to be refrigerated, wrapped in plastic or aluminum foil, and kept far away from other foods with strong smells, as the butter will absorb these odors. I look for store specials and pick up five to ten pounds of sweet butter (after carefully checking the expiration date); I store the butter in the freezer, then I pull it out the night before and defrost it at room temperature on the kitchen counter.

The easiest way to soften a stick of butter is to cut it into 8 pieces, place the pieces in a 2-cup glass measure, cover with a small glass plate (better than plastic wrap, which tends to explode), and microwave on high for 30 seconds. Stir it, then microwave on high again for 15 seconds, or until some of the butter has melted and the rest is in soft lumps. Stir until it is smooth, but don't heat it until it has turned to a liquid. Sometimes when you melt butter, a milky-white residue separates out. This residue is the milk solids, the part of the butter that can burn if heated to too high a temperature. If you are making something that calls for butter to be cooked at high heat (pastries made with phyllo dough, for instance) and you want to prevent burning, melt the butter, skim off the foam, then spoon off the clear yellow butter, leaving the milky residue in the pan. You can use this "clarified butter" in either liquid or solid form for cooking, browning, and basting.

About substituting fats: Invariably someone asks, "Can I use margarine instead of butter in your recipes?" (Funny, no one ever asks about lard.) I have to say that the only, and

I mean only, excuses for making this substitution are serious health considerations, or the fact that you keep kosher and want to serve meat during the meal, or dedicated vegetarianism. The difference is palpable, so if you don't fit into one of the above categories, use butter.

You can use vegetable, canola, corn, peanut, and safflower oils interchangeably in these recipes. Olive oil should not be used in place of vegetable oil unless it is labeled "Extra Light." All other varieties of olive oil have a degree of olive taste that will compete with or overpower other ingredients.

About Sweeteners

The list is long: granulated sugar, superfine sugar, light and dark brown sugars, coarse (baker's) sugar, confectioners' (powdered) sugar, honey, maple syrup, molasses, light and dark corn syrups. Their primary function is to add flavor in the form of sweetness to foods. Since we are interested here in the function of sweeteners in baking, you should know that sugar (primarily the first six items in the list) makes your cookies and cakes tender and moist. It stabilizes mixtures during the beating process, which means that eggs or soft butter beaten with sugar will whip up lighter and stay fluffier longer. Sugar helps things turn brown during the baking process through caramelization. The beautiful golden-brown crust on the top of your cake results from the sugar cooking. Brown sugars give a more assertive flavor than granulated sugars. Liquid sweeteners (the last five items in the list) do some of the above, and they also lengthen the time a baked good stays fresh. Corn syrup keeps fudge or frosting from getting hard, and keeps sweet sauces flowing. Be very careful when using molasses—the taste is very strong, especially the blackstrap variety—and will overpower all other flavors. Artificial sweeteners behave in completely different ways from "natural" sugars and cannot be substituted for them in these recipes.

About Salt

Even though we're making desserts, you still need to add just a pinch of salt. Salt improves the taste of all the foods in which it's used, deepening, enhancing, and intensifying the other flavors. Salt acts not only to balance the other flavors, it brings depth and complexity to the finished dish. It strengthens the protein in flour and stabilizes beaten egg whites. Food without salt is boring, but be careful always to measure accurately, since too much salt will ruin a dish. Don't measure any dry ingredient with the spoon poised over the mixing bowl. Also be careful not to store salt and sugar in similar canisters or bowls; visually they are impossible to tell apart. Use regular supermarket salt, not kosher or sea salt, unless the recipe specifies another kind. Coarse sea salt or kosher salt may not dissolve completely and may affect the taste and texture of the final product.

About Flour

For the most part, you'll be using two kinds of flour in this book. The first is all-purpose flour, which has a protein content of around 12 grams per cup. Check the nutritional panel on the side of the bag (remember that it's written for a ¼-cup measure, so you'll have to multiply by 4). While you're checking the bag, make sure that the flour is unbleached and unbromated, two chemical processes that rob flour of nutrients. You'll use this flour for most quick breads, cookies, bars, piecrusts, and some cakes. You'll also use cake flour, which has a somewhat lower protein level and is more finely milled and imparts a very tender, delicate texture to recipes that call for it. Typically cake flour is bleached, making it slightly acidic, which strengthens the flour without adding to the gluten (protein). This adds to its ability to produce lighter results. All-purpose flour and cake flour are not the same and cannot be used interchangeably. Store all-purpose flour in a cool, dry place in a covered container. I strongly recommend removing it from the bag and placing it in a heavy-duty plastic tub with a snap-on lid. Cake flour comes in a bag or in a box with an inner bag that should be tightly closed after the initial opening. Store cake flour in a cool, dry place as well. Unless you live in an incredibly humid climate, it's not necessary to refrigerate flour.

You don't often see desserts made completely with whole wheat flour, as it is heavier than all-purpose flour, which makes for rather leaden results (as in carrot cake from the health food store that could be used for a door stop). Whole wheat flour still contains the bran, which accounts for the weight. Used in combination with all-purpose white flour, it can give a sweet, nutty taste to things like cookies.

About Eggs

Without eggs you'd be eating fruit for dessert. Eggs bind other ingredients together and give texture, color, and flavor to whatever you're baking. Air bubbles beaten into eggs expand in the oven, causing cakes and cookies to rise. The fat in egg yolks gives moisture to things baked with them and lengthens their shelf life. Eggs have nutritional value, as they are rich in protein as well as essential minerals. I have used egg substitutes in one recipe that originally called for uncooked eggs to prevent the danger of salmonella, a bacterial illness that leads to food poisoning, caused in some cases by eating contaminated raw or undercooked eggs.

All the recipes in this book were created using extra-large eggs. It's essential to use this size of egg if you want to end up with the same results I did. When you shop for eggs, first check the expiration date on the box, then open the carton to look for cracked or soiled eggs (this is how salmonella gets a leg up). Don't buy a carton with cracked or soiled eggs. Store eggs in the refrigerator in the carton—this will keep them fresh and out of harm's way. You can tell if an egg is stale—and therefore unusable—by placing it in a glass of water. If it floats, throw it out (or scramble it up for the dog's dinner).

About Meringue

Meringue is a miracle that happens when you whip egg whites with sugar until they look like shiny, white, thick puffs of clouds as seen from an airplane.

You can whip egg whites without sugar to lighten things like a savory soufflé, for as the air bubbles expand in the oven, the soufflé will rise. When the soufflé is removed from the oven, it must be eaten quickly because as it cools, the air bubbles deflate and so does the soufflé.

Egg whites beaten with sugar can be used to cause certain kinds of cakes and sweet soufflés to rise. The action of getting the meringue incorporated into the batter or soufflé base without deflating the air bubbles is called "folding" (see page 14).

When egg whites are beaten with sugar and then baked at a low temperature, the liquid in the eggs evaporates, leaving a crisp sugar shell. That shell will remain crisp and hard if it is stored in a dry place. As soon as it is exposed to moisture, whether in the air or from coming in contact with other ingredients (a filling, for example), it will soften and become tacky. This doesn't mean it's no longer fit to eat; on the contrary, soft meringue is delicious—it's just a relaxed version of its rigid cousin.

It takes a little practice not to overbeat meringue. It's important to stop beating before the point where the mixture looses its sheen and starts to look dull, because at this point the structure of the air bubbles is tired and beginning to disintegrate.

Using superfine sugar, which dissolves quickly, will help to prevent a granular texture.

"Weeping" is what we call those tiny beads of moisture that sometimes form on the surface of baked meringue. When overcooked, meringue structure is compromised and water leaks out of the egg whites, according to my friend Shirley Corriher (a.k.a., the Kitchen Doctor) in her book *Cookwise* (William Morrow, 1997). Shirley suggests adding a "slurry"—a cooked mixture of cornstarch and water—to the egg whites during the beating process. However, an easier solution comes from Howard Hillman's book *Kitchen Science* (Houghton Mifflin, 1981). Howard recommends using confectioners' sugar in place of granulated when making meringue, since confectioners' sugar not only distributes itself more evenly, but also contains cornstarch, which eliminates the need to melt the sugar before it is added to the egg whites.

About Leavening Agents

What turns an inch of batter into a 2½-inch-high cake layer or a beautifully domed muffin, or a ball of dough into a puffy cookie? One or a combination of several things: beating eggs (whole, or yolks or whites separately) either by themselves or with sugar; or beating butter, either alone or with sugar, so that air bubbles incorporated in the mass will expand during the baking process, causing the baked goods to rise. Most of the rise, however, will deflate within minutes of cooling as the air bubbles shrink to close to their original size. Baking powder and baking soda to the rescue.

Baking powder is a mixture of an acid, an acid-reacting salt or a combination of acid-reacting salts, and bicarbonate of soda. Double-acting baking soda (which is what practically everyone uses) reacts first to liquid (like baking soda does), then to heat—thus the name "double acting." In the presence of moisture and heat, the acid-reacting salts act upon the bicarbonate of soda to release carbon dioxide. Part of the carbon dioxide is absorbed by the liquid ingredients in whatever you are baking. The rest gradually pushes into the air cells that you created by beating the eggs/sugar/butter, and helps them expand until the batter or dough is stabilized or set during the baking process. These air bubbles keep their shape after cooling, thus your cake and muffins stay high and your cookies are fluffy and soft.

Baking soda (sodium bicarbonate) contains carbon and oxygen, which together form carbon dioxide, the same gas in baking powder that expands and stabilizes the air bubbles. However, baking soda is an alkali and needs an acid to get it going. That's why you'll usually find things like buttermilk, yogurt, chocolate, brown sugar, molasses, or lemon juice— all with an acid pH—in recipes calling for baking soda. Baking soda starts acting as soon as it is combined with liquid, as opposed to baking powder, which must be heated first. So, if baking soda is the only leavening in your recipe, don't waste time getting the item into the oven.

About Extracts and Flavorings

Vanilla extract masks the "eggy" taste of eggs, gives depth and intensity to other flavors, and adds sweet, mellow richness to baked goods. Pure vanilla extract is made by soaking vanilla beans—the dried pods of an orchid grown in places such as Tahiti and Madagascar—in alcohol and water. When sniffed alongside real vanilla, artificial vanilla flavoring smells like the poor imitation it is. Many of the chocolate recipes in this book do not call for vanilla, since the chocolate is such an assertive flavor by itself and would overpower any added vanilla.

You can make your own very good vanilla extract by using a fresh vanilla bean, which can be found in gourmet shops or purchased by mail order from the King Arthur Flour Baker's Catalogue (see page 316). Slit the vanilla bean lengthwise to expose the seeds, then insert it into a small jar containing about 1 cup brandy or cognac. Bend the bean, if necessary, to immerse it in the liquid. Cover the jar and let it sit at room temperature for at least two weeks or as long as several years.

Almond extract, another commonly used infusion, is made from bitter almond oil and alcohol. It gives added punch to recipes that contain ground almonds. You can find hundreds of flavorings both on the supermarket shelf and through mail-order catalogs. Mocha, hazelnut, cinnamon, anise, peppermint, raspberry, wintergreen, blackberry, and maple are just a few. The very best flavors come from natural essences—as opposed to the artificial kinds—hence the words "pure" and "imitation" on the labels.

There is nothing like freshly grated orange, lemon, or lime zest to add spark and flavor to recipes. Zest is the bright, colored skin of citrus fruit. It's important not to include the white pith under the zest, which has a bitter, unpleasant taste. The easiest way to remove the zest and leave the pith is to use a citrus zester (see page 41). Citrus juice also gives terrific flavor, and brings out other flavors as well. When a recipe calls for freshly squeezed citrus juice, don't even think about using anything from a bottle or a plastic, lemon-shaped container.

Another flavoring option is citrus oils: lemon, lime, orange, and tangerine. Used in tiny amounts, they add a flavorful brightness to any dessert (see Boyajian Boston, page 316). As a rule, a scant ¼ teaspoon of an oil is equal to the zest of one whole fruit.

About Substituting Pans

Each recipe in this book calls for a specific size and type of pan. If you alter the size of the pan, several things can happen. You will have too much batter or dough, so you'll be forced to overfill the pan. If the pan is too small, the batter or dough will rise in the oven and over-flow the pan, making a mess on the sides of the pan and on the bottom of the oven. If the pan is too large, the batter or dough will be so thin that it will burn before the baking time is over. If you use a layer cake pan to make a quick bread, you won't have a moist interior. Making a recipe that calls for a 9-inch square pan in a 9 by 13-inch pan will not give you more brownies. When recipes can be converted to other pans, the recipe will indicate that along with the revised cooking time.

About Substituting Ingredients

I still vigorously object to substituting margarine for butter. My friend and literary agent, Susan Ginsburg, however, showed me that it *can* be done. Susan keeps a kosher home, and serves the Flourless Chocolate Cake on page 156. While I still prefer the taste of butter, if using margarine means the difference between making one of my recipes and serving fruit salad, I say go for it. I've begun to experiment with egg substitute (Coffee Toffee Pie, page 304), especially in recipes that call for uncooked eggs. Salmonella is a grave concern, so it's good news that egg substitute works in these recipes. As for using the substitute in recipes in which the eggs are cooked, you'll have to let me know your results.

Some ingredients can be substituted for each other without any problem: dark brown sugar for light brown sugar (the taste will be different, but not substantially); whole milk for 2% milk; regular yogurt for low-fat yogurt; milk chocolate chips for dark chocolate chips, when used whole. (Milk chocolate and dark chocolate cannot be substituted for one another when a recipe specifies melted chocolate.) You can use dried cranberries, currants, or bits of dried apricots or dried apples in place of raisins. You can use almonds, walnuts, and pecans interchangeably in these recipes.

About the Temperature of Ingredients

Room temperature: Unless specified, all ingredients should be at room temperature before you start to make these recipes. When ingredients are at room temperature and the butter is soft, it's easier to combine and aerate the butter, thus reducing the amount of time spent mixing batters and doughs. The easiest way to judge whether or not something is at room temperature is to touch it. If it doesn't feel cold or cool, then you can assume it's fine. The simplest way to bring things to room temperature is to remove the butter, eggs, milk, cream cheese, sour cream, yogurt, and other refrigerated ingredients from the refrigerator about an hour before you start to bake. If you haven't done this, you can bring the eggs to room temperature by placing them in water that's hot—but not hot enough to burn your hand—for five minutes. Other ingredients such as yogurt, sour cream, and cream cheese can be microwaved for 10 to 12 seconds, stirred, and then microwaved again until they are tepid. Cold butter should be cut into tablespoons, half melted in the microwave (20 to 30 seconds per stick), then stirred with a rubber spatula until soft. Egg whites whip up much faster when they are at room temperature.

Hot: Some recipes call for simmering or boiling ingredients either separately or in combination. Usually the amount of cooking time is given along with a visual cue ("Simmer the egg yolks, lemon juice, and cornstarch for 4 minutes, or until the mixture is very thick and looks like warm pudding"). It's important to make sure that you cook the ingredients for as long as the recipe indicates; otherwise, as in the above example, you'll have filling that won't set up after cooling.

Cold: Sometimes the success of the recipe depends on ingredients being cold. Heavy cream whips best when it's cold (40° to 45°F) and whipped in a bowl that's been chilled using chilled beaters. When the fat in heavy cream is cold, it surrounds the air bubbles and keeps them stable—almost exactly the opposite of whipped egg whites. Piecrusts should be chilled during the rolling process for two reasons: Chilling allows the gluten (protein) in the flour to relax, which makes rolling easier, and chilling solidifies fat that might have gotten soft during the rolling process. When the fat gets soft, the dough becomes difficult to handle.

About the Order of Ingredients

The ingredients for each recipe are listed in the order in which they are used in the recipe. Sometimes an ingredient has to be dealt with first, then set aside to be added later; almonds, for example, may need to be toasted then cooled before they are added. The best way to organize yourself to make sure that all the ingredients are used (did I put the baking soda in or not?) is to line up the ingredients in the order in which they are listed. As each one is used, either put it away or put it on another counter. Even though a casual observer might think you are crazy, I suggest you say the name of the ingredient as it is used in addition to moving it, lest you lose track of what you've done.

About Cooling

When hot things come out of the oven, they need to be cooled. Whether it's for 5 minutes or 5 hours, this step makes a difference. Foods continue to cook for several minutes after they are removed from the oven, so a cake that tested done with a cake tester will still be too moist and fragile inside to survive cutting. Most bars (brownies and others) are almost liquid right out of the oven, and will ooze out of shape if they are cut before cooling. Things that should be cooled in the pan will fall apart if they are removed too soon; cheesecake is the perfect example. While a chocolate chip cookie hot from the oven is heaven, that cookie will not hold its shape unless it's allowed to cool slightly before removing it from the baking sheet.

Many recipes instruct you to cool things off on a wire cooling rack. This allows the air to circulate underneath the pan so that moisture doesn't accumulate, causing soggy bottoms. Think of what happens when you put a piece of hot toast down on a plate—the underside gets soft because of the hot air condensing there.

About Storage and Freezing

The worst place to store baked goods for any length of time is in the refrigerator, where they will get soggy and pick up the smell of any other foods stored nearby. They will also get stale more quickly than at room temperature, due to the starches contracting and releasing their liquids. As a rule of thumb, cookies and bars can be stored at room temperature in a covered container for at least a week before getting stale. Otherwise you can freeze them. The easiest way to do this is to allow them to cool completely, then place them on a baking sheet and place the sheet in the freezer. After the cookies or bars are frozen solid (at least 3 hours) stack them in a freezer-strength recloseable plastic bag. Remember to use a waterproof marker to note the contents on the bag and the date the contents were frozen. Refer to the individual recipe to know how long you should freeze them. Defrost in the bag at room temperature on a counter for 1 to 2 hours. Some cookie dough can also be formed into a roll, frozen, sliced, and baked. See page 95 for a recipe and instructions.

Assuming that you're not going to polish off two dozen muffins within hours of removing them from the cooling rack, you're going to need to put them someplace to stay fresh. I like to freeze muffins and scones in individual plastic bags so I can pull one at a time out of the freezer and let it defrost overnight on the counter to be ready to eat in the morning.

For short-term room-temperature storage of scones, perforated plastic bags work really well. Moisture cannot get trapped inside, so the scones do not get soggy. These are sold as vegetable refrigerator storage bags in the supermarket, and are available as perforated bread bags from the King Arthur Flour Baker's Catalogue (see page 316). Freeze scones as you would muffins. Biscuits cannot withstand the freezing process—it's better to eat them fresh.

Tea cakes and quick breads can be frozen whole or sliced. Cool them completely, wrap them airtight in plastic wrap, then place them in a freezer-strength recloseable plastic bag. Again, mark the name of the recipe and the date on the bag. Layer cakes are best frozen unfrosted in the same manner as tea cakes. Refer to the individual recipe to know how long you can freeze them.

Fruit pies, except pumpkin, which shouldn't be frozen, should be frozen before baking, then defrosted, covered, at room temperature for 1 hour before baking according to recipe directions.

Crumbles, crisps, and cobblers should not be frozen or even refrigerated. The fruit gets mushy and the toppings get soggy.

Custard-based and meringue-topped pies such as lemon meringue and Key lime should not be frozen. The Pumpkin Cheesecake (page 171) freezes fine.

Cheesecakes freeze beautifully, but without any fruit topping, which should always be added just before serving. Cool the cake completely. If it was baked in a springform pan, remove the sides of the pan, then transfer the cake to an aluminum foil–covered cardboard cake round. (If the cheesecake was baked in a pie plate, leave it in the plate.) Wrap the cake in several thicknesses of plastic wrap, then place in a freezer-strength recloseable plastic bag, noting the contents with a waterproof marker. As a rule, cheesecakes can be frozen for 3 months. Defrost, still wrapped, either overnight in the refrigerator or at room temperature for 3 to 4 hours.

Self-defrosting freezers can dry food out and cause freezer burn, which is why it's so important to wrap frozen food well, especially if you plan to freeze it for several months. Defrosting food with the wrapping in place means that any moisture that has accumulated on the outside of the package will remain on the outside and will not cause the food to become soggy.

Equipment (and Other Stuff You Really Need to Have to Make These Recipes Work)

Oh, man, you just spent money buying this book, you're itching to get going on those brownies, and now I'm telling you that you have to get all this stuff first? Patience. You need to give me a few more minutes. Unless you've been eating exclusively takeout or at

Mom's until this very minute, you already probably own some of these things. No doubt there are a few you don't own, but if you are going to take the time and spend good money on ingredients you're going to have to invest in a bunch of this equipment. I'm hoping you already own the first two items, and perhaps the third. Without them your ship is sunk and at best this book will become bedtime reading. If you need any inspiration, think how good those brownies will taste if they are made the right way.

Oven: Your oven should be clean; burned-on food will smoke during baking and affect the taste of delicate things such as cakes and meringues. The door should close securely; a poorly sealed door will drastically affect the thermostat. The racks should be level; this will affect the evenness of cooking as well as the level of batter-based cakes, loose pie fillings, and cupcakes. The temperature should be accurately calibrated; the dial should represent what the actual oven temperature is. If you have any doubts, use a mercury oven thermometer to check the temperature.

These recipes were not tested in a convection oven. A convection oven has a fan that blows hot air around, which speeds up the cooking time. If your oven can be used in both convection and conventional modes, then use the conventional mode for these recipes. If you have an oven that bakes in convection mode only, the rule of thumb is to reduce the oven temperature specified in the recipe by 25°F and the cooking time by 5 to 10 minutes.

Work surface: You don't need a fancy granite or marble countertop to make any of these recipes. Any smooth, nonporous surface will do. If you have a grouted tile countertop you might want to consider buying an acrylic cutting board, available in every kitchenware and hardware store. Buy the largest one that can fit in your dishwasher.

Electric mixer: I know Great-Grandma did all her baking by hand, but she didn't have three carpools to drive, a brief due, or seventy-five e-mails to answer. You want to make these by hand? Of course you can, and when you're finished perhaps you could answer my e-mails.

In a departure from other books that have you use heavy-duty mixers or food processors, I've created all these recipes using a hand-held electric mixer (I use a five-speed KitchenAid® that costs about thirty dollars). While some of you may own heavy-duty mixers, it's my experience that novice bakers will have significantly more success with a mixer that puts them directly in touch with the ingredients in the bowl. The food processor removes you almost completely from the ingredients as they are being mixed. It's incredibly easy to overmix batters and doughs; the difference between 30 and 60 seconds of mixing in a heavy-duty mixer (where you have to stop and lift the paddle to check the contents of the bowl) or 10 to 15 seconds in the food processor can mean rubbery cakes and muffins; dry, overworked meringues; and separated whipped cream. It will take slightly longer to mix things with a hand-held mixer, but the control, plus the cook's ability to "feel" the consistency of the ingredients while they are being mixed, beaten, or whipped, are worth it and will be evident in the final product.

Some Thoughts on Baking Pans and Sheets

One of the most important keys to success in baking is to use heavy-duty baking pans and baking sheets. Cheap pans conduct heat poorly and unevenly, and warp when subjected to high heat, so your cake ends up not only lopsided, but burned on one side and raw on the other. The extra cost of good pans is worth it. They will last a lifetime—especially if you use them only for baking (you'd be surprised at what some folks use their kitchen equipment for). Take the time to wash them by hand, since repeated trips through the dishwasher will eventually mar and dull even the most durable surfaces, including those which are nonstick.

Take the time to clean every speck of grease, spills, and what-have-you off your pans each time you use them. Besides aesthetics, there is a very practical reason for doing this: burned-on food gets more burned on every time you bake; and soon becomes part of your pan. Every time you wash the pan, the burned-on food gets wet and absorbs new grease along with detergent. In no time at all there's a blob of really gross stuff stuck to your pan. This not only ruins the surface of the pan, but ultimately affects the taste of whatever you are baking.

Numbers 1 through 12 (listed on pages 39–40) are the pans you will need to make all the recipes in this book. I prefer the commercial-weight nonstick aluminum pans made by both Chicago Metalic and Kaiser Bakeware. The pans never warp, the heat is evenly distributed, and the designs are classic and elegant. These pans can be found in almost any serious kitchenware store, by mail order, and on the Internet (see page 315). It certainly helps to buy equipment from a knowledgeable salesperson—one who uses the equipment and can give you personal advice. I find that Williams-Sonoma and most independent cookware shops are staffed by people who have been trained well and have used the equipment they are selling. I haven't had this experience in large department or discount stores.

If you are shopping for equipment, don't be seduced by the Ferrari equivalent—you absolutely do not have to pay sixty dollars for a baking pan. Twenty dollars is more like it. The King Arthur Flour Baker's Catalogue is a fine source of good-quality, heavy-duty bakeware (see page 316). Before you go shopping, be sure to note the inside dimensions of your oven. A baking sheet, the longest and widest piece of baking equipment that will go in your oven, should fit on the rack so that there are at least 1½ inches of clear space between the baking sheet, the oven walls, and the closed oven door.

I started out using glass baking dishes and then, with the exception of my pie plates, I shifted to metal. Metal browns more evenly than glass, and it doesn't shatter if you drop it on the floor or place it on a cold surface. I once saw my life pass before me when I pulled a 17 by 11-inch glass baking pan out of the oven and placed it on a granite counter. The dish not only shattered into a million lethal shards, but it sprayed the entire kitchen and everything else I had cooked. Months later I was still sweeping glass from the corners of the room. I also find that metal cleans up faster and better than glass. Those stubborn stains on glass never seem to give way to even the most enthusiastic scrubbing.

The Equipment List

1. Two round heavy-duty aluminum layer cake pans, 9 inches in diameter and 2 inches deep, preferably nonstick

2. One heavy-duty aluminum springform pan, 9 inches in diameter and 3 inches deep, preferably nonstick

3. One 12 by 17 by 1-inch heavy-duty aluminum half-sheet pan, which I call a baking sheet. In addition to making the cake part of jelly rolls, this rimmed baking sheet can be used as a cookie sheet (which does not have a lip or rim), for setting under a smaller pan to catch baking spills, and as the base for a water bath.

4. Two heavy-duty baking (cookie) sheets

5. One 9 by 13-inch baking pan, 2 inches deep, for bars, squares, and cakes

6. One 9 by 9-inch baking pan for brownies, bars, and squares

7. One glass or heavy-duty metal pie plate, 9 inches in diameter and 1¼ inches deep

8. One deep-dish pie plate, 9 inches in diameter and 2 inches deep

9. One 12-hole standard muffin tin with ⅓-cup-capacity holes, heavy-duty aluminum, preferably nonstick. These recipes were tested in this size muffin tin. You can use a tin with slightly larger holes; your muffins, however, won't be as high or you may get 10 muffins when our recipe says 12.

10. One 6-hole jumbo muffin tin with ¾-cup-capacity holes, heavy-duty aluminum, preferably nonstick

11. One 8½ by 4½ by 1½-inch loaf pan, glass or metal

12. One 10-inch heavy-duty bundt-style pan with a 12-cup capacity and with a center core and fluted sides, preferably nonstick

13. Mixing bowls: 2-quart, 1½-quart, and 1-quart; heavy-duty metal or dishwasher-safe molded plastic

14. Saucepans: 2-quart and 1-quart, with lids

15. A set of microwave-safe glass bowls with tops or covers

16. A sauté pan, 10 to 12 inches in diameter

17. A kitchen timer with a loud ring. A digital timer is the most accurate, and one that you can clip on your apron or fit in your pocket in case you have to leave the kitchen is great.

18. Two wire cooling racks

19. A set of dry measures: 1 cup, ¾ cup, ⅔ cup, ½ cup, ⅓ cup, ¼ cup

20. Liquid measures with a pouring spout: 4 cup and 2 cup, in glass or clear plastic. These measures are larger than you might think you need, but recipes frequently call for combining liquid ingredients in a measuring cup and then pouring them into the dry ingredients, so a large size is more useful.

21. Metal measuring spoons: 1 tablespoon, 1 teaspoon, ½ teaspoon, ¼ teaspoon

22. A dishwasher-safe cutting board, as large as will fit in your dishwasher

23. A heavy rolling pin: I like the heavy wooden kind with handles and ball bearings, as opposed to the French, tapered variety, because it's easier to manipulate.

24. A citrus reamer: An inexpensive hand model is fine—you don't need a fancy electric version.

25. A ladle

26. Two heatproof rubber spatulas, one large, one small

27. One wire whisk

28. Two long-handled wooden spoons

29. A citrus zester to remove the thin, colored outer layer from citrus fruit

30. A 10-inch medium-mesh sieve for sifting dry ingredients

31. 1-gallon and 1-quart recloseable plastic bags for food storage, and jumbo-size (2 gallon) recloseable bags for rolling piecrust and for storage of whole cakes

32. A paring knife

33. A serrated knife, at least 12 inches long, for slicing cake layers in half

34. A pastry brush

35. Two offset metal spatulas, one small, one large, for lifting bars and cookies and for frosting cakes in the pan

36. Parchment paper in 12 by 17-inch rectangles and 9-inch rounds or in a tear-off roll, and/or 11 by 17-inch reusable silicone panliners (Silpat™ or Exopat™). The latter are marvelous inventions and should be considered if you go through a large quantity of parchment paper or if you are sick of scrubbing pans that have been greased and floured before baking. Silicone pan liners are available from the King Arthur Flour Baker's Catalogue (see page 316).

37. Cardboard cake rounds: 10-inch-diameter for placing under 9-inch-round cakes for serving or freezing, and 9-inch-diameter to be covered with heavy-duty aluminum foil and used to replace springform pan bottoms during baking

38. Paper doilies in assorted sizes

39. A wire cake tester

40. Kitchen scissors

41. Serving spoons

42. A wedge-shaped cake/pie server

43. Pot holders and oven mitts

44. An apron

45. Dish towels

46. Plastic wrap, wax paper

47. Heavy-duty aluminum foil

48. A waterproof marker

49. A food grater

50. Plastic cake/pie carriers: a high, round container for storing cookies and all 9-inch round cakes, and a rectangular one to store cupcakes, cookies, and 9 by 13-inch cakes.

51. Airtight canisters in assorted sizes for food storage

52. A food processor

53. Pie weights

Other Stuff You Might Consider

1. A dough scraper: a handy, straight-edged metal device with a wooden or plastic handle, perfect for moving dough around on a work surface and for scraping down counters during cleanup. It is also called a bench knife.

2. A bowl scraper: a handy plastic gadget for getting the last bit of ingredients out of the bottom of a mixing bowl

3. An oven thermometer

4. An instant-read thermometer

5. A candy thermometer

6. A double boiler, if you don't feel comfortable using a metal bowl perched over a pan of simmering water

7. A flame tamer to control the heat of the burner

8. A second set of dry and liquid measures and measuring spoons

9. A pastry blender: a gadget used for working fat into dry ingredients. It is sometimes called a "pastry cutter." Two table knives are also fine for this job.

10. An icing spatula, so you can spread those swirls just like Betty Crocker.

11. A small fine-mesh sieve for sifting confectioners' sugar or cocoa onto the top of cakes; also great for straining seeds and pulp from citrus juice.

12. A 2-tablespoon and a ¼-cup ice cream scoop, for forming cookies.

13. Paper or aluminum foil cupcake liners

14. A piping bag and pastry tips

15. Extra mixing bowls

16. A cookbook holder to keep this book open and free of splatters and spills

17. Cookie cutters: 1½-inch, 2-inch, 2½-inch, and 3-inch rounds, as well as assorted shapes

18. A vegetable peeler

19. A kitchen scale

20. A food mill (I use a Foley mill)

21. A domed cake cover for protecting cakes stored at room temperature

Pantry

Obviously you're not going to have every ingredient on hand for every recipe in this book. When the brownie or chocolate chip cookie craving strikes you, however, it's nice if the few things necessary to make them are located no farther than your kitchen cupboard. You'll notice that I suggest storing many of these items, once opened, in recloseable plastic bags on the pantry shelf. This way you can see what's in them without opening them up, they take up much less room than canisters or plastic containers, and they protect from meal moths (pesky little winged creatures that love grains, seeds, herbs, and nuts). Unless specified, the following ingredients are stored at room temperature, not in the refrigerator, unless you live in a climate where all foods need to be stored in the refrigerator.

About Quality of Ingredients

You know the expression "garbage in, garbage out"? It means that no alchemy takes place in a 350°F oven that turns chocolate your kids rejected two Halloweens ago, rancid butter, and poor-quality flour into something you'd want to eat. This doesn't mean that you have to send to France for thirty-dollar-a-pound designer cocoa or buy organic butter. It means reading labels to make sure the chocolate you use is made with cocoa butter and not palm kernel or coconut oil. It means smelling and/or tasting that peanut butter you've kept on the back shelf for two years, to make sure it's still good. It means reading expiration dates on perishables such as butter and eggs. It means using unbleached, unbromated flour and not the deeply discounted no-name brand that was on special in the warehouse superstore. It means using the ingredient specified in the recipe (see About Substituting Ingredients, page 33).

Essential Ingredients

Baking powder: Store this tightly covered in its *original* container; you need to know that this is baking powder, not baking soda.

Baking soda: Store the opened box in a recloseable plastic bag in a dry place to prevent lumps. Place a second open box in the refrigerator where it will absorb odors.

Salt: Store tightly sealed, away from dampness.

All-purpose unbleached white flour: Remove flour from the original bag and place in a canister or large, tightly covered plastic container. Store in a cool, dry place and check occasionally for meal moths, especially if you buy organic flour.

Cake flour: Store in a cool, dry place. After opening, close the inner plastic bag securely and store it in the closed box.

Cornstarch: Place the opened box in a recloseable plastic bag and seal it shut.

Cream of tartar: Store in a tightly sealed container in a cool, dark place.

Granulated sugar: Remove this from the original bag and place in a canister or a large, tightly covered plastic container.

Confectioners' sugar: Place the opened box in a recloseable plastic bag and seal it.

Dark brown and **light brown sugar:** Place the open box in a large, recloseable plastic bag, squeeze out the air, and seal it. If the sugar gets hard, place a slice of apple in the bag, close the bag, and leave it for a few hours or overnight, then discard the apple.

Honey: Take care to wipe drops from the lid and jar opening to prevent sticking. Store opened honey in the refrigerator.

Maple syrup: Buy the real stuff—not the flavored sugar syrup. Take care to wipe drops from the lid and jar opening to prevent sticking. Store opened maple syrup in the refrigerator.

Molasses: Buy regular, mild-tasting molasses for these recipes, not blackstrap. Take care to wipe drops from the lid and jar opening to prevent sticking and ants.

Light and **dark corn syrup:** Wipe drops from the cap and opening to prevent sticking, then secure the cap well.

Spices: Ground cinnamon, nutmeg, cloves, ginger, and allspice play a big part in American baking. Buy all ground spices in small quantities and replace them every 6 to 8 months, as they lose their potency over time. You can maximize their shelf life by storing them in tinted jars with lids tightly closed, in a cool, dry place—not in clear jars on top of your stove.

Chocolate: When buying chocolate and chocolate products, think quality. Chocolate has such a dominant flavor that you want that dominant flavor to taste great. This is not the time for no-name brands.

Unsweetened cocoa powder: This is the ground nib of the roasted cocoa bean, with most of the cocoa butter (the vegetable fat in chocolate) removed. Store it in a tightly sealed container.

Unsweetened baking chocolate: This is the nib mixed with cocoa butter, which provides a very intense chocolate taste in baking. It's best to buy it in a box of 1-ounce squares, which will save your having to measure or weigh it for recipes. Store it wrapped securely in plastic wrap or in a tightly sealed container, away from sunlight, dampness, and strong odors. It will keep for up to three years.

Dark sweet chocolate (semisweet or bittersweet): This is a mixture of chocolate, sugarcane, vanilla extract or artificial vanilla flavoring, and cocoa butter; it is processed (conched) to make it smooth and palatable. It is available as baking bars and blocks. Look for such names as Ghirardelli, Lindt, Perugina, Valrhona, or Callebaut. Wrap securely in plastic wrap or place in a tightly sealed container, away from sunlight, dampness, and strong odors. It will keep for up to three years.

Milk chocolate: This is dark sweet chocolate with dry milk solids added to it, which gives it a creamier and more mellow taste than sweet dark chocolate. Wrap securely in plastic wrap or place in a tightly sealed container, away from sunlight, dampness, and strong odors. It will keep for four to six months.

White chocolate: This is made from cocoa butter (which gives it a mild chocolate flavor), dry milk solids, and sugar. Wrap securely in plastic wrap or place in a tightly sealed container, away from sunlight, dampness, and strong odors. It will keep for four to six months.

Chocolate chips: These are made with less cocoa butter than bar chocolates, which helps them retain their distinctive shape during baking. As a rule it's better, for both taste and texture, to use chips in chocolate chip cookies and bars where you want the shape intact than to melt them for use in place of bar or chunk chocolate. Check the package to make sure that the product contains some cocoa butter. Store opened bags in recloseable plastic bags or in tightly sealed containers, away from sunlight, dampness, and strong odors.

Peanut butter: Store this in the refrigerator after opening. Always taste before using to make sure it's not rancid.

Oats, quick-cooking and old-fashioned: The only difference between these is that quick-cooking oats have been rolled and cut into several pieces to shorten the cooking time, and old-fashioned oats have been rolled but not cut. In the recipes in this book they can be used interchangeably. Do not confuse them with instant oats, which are preprocessed, or with steel-cut oats, known as Scotch or Irish oatmeal, which are unprocessed and need a very long time to cook. Oats are always added to recipes uncooked, unless otherwise specified. Store oats in the refrigerator after opening.

Vanilla extract: Use pure vanilla extract, not imitation vanilla. Store tightly sealed, away from sunlight.

Nonstick vegetable spray: Don't use a flavored or olive oil variety. Store away from heat.

Powdered buttermilk: This comes in a cardboard canister with a tight-fitting plastic lid. Store it in the refrigerator after opening.

White vinegar: Store this tightly closed at room temperature.

Solid vegetable shortening, such as Crisco: This can be purchased in a can with a tight-fitting lid, or in bars that must be sealed in plastic wrap to protect from absorbing other food smells in the refrigerator. Store at room temperature until opened, then refrigerate.

Vegetable oils, such as canola, safflower, corn, peanut, or olive oil: Store tightly closed in a cool, dark place.

Nuts: Pecans, almonds, and walnuts can for the most part be used interchangeably in these recipes. Almonds are available whole, sliced, and slivered, as well as unblanched (with the thin, dark skin left on) and blanched (with the skin removed). These recipes use the blanched variety, as the skin can be bitter and tough. Unless otherwise specified, nuts are unsalted. Nuts stored at room temperature will become rancid fairly quickly; you can tell by their unpleasant taste and smell. Nuts should be placed in recloseable plastic bags or tightly sealed containers and stored in the freezer, where they can keep for up to one year.

Toasted nuts are often specified in these recipes. You can toast large quantities at one time, then package them and store them as you would fresh ones.

Jelly, jam, and preserves: Jelly is a mixture of fruit juice that has been boiled with sugar and, in some cases, with a thickening agent such as pectin added. Jam and preserves are made in a similar fashion but contain whole fruits or pieces of fruit. Pectin, a carbohydrate found in the cell walls of plants, produces a natural gel when combined with fruit acids and sugar over heat; the gel causes the cooked mixture to thicken and set. Store unopened jars in the pantry; once opened, store the jars in the refrigerator.

Dried fruit, such as raisins, currants (which look like tiny raisins), prunes, dates, apricots, apple rings, cranberries, and cherries: These add bursts of flavor to muffins, quick breads, cookies, bars, and cakes. As a rule of thumb, these dried fruits can be used interchangeably. To cut up large pieces of fruit for baking, spray scissor blades with nonstick vegetable spray and snip the fruit with the scissors. For easy identification of dried fruits on the shelf once they have been opened, keep them in the original bag or box, place that in a recloseable plastic bag, then seal tightly.

Dried cranberries are a useful substitution for fresh or frozen cranberries in recipes. Use ¾ cup of the dried product for 1 cup of the fresh.

Nonessential Ingredients

Whole wheat flour: This flour contains the bran and germ, which can become rancid if stored improperly. Buy it in small quantities and store it in the freezer, in a recloseable plastic bag or in a tightly sealed container.

Wheat germ: Place in a recloseable plastic bag or a tightly sealed container and store in the refrigerator or freezer.

Lora Brody's Dough Relaxer: Use this for light and tender biscuits, easy-to-roll piecrusts and cookie dough, rich tea cakes, and coffee cakes. Visit my website (see page 315) or call our toll-free number, 888-9-BAKEIT, to receive a free sample.

Sweetened condensed milk: Once opened, store leftover quantities in a sealed container and store in the refrigerator for up to 1 week.

Coconut: This is dried coconut, and may be shredded or flaked, and sweetened or unsweetened. Once opened, store it in a recloseable plastic bag.

Coconut milk: Once opened, pour unused coconut milk into a plastic container and store, tightly covered, in the refrigerator for up to 1 week or in the freezer for up to 6 months.

Peanuts, pine nuts, macadamia nuts, and hazelnuts: Place these in recloseable plastic bags or tightly sealed containers and store in the freezer for up to 1 year. You may toast these nuts before freezing.

Preground almonds: These are available from the King Arthur Flour Baker's Catalogue (see page 316). Store them in the freezer in a recloseable plastic bag or tightly sealed container. They may be toasted before freezing.

Caraway seeds, poppy seeds, anise seeds, and star anise: Buy these in small quantities and store in tightly sealed jars in a cool, dry place. Replace every 6 to 9 months, as they lose their potency over time.

Candied (or crystallized) sugar: Store in a recloseable plastic bag or an airtight container at room temperature.

Espresso powder or granules: Store tightly covered in a cool, dark place.

Citrus oils, such as lemon, orange, and lime: Once opened, store in the refrigerator in tightly sealed containers.

Minute brand tapioca: This is available in the baking aisle of the supermarket. Store the opened box in a recloseable plastic bag.

Peppermint and almond extracts: Store tightly closed and away from light.

Food coloring: Tightly capped, it will last indefinitely.

Canned pumpkin puree: Be sure to buy plain pumpkin puree, not pumpkin pie filling, which has spices added.

Superfine sugar: This is also called bar sugar, as it is used in making mixed drinks. Use this when you want to make sure the sugar in your recipe dissolves fast and completely.

Baker's (coarse) sugar: This adds special crunch to the tops of baked goods. It is available through the King Arthur Flour Baker's Catalogue (see page 316).

Spirits: Several of the recipes in this and other baking books call for the addition of alcohol in some form or another. If you prefer not to use alcohol, it's usually fine to substitute an equal amount of orange juice. If the addition is "optional" you can eliminate some or all of it. If you do choose to add it, remember that the flavor of alcohol is strong and will, if used in excess, overpower other flavors. I suggest that you add half the suggested amount, taste it, and add more if you want a stronger taste. I usually have on hand Grand Marnier or other orange-flavored liqueur, Chambord or other raspberry-flavored liqueur, brandy, and dark rum.

Perishable Ingredients (These go in the refrigerator.)

Extra-large eggs: All the recipes in this book were tested with extra-large eggs; it's important to use this size to get good results. When buying eggs, check the expiration date, then open the carton to make sure no eggs are cracked or soiled. Refrigerate eggs in their carton, not on the refrigerator door; they will stay fresh longer and won't be subject to breakage.

Dairy products, such as milk (whole and 2%), buttermilk, yogurt, heavy cream, sour cream, and cream cheese: These tenderize the texture of cakes, cookies, and other baked goods. They extend shelf life and add richness and flavor, and they are a valuable source of calcium as well. Keep milk in the coldest part of the refrigerator; it has the shortest shelf life of the products listed.

If you're not a milk drinker and don't keep a fresh quart on hand, think about buying a box of powdered milk. You don't need to reconstitute it before adding it to a recipe. Follow the directions on the package for how much powder to use for a given quantity of milk, add the powder along with the other dry ingredients in the recipe, then substitute water for the amount of liquid milk called for in the recipe. Powdered buttermilk is another good thing to have on hand. It is available in health and natural food stores, and in many supermarkets. Substitute powdered buttermilk for fresh in the manner described for regular milk.

Unsalted (sweet) butter: Check the label to make sure it's unsalted. Check the expiration date, too. Some butter comes in 1-pound blocks, but you want to buy it in sticks (4 sticks to a pound). Store it in the freezer if you don't plan to use it in a few days. Wrap it securely and store it away from strong odors. For more on butter, see page 17.

Fresh fruit: Fruit adds texture, flavor, and moisture to baked goods. High-moisture fruits such as oranges and bananas will become mushy and fall apart during baking, unlike apples, pears, and slightly underripe peaches and nectarines. Berries need to be handled gently, since mixing them too vigorously will crush them and make them part of the batter, and thus unrecognizable. Although many people prefer to eat fruit at room temperature for optimum flavor, fruit ripens quickly at room temperature; refrigeration slows the ripening process and prolongs the life of the fruit you want to use in baking.

It's fine to use frozen berries in place of fresh in muffins and fruit pies. Generally neither frozen berries nor peaches need to be defrosted before using; check the recipe for any special instructions. If you have picked a windfall of fresh berries, freeze them for later use by rinsing them (only if absolutely necessary), patting them dry, and placing them in a single layer on a baking sheet. Freeze for several hours or overnight, then place the berries in freezer-strength recloseable plastic bags and freeze for up to 6 months.

Glossary

Permission has been generously granted by the publishers and editors of the *Webster's New World Dictionary of Culinary Arts* (Prentice-Hall, 1997) for use of the following information.

What does it mean when you say . . . ?

Beat: To mix by stirring rapidly and vigorously in a circular motion.

Blanch: To cook food very briefly and partially in boiling water or hot fat; generally used to assist preparation (as in loosening peach skin), as part of a combination cooking method, to remove undesirable flavors, or to prepare a food for freezing.

Blend: To mix two or more ingredients together until uniformly combined.

Boil: To cook by boiling, a moist heat cooking method that uses convection to transfer heat from a hot (approximately 212°F [100°C]) liquid to the food submerged in it; the turbulent waters and higher temperatures cook foods more quickly than do poaching and simmering.

Chop: To cut food into small pieces where uniformity of size and shape is neither necessary nor feasible.

Core: To remove the central seeded area from a fruit; the center part of pomes (fruits from the family *Rosaceae* such as apples, pears, and quince); sometimes tough and woody, it contains the fruit's small seeds (called pips).

Cream: To mix softened fat and sugar together vigorously to incorporate air, used for making some quick breads, cookies, and high-fat cakes.

Curdle: The separation of milk or egg mixtures into liquid and solid components, generally caused by excessive heat, overcooking, or the presence of acids.

Cut in: To mix a solid fat into flour and other dry ingredients until only small pieces of the fat remain.

Dice: To cut food into cubes; or the cubes of cut food.

Double boiler: An assemblage used to cook heat-sensitive foods such as sauces, chocolate, or custards. One pot sits partway down a second pot, simmering water in the bottom pot gently heats the top pot's contents. Also known as a double saucepan.

Drizzle: To pour in a very fine stream of liquid over a food or plate.

Dust: To coat a food or utensil lightly with a powdery substance such as flour or confectioners' sugar.

Flute: To make a decorative pattern on the raised edge of a piecrust.

Fold: To incorporate light, airy ingredients into heavier ingredients by gently moving them from the bottom up over the top in a circular motion.

Glaze: To apply a shiny coating to a food; any shiny coating applied to a food or created by browning; a thin, flavored coating poured or dripped onto a cake or pastry.

Grate: To reduce food to small pieces by scraping it on a rough surface.

Grease: To rub fat or a fat substitute on the surface of a cooking utensil.

Knead: To work a dough by hand or in a mixer to distribute ingredients and develop gluten, or to press, rub, or squeeze with the hands.

Mince: To cut or chop a food finely.

Peel: To remove rind or skin; the rind or skin of a fruit or vegetable.

Pinch: The amount that can be held between the thumb and forefinger.

Preheat: To bring an oven, broiler, or pan to the desired temperature before putting in the food.

Pulse: The action of breaking up a food in a food processor using quick bursts of power until the desired size and texture are achieved.

Puree: To process food to achieve a smooth pulp; food that is processed by mashing, straining, or fine chopping to achieve a smooth pulp.

Rest: The period during which a food (for example, bread or a roasted turkey) is allowed to lie undisturbed immediately after cooking and before slicing or carving.

Room temperature: Generally 72°F (22.2°C).

Scald: To heat a liquid, usually milk, to just below the boiling point.

Scant: An amount just shy of what the measuring cup or spoon will hold when full.

Seed: To remove seeds, as from citrus fruits and apples.

Set up/set: To allow a mixture to thicken or congeal, usually by chilling, as with gelatin.

Shred: To shave, grate, cut, or otherwise reduce a food to relatively long, narrow pieces.

Sift: To pass dry ingredients, such as flour and baking powder, through a sieve or sifter to remove lumps and blend and aerate the ingredients.

Simmer: To cook by moist heat, using convection to transfer heat from a hot liquid (approximately 185° to 205°F, 185° to 96°C) to the food submerged in it; to maintain the temperature of a liquid just below the boiling point.

Soften: To change the consistency of an ingredient from hard to soft, usually by the application of heat or movement.

Sprinkle: To scatter small amounts of a dry substance or drops of liquid over the surface of a food.

Stir: To mix ingredients gently until blended, using a spoon, whisk, or rubber spatula.

Strain: To pour foods through a sieve, mesh strainer, or cheesecloth to separate or remove the liquid component from solids.

Unmold: To remove food from the container (usually a decorative dish) in which it was prepared, usually done by inverting it over a serving plate.

Water bath: A hot-water bath used to cook foods gently or to keep cooked foods hot (also known as a *bain-marie*); a container for holding foods in a hot-water bath.

Whip: To mix foods by vigorously beating to incorporate air; a whisk or an electric mixer with its whip attachment is used.

Whisk: A utensil consisting of several wire loops joined at a handle, the loops generally create a round or teardrop-shaped outline and range in sizes from 8 to 18 inches (20.3 to 45.7 cm). It is used to incorporate air into foods such as eggs, cream, or sauces; to mix by beating with a whisk.

Work in: To combine two unlike ingredients, usually by the application of pressure.

Yield: The total amount of a product made from a specific recipe.

Zest: To remove strips of rind from a citrus fruit; the colored, outermost layer of citrus rind, used for flavoring creams, custards, and baked goods. Can be candied and used as a confection or decoration.

Conversion Chart

A pinch	=	⅛ teaspoon, or as much as you can hold between your thumb and forefinger
1 teaspoon	=	⅓ tablespoon
3 teaspoons	=	1 tablespoon
2 tablespoons	=	1 fluid ounce
4 tablespoons	=	¼ cup or 2 fluid ounces
5⅓ tablespoons	=	⅓ cup or 2⅔ fluid ounces
8 tablespoons	=	½ cup or 4 fluid ounces
16 tablespoons	=	1 cup
2 cups (liquid)	=	1 pint
4 cups (liquid)	=	1 quart
4 quarts	=	1 gallon
¼ cup	=	4 tablespoons
⅜ cup	=	¼ cup plus 2 tablespoons
⅝ cup	=	½ cup plus 2 tablespoons
⅞ cup	=	¾ cup plus 2 tablespoons
1 pound	=	16 ounces
½ pound	=	8 ounces
¼ pound	=	4 ounces

BUTTER

32 tablespoons (4 sticks)	=	16 ounces (1 pound)
16 tablespoons (2 sticks)	=	8 ounces (½ pound)
8 tablespoons (1 stick)	=	4 ounces (¼ pound)
4 tablespoons (½ stick)	=	2 ounces
2 tablespoons (¼ stick)	=	1 ounce

Bars and Squares

This is the chapter to start with if you are a novice baker. Bars and squares are the most forgiving desserts you can make. They are meant to look homey and just a bit unsophisticated. Slightly overmixing or overcooking them will give you a chewier, crustier result, while undercooking will make them a little moister inside. You don't expect bars and squares to rise very much, so you don't have to worry if they are puffy or flat. After you cut them and trim the edges they will look beautiful no matter what you've done to them—and they will taste just as good.

Like cookies, you can freeze bars and squares, pulling just what you need out of the freezer—they defrost in no time. One more thing: If you see a recipe that appeals to you except for the nuts (a good number of these recipes do contain nuts), you can leave them out in most cases. Here's a good rule of thumb: If the name of the nut is in the recipe title, it's probably not a good idea to leave the nuts out; otherwise, go for it. Also, feel free to substitute the kinds of nuts called for in the recipe; if you don't like pecans (or don't have any on hand), use walnuts or hazelnuts or even macadamia nuts.

Bar Talk
What Should I Do If . . .

The edges are hard? The bars may have overbaked. Next time set the timer for 10 minutes less than the baking time stated in the recipe. If the edges look crusty, but the middle is wet and jiggles slightly, cover the top loosely with aluminum foil and continue baking. The oven temperature may be too high. Make certain that you've set the oven to the right temperature. Use an accurate oven thermometer to make sure the oven thermostat is accurate—that what it says on the dial is the temperature of the oven. You may have used the wrong-size pan. This may have caused the batter to be spread too thin so that the edges cooked too fast and became brittle.

They're raw in the middle? Bars that are soft in the center will harden after they have cooled. On the first go-around, wait until the bars are cooled and cut. Then, if the batter is still raw-looking (oozing and semiliquid) after the bars have been thoroughly cooled, increase the baking time by 5 to 7 minutes next time. Don't let underbaked bars sit around—eat them right away, because you don't want the undercooked eggs in the batter to grow bacteria. You can try rebaking them in a preheated 375°F oven for 15 to 20 minutes, even after they are cut (but still in the pan). The edges might get a bit hard, but it's better than food poisoning.

I want to cut the bars into the same size? I have to confess that I'm not as compulsive as many of my peers who want each brownie exactly the same size. Maybe that's because I liked fighting with my sibling over who got the biggest one. The secrets to same-size bars are some math skills and a ruler (some folks stick toothpicks in to mark the measurements before cutting. I don't have time for that; I'd rather eat uneven brownies). A 9-inch pan is easy. You just measure nine 3-inch squares; you can do this by making two equidistant cuts from top to bottom and two from side to side. If those are too big, you can cut them in half to make 18 rectangles. With a 9 by 13-inch baking pan, cut off that last inch on the long side and eat it so that the cake measures 9 inches by 12 inches. Then you make four cuts at 3-inch intervals on the long side and three 3-inch cuts on the short side. This will give you twelve 3-inch squares. If you wish, cut the squares in half to make twenty-four 3 by 1½-inch bars. Whew!

I want to make smaller or larger bars? See above.

I'm having trouble getting them out of the pan? You know the saying "the first cut is the deepest"? Well, in baking it's "the first cut is the hardest." After running the tip of a knife around the rim to free the sides, cut the bars, then use an offset spatula to dislodge the first bar. The rest should be easy to remove. A helpful hint: Be sure to cut the bars all the way through to the bottom of the pan. If you are afraid of scratching the pan, use the bottom edge of a metal spatula (the offset one is perfect) to cut the bars, instead of a knife.

The bars crumble or fall apart when I cut them? Overcooked and dry bars will crumble, and cutting bars while they are still warm will make them fall apart.

I want to make them look fancy? After the bars have cooled and before they are cut, you have several options for dressing them up. You can place some cocoa powder or confectioners' sugar in a fine-mesh sieve and dust the surface lightly. Hold the sieve over the pan and tap your fingers against the rim. Resist the temptation to shower on a heavy coating, as most of it will fall off. Another option is to drizzle melted dark or white chocolate over the surface. The easiest way to do this is to melt 1 cup semisweet chocolate or white chocolate chips plus 4 tablespoons unsalted butter in the microwave or in a double boiler (see page 16). When melted, stir or whisk until smooth, then dip the end of the whisk into the chocolate and tap it with your hand so the chocolate splatters and drips over the surface of the uncut bars. Allow the chocolate to cool and harden before cutting the cake into bars. Another really easy trick to making plain squares and bars (and cookies, too, for that matter) look fancy is to place them on a doily-covered serving plate or pretty tray.

I want to make them now and eat them later? Bars and squares will keep at least a week in an airtight container stored at room temperature. They can also be frozen in plastic containers with snap-on lids for several months. Defrost them, still covered, at room temperature. Refrigeration is not a good idea, since they will pick up the odors of other food in the refrigerator, and they may become soggy as well.

I want to leave out the nuts/raisins/coconut? My youngest son hates anything with a crunchy texture—mostly nuts—so I simply leave them out. You can do the same with raisins and coconut if they are not an essential part of the recipe. In other words, leaving walnuts out of chocolate chip cookies is fine, but it's not a good idea to leave the ground almonds out of a cookie recipe that uses nuts in place of, or in addition to, flour. Leaving raisins out of hermit bars won't make a big difference, and leaving coconut off fluffy white frosting is fine. It's probably not such a great idea to leave the coconut out of the bars that have coconut in the name of the recipe. It's better to pick another recipe.

I want to make them chewy, fudgy, or cakelike? Some people like their bars chewy, some like theirs cakey, some like them rich and sweet and, when chocolate is one of the key ingredients, many like them fudgy. Have you ever wondered what makes the consistency of bars different one from another? Probably not. But now that I've mentioned it, once you know what makes those differences, you can look at a recipe and, more often than not, tell if it's going to result in a cakey, chewy, rich, or fudgy bar or square.

The cakelike consistency in Birthday Cake Brownies, page 61, is due to the fact that there is less chocolate, butter, and sugar than you'll find in Fantasy Brownies, page 59. Also, a longer time spent creaming the butter and sugar before adding the eggs gives these brownies a lightness you won't find in their fudgy or rich cousins.

Chewy bars, such as Cranberry Granola Bars, page 72, have a higher ratio of flour to fat (oil in this case), less sugar, and fewer eggs than the rich or fudgy bars. Ingredients such as dried fruit, oats, liquid sweeteners (molasses, corn syrup, honey), and light and dark brown sugars contribute to the chewiness, as well.

The rich (or fudgy) personality of the Fantasy Brownie, as well as the Lemon Squares, page 67, and Pecan Mini Pies, page 79, is directly related to the higher amounts of butter and sugar and the lower amount or absence of flour and other dry ingredients such as oats or nuts. Baking time can be a factor too: The longer the bars bake, the drier they will be. Sometimes bars will be intentionally underbaked, which means they will remain gooey in the center, even after they have cooled.

Fantasy Brownies

Makes: 18 brownies

What you'll need:

9 × 13-inch baking pan

sharp, heavy knife for chopping chocolate

microwave or small metal bowl and pan of simmering water, for melting chocolate and butter

whisk or mixing spoon

hand-held electric mixer

Baking time: 20 minutes

Everyone has a favorite brownie—the one by which all others are judged. My fantasy brownie has to glow with a pure chocolate taste, be heartbreakingly rich, creamy to the point of almost melting, and satisfying enough that one (okay, two) is enough to subdue any cravings. My fantasy brownie doesn't have nuts to interrupt the chocolate experience. Well, after that buildup, you're thinking that I'd better deliver the goods. You can e-mail me at *Blanche007@aol.com* if you want to tell me how close to your mark I've come.

FOR PREPARING THE PAN

1 tablespoon unsalted butter or solid vegetable shortening, softened

FOR THE BROWNIES

6 ounces (6 squares) unsweetened chocolate, chopped (see Lora Says and page 16)

2 sticks (16 tablespoons) unsalted butter

4 extra-large eggs

1 cup granulated sugar

1 cup packed light brown sugar

1 cup all-purpose flour

Scant ½ teaspoon salt

1. Preheat the oven to 375°F with a rack in the center of the oven. Coat the inside of the baking pan with the butter or solid vegetable shortening. Set aside.

2. Melt the chocolate with the butter either in the microwave or in a small metal mixing bowl set over, but not touching, a pan of gently simmering water. Use a whisk or a mixing spoon to combine the two, then set aside to cool slightly.

3. Break the eggs into a large mixing bowl. Stir in the granulated and light brown sugar. With the mixer on high speed, beat the eggs and sugars together until light and fluffy, 3 to 4 minutes. Move the beaters around the bowl, and scrape down the sides of the bowl with a rubber spatula several times while mixing. On low speed, beat in the flour and salt, and mix together only until all traces of white disappear. Mix in the chocolate and butter mixture on low speed until the chocolate is just incorporated.

4. Pour and scrape the batter into the prepared pan and smooth the top with a rubber spatula. Bake for 20 minutes, or until the brownies are cooked around the edges and just firm in the center. Remove the brownies from the oven and allow them to cool in the pan before cutting into 18 portions.

5. The bars can be stored in a covered tin at room temperature for up to 1 week. To freeze, allow them to cool completely after baking, then spread them on a baking sheet and place in the freezer for at least 3 hours. When the bars are thoroughly frozen, stack them in a freezer-strength recloseable gallon-size plastic bag for up to 3 months. Use a waterproof marker to note the contents of the bag and the date. Defrost them in the bag at room temperature for 1 to 2 hours.

LORA SAYS: Unsweetened chocolate delivers the biggest flavor, which can be diluted when sugar, milk, or flavorings are added to chocolate. These days, you have choices in brands of unsweetened chocolate. Callebaut and Valrhona are two of my favorites; they can be found in many gourmet food stores and by mail order from Dairy Fresh Candies (see page 316). Unsweetened chocolate will keep in a cool, dry place—but not the refrigerator or freezer—for several years.

LORA SAYS: Eggs get beaten for a long time here because they are the only leavening in the recipe. The air bubbles caused by the mixing expand during baking, causing the bars to rise ever so slightly.

Birthday Cake Brownies

Makes: 16 bars

What you'll need:

9-inch square baking pan

scissors for cutting parchment paper or aluminum foil for lining the pan

parchment paper or aluminum foil for lining the pan

mesh sieve

Microwave or small metal bowl and pan of simmering water, for melting chocolate

hand-held electric mixer

cake tester

wire rack

Baking time: 25 to 30 minutes

If you are looking for lighter, more delicate brownies, then try these. I like to serve them under a scoop of vanilla ice cream with some hot fudge sauce dribbled on top. They got their name from a friend of mine who wanted a huge brownie for a birthday cake.

FOR PREPARING THE PAN

1½ tablespoons unsalted butter or solid vegetable shortening, softened

FOR THE BROWNIES

2⅓ cups all-purpose flour

½ teaspoon baking powder

½ teaspoon salt

4 ounces (4 squares) unsweetened chocolate

½ stick (4 tablespoons) unsalted butter, softened

¾ cup granulated sugar

1 tablespoon light corn syrup

2 extra-large eggs

2 teaspoons pure vanilla extract

¼ cup milk

1. Preheat the oven to 350°F with a rack in the center of the oven. Coat the inside of the baking pan with some of the butter or solid vegetable shortening. Cut a piece of parchment paper or aluminum foil to fit neatly into the bottom of the pan, place it in the pan, then coat the parchment paper or aluminum foil liner. Set aside.

2. Place a mesh sieve over a medium mixing bowl and add the flour, baking powder, and salt. Shake the contents into the bowl and set aside.

3. Melt the chocolate either in the microwave or in a small metal mixing bowl set over, but not touching, a pan of gently simmering water. Set aside to cool slightly.

4. Place the butter and sugar in a large mixing bowl. With the mixer on high speed, beat the butter with the sugar for 5 minutes until it is light and fluffy. Beat in the corn syrup, then add the eggs, one at a time, making sure the first is completely incorporated before adding the second. Move the beaters around the bowl, and scrape down the sides of the bowl with a rubber spatula while mixing. Add the vanilla and milk. The mixture may look curdled, but that's okay. Reduce the mixer speed to low and beat in the melted chocolate. Continue beating for 1 minute so that the mixture thickens slightly.

5. Use a rubber spatula to fold the flour mixture into the chocolate mixture. Mix only until no traces of flour remain. Pour and scrape the batter into the prepared pan and smooth the top with a rubber spatula. Bake for 25 to 30 minutes, or until the top is dry and a cake tester inserted into the center of the cake comes out clean and dry. Remove the pan from the oven and set it on a wire rack to cool completely. You may cut the brownies in the pan, or invert the pan onto a cutting board, remove the parchment paper or aluminum foil liner, and cut them into 16 squares with a long, serrated knife.

6. The bars can be stored in a covered tin at room temperature for up to 1 week. To freeze, allow them to cool completely after baking, then spread them on a baking sheet and place in the freezer for at least 3 hours. When the bars are thoroughly frozen, stack them in a freezer-strength recloseable gallon-size plastic bag for up to 3 months. Use a waterproof marker to note the contents of the bag and the date. Defrost them in the bag at room temperature for 1 to 2 hours.

Blondies

● ●

Makes: 16 bars

What you'll need:

9-inch square baking pan

scissors for cutting parchment paper or aluminum foil for lining the pan

parchment paper or aluminum foil for lining the pan

baking sheet for toasting pecans

sharp, heavy knife for chopping pecans

mesh sieve

medium saucepan

whisk

mixing spoon

cake tester

wire rack

Baking time: 25 to 30 minutes

Blondies are brownies that don't have any chocolate. The combination of light and dark brown sugars combines with toasted pecans to make a butterscotch bar that is both rich and sweet.

FOR PREPARING THE PAN

1½ tablespoons unsalted butter or solid vegetable shortening, softened

FOR THE BLONDIES

1¼ cups all-purpose flour

½ teaspoon salt

1 stick (8 tablespoons) unsalted butter

1 cup packed light brown sugar

½ cup packed dark brown sugar

2 extra-large eggs

1 tablespoon pure vanilla extract

1 cup pecans, toasted and coarsely chopped (see pages 18–19)

1. Preheat the oven to 350°F with a rack in the center of the oven. Use some of the butter or solid vegetable shortening to coat the inside of the baking pan. Cut a piece of parchment paper or aluminum foil to fit into the bottom of the pan, place it in the pan, then coat the parchment paper or aluminum foil liner. Set aside.

2. Place a mesh sieve over a small mixing bowl and add the flour and salt. Shake the contents into the bowl and set aside.

3. Place the butter and the light and dark brown sugar in a medium saucepan set over medium heat. Whisk the mixture until the sugar dissolves, and continue to whisk until the mixture starts to bubble and becomes smooth. Remove the saucepan from the heat and let it cool for about 15 minutes, stirring occasionally, until you can touch the pan surface with your hand. Use a wooden spoon to stir in the eggs, vanilla, flour mixture, and nuts. Make sure that all the ingredients are well incorporated, but don't overbeat the mixture. Pour and scrape the batter into the prepared pan and smooth the top with a rubber spatula.

4. Bake the blondies for 25 to 30 minutes, or until a cake tester inserted into the center comes out clean, but with a few moist crumbs. Remove the pan from the oven and place it on a wire rack so that the blondies cool completely in the pan. You may cut the blondies in the pan, or invert the pan onto a cutting board, remove the parchment paper or aluminum foil liner, and cut them into 16 squares.

5. The bars can be stored in a covered tin at room temperature for up to 1 week. To freeze, allow them to cool completely after baking, then spread them on a baking sheet and place in the freezer for at least 3 hours. When the bars are thoroughly frozen, stack them in a freezer-strength recloseable gallon-size plastic bag for up to 3 months. Use a waterproof marker to note the contents of the bag and the date. Defrost them in the bag at room temperature for 1 to 2 hours.

Sticky Hands Caramel Bars

Makes: 18 bars

What you'll need:

9-inch square baking pan

baking sheet for toasting pecans

sharp, heavy knife for chopping pecans

hand-held electric mixer

wire rack

Baking time: 45 minutes

Talk about buttery, sweet, melt-in-your-mouth caramel madness. These bars have no leavening, so they are as dense as can be. Don't be tempted to cut them until they've had a chance to set up in the refrigerator.

FOR PREPARING THE PAN

1 tablespoon unsalted butter or solid vegetable shortening, softened

FOR THE CARAMEL BARS

2 sticks (16 tablespoons) unsalted butter, softened

2 cups packed dark brown sugar

2 extra-large eggs

1 tablespoon pure vanilla extract

1¼ cups all-purpose flour

1½ cups pecan halves, toasted and coarsely chopped (see pages 18–19)

1. Preheat the oven to 350°F with a rack in the center of the oven. Use the butter or vegetable shortening to coat the inside of the baking pan. Set aside.

2. Place the butter and dark brown sugar in a large mixing bowl. With the mixer on high speed, beat the butter and sugar together until the mixture is light and fluffy, about 2 minutes. Add the eggs, one at a time, making sure the first is completely incorporated before adding the second. Move the beaters around the bowl and scrape down the sides of the bowl with a rubber spatula several times while mixing. Reduce the speed to low and mix in the vanilla and flour, and mix just until there are no traces of flour remaining. Add the nuts and mix them in.

3. Pour and scrape the batter into the prepared pan and smooth the top with a rubber spatula. Bake for 45 minutes, or until the sides of the batter have risen up slightly more than the center and the top is shiny and dry. The interior of the batter will still be quite soft—almost liquid. Remove the pan from the oven and place the pan on a rack to cool for 30 minutes, then place it in the refrigerator for 2 hours, or until it is very cold. Use a sharp knife to cut the bars into a 3 by 3-inch grid, and then cut each bar in half to make 18 bars.

4. The bars can be stored in a covered tin at room temperature for up to 1 week. To freeze, allow them to cool completely after baking, then spread them on a baking sheet and place in the freezer for at least 3 hours. When the bars are thoroughly frozen, stack them in a freezer-strength recloseable gallon-size plastic bag for up to 3 months. Use a waterproof marker to note the contents of the bag and the date. Defrost them in the bag at room temperature for 1 to 2 hours.

LORA SAYS: It's important to resist cutting into these until they have had a chance to cool completely. If you're in a big hurry, you can stick the pan in the freezer after it's cooled for 15 minutes at room temperature. It will take about 40 minutes in the freezer or 3 hours at room temperature to cool the inside enough so the bars can be cut.

Lemon Squares

Makes: 16 squares

What you'll need:

9-inch square baking pan

food processor or recloseable gallon-size plastic bag and heavy rolling pin or saucepan for crushing crackers

microwave or small saucepan for melting butter

citrus zester

citrus reamer

fine-mesh sieve for straining lemon juice

mixing spoon and rubber spatula

hand-held electric mixer

small sieve for dusting with confectioners' sugar

Baking time: 35 minutes

A friend of my mother's would serve these lemon squares at their bridge games. My mother, knowing how I loved them, would bring some home for me. I thought they were the most sophisticated pastries I'd ever seen; they conjured up images of ladies drinking tea from delicate china cups with pinkies in the air, and doilies on polished silver trays. I still reserve them for slightly more formal occasions, but if you're craving a tart, lemony, butter-rich treat, go for it.

FOR THE CRUST

1½ cups graham cracker crumbs (about 10 whole crackers, crushed)

1 stick (8 tablespoons) unsalted butter, melted

FOR THE FILLING

3 extra-large eggs

1 cup granulated sugar

1 teaspoon baking powder

Pinch of salt

Finely grated zest of 2 lemons

⅓ cup fresh lemon juice, strained

About ¼ cup confectioners' sugar

1. Preheat the oven to 350°F with a rack in the center of the oven.

2. Place the graham cracker crumbs and the melted butter in a medium mixing bowl. Use a wooden spoon or a rubber spatula to mix them together thoroughly. Scrape the mixture into the baking pan, and use your fingers to press the mixture evenly onto the bottom of the pan. Bake for 10 minutes, then remove the pan from the oven to cool while you make the lemon filling. Keep the oven at temperature setting.

3. Break the eggs into a large mixing bowl, then add the granulated sugar. With the mixer on high speed, beat the mixture until it is light yellow and almost doubled in volume, about 3 minutes. Move the beaters around the bowl and scrape down the sides with a rubber spatula several times while mixing. Add the baking powder and salt, and beat on low speed until just mixed, scraping down the sides of the bowl. Beat in the lemon zest and juice.

4. Pour and scrape the filling into the crust and smooth the top with a rubber spatula. Bake for 25 minutes, or until the top is golden brown and wiggles only slightly when the pan is moved. Remove the pan from the oven and allow it to cool. Place confectioners' sugar in a small sieve and sprinkle generously over the top of the cooled filling. Cut into 16 squares.

5. The squares can be refrigerated, covered securely with plastic wrap, for up to 1 week. To freeze, allow them to cool completely after baking. Do not dust with confectioners' sugar. Spread them on a baking sheet and place in the freezer for at least 3 hours. When the bars are thoroughly frozen, stack them in a plastic bag for up to 3 months. Use a waterproof marker to note the contents of the bag and the date. Defrost them in the bag at room temperature for 1 to 2 hours. Dust with confectioners' sugar before serving.

LORA SAYS: Using only the colored zest of a lemon or any citrus fruit will give you the most assertive taste. The white part right under the zest, called the pith, has a bitter taste, and that's why it's important to grate only the outermost surface.

LORA SAYS: When a recipe calls for both zest and juice of a lemon, lime, or orange, it's easier to use a citrus zester to remove the zest before you cut the fruit and squeeze it. You can get more juice out by first rolling the fruit on the counter several times with the flat of your hand. There is no substitute for the taste of freshly squeezed lemon juice. Don't even think about using anything from a bottle or a plastic, lemon-shaped container.

Apricot-Nut Bars

Makes: 20 bars

What you'll need:

9-inch square baking pan

scissors for cutting parchment paper or aluminum foil for lining the pan

parchment paper or aluminum foil for lining the pan

food processor or sharp, heavy knife for finely chopping nuts

mesh sieve

hand-held electric mixer

wire rack

small sieve for dusting with confectioners' sugar

Baking time: 40 minutes

If you need something on the elegant side with a hint of sophistication, then look no further.

FOR PREPARING THE PAN

1½ tablespoons unsalted butter or solid vegetable shortening, softened

FOR THE BARS

1½ cups walnuts or slivered blanched almonds (see page 47)

½ cup plus 3 tablespoons granulated sugar

1 cup all-purpose flour

½ teaspoon baking powder

½ teaspoon ground cinnamon

⅛ teaspoon ground cloves

⅛ teaspoon salt

1½ sticks (12 tablespoons) unsalted butter, softened

¾ teaspoon pure vanilla extract

2 extra-large egg yolks (see page 12)

1 cup apricot preserves (one 10- to 12-ounce jar)

Confectioners' sugar

1. Coat the inside of the baking pan with the butter or solid vegetable shortening. Cut a piece of parchment paper or aluminum foil to fit into the bottom of the pan, place it in the pan, then coat the parchment paper or aluminum foil liner. Set aside.

2. Place the nuts and 3 tablespoons sugar in the bowl of a food processor fitted with the metal blade. Pulse several times to coarsely chop the nuts, then process the nuts until they are finely ground. Watch carefully, as you do not want to pulverize the nuts into nut butter. Set aside. (You may chop the nuts by hand, with a knife; see page 19 for instructions. It will take some time, because you need to chop the nuts as finely as possible.) Mix in the 3 table-spoons of sugar after chopping the nuts.

3. Place a mesh sieve over a small mixing bowl and add the flour, baking powder, cinnamon, cloves, and salt. Shake the contents into the bowl and set aside.

4. Place the butter, ½ cup sugar, and the vanilla in a large mixing bowl. With the mixer on high speed, beat the ingredients together until the mixture is light and fluffy, about 2 minutes. Move the beaters around the bowl and scrape down the sides of the bowl with a spatula several times while mixing. Reduce the mixer speed to medium and add the egg yolks. Beat until they are thoroughly incorporated, scraping the bowl as you work. With the mixer on low speed, beat in the reserved nut mixture and the flour mixture. Beat just until blended.

5. Measure out half of the batter and spread it in the prepared pan. Spread the preserves carefully over the top, using a rubber spatula or a small offset spatula to smooth them evenly. Use your fingers to drop teaspoon-size bits of the reserved batter over the surface of the preserves. Refrigerate the pan for 20 minutes.

6. When you are ready to bake the bars, preheat the oven to 350°F with a rack in the center of the oven. Remove the pan from the refrigerator and bake for about 40 minutes until the preserves begin to bubble and the crust is just firm to the touch. Remove the pan from the oven and place it on a wire rack to cool completely. Cut the cake into a 4 by 5 grid, to make 20 bars. Remove the bars from the pan and place them on a serving plate. Dust the tops with confectioners' sugar.

7. The bars can be stored in a covered tin at room temperature for up to 1 week. To freeze, allow them to cool completely after baking. Do not dust with confectioners' sugar. Spread them on a baking sheet and place in the freezer for at least 3 hours. When the bars are thoroughly frozen, stack them in a freezer-strength recloseable gallon-size plastic bag for up to 3 months. Use a waterproof marker to note the contents of the bag and the date. Defrost them in the bag at room temperature for 1 to 2 hours.

LORA SAYS: Ground spices lose their potency and flavor within a few months after opening the jar or can. You can maximize their shelf life by storing them in tinted jars with lids tightly closed in a cool, dry place—not in clear jars on top of your stove.

LORA SAYS: Jams and preserves can be removed from the jar and will spread easier when warm. Place the open jar in the microwave for 15 to 20 seconds, or just until the contents feel warm.

LORA SAYS: You can buy ground almonds in gourmet stores and from catalogs such as the King Arthur Flour Baker's Catalogue (see page 316).

LORA SAYS: The key to grinding nuts in the food processor is to do about a cup at a time, and not to grind the point where the oil starts separating from the nuts and you end up with nut butter. Use the pulse button for more control; it flings the nuts upward with each pulse, which aerates the mass and prevents overgrinding.

LORA SAYS: If a recipe calls for dusting the surface with confectioners' sugar and you plan to refrigerate the dessert before you serve it, hold off on adding the confectioners' sugar until just before serving. The sugar will melt from the condensation in the refrigerator.

Cranberry Granola Bars

Makes: 24 bars

What you'll need:

9 × 13-inch baking pan

scissors for cutting the parchment paper or aluminum foil for lining the pan

parchment paper or aluminum foil for lining the pan

baking sheet for toasting wheat germ

mesh sieve

mixing spoon

wire rack

small, sharp knife for loosening bars from pan

baking pan for inverting bars

long, sharp knife for cutting bars

Baking time: 35 minutes

What could be more American (besides brownies, of course) than granola bars? These are a million times better than the packaged kind you find in the health food store. If you wish, substitute an equal amount of raisins or dried cherries for the cranberries, and add ½ cup of chocolate chips to the batter as well.

FOR PREPARING THE PAN

1½ tablespoons unsalted butter or solid vegetable shortening, softened

FOR THE BARS

1¼ cups all-purpose flour

1 teaspoon salt

½ teaspoon ground cinnamon

½ teaspoon ground nutmeg

2 cups oats, old-fashioned or quick-cooking (see page 46)

1 cup packed dark brown sugar

1 cup dried cranberries

½ cup slivered blanched almonds

½ cup toasted wheat germ (see Lora Says)

½ cup vegetable oil

½ cup honey

2 teaspoons almond extract

2 extra-large eggs, lightly beaten

1. Preheat the oven to 350°F with a rack in the center of the oven. Coat the inside of the baking pan with butter or solid vegetable shortening. Cut a piece of parchment paper or aluminum foil to fit into the bottom of the pan, place it in the pan, then coat the parchment paper or aluminum foil liner. Set aside.

2. Place a mesh sieve over a large mixing bowl and add the flour, salt, cinnamon, and nutmeg. Shake the contents into the bowl. Add the oats, dark brown sugar, cranberries, almonds, and wheat germ. Stir the ingredients together well with a wooden spoon. Place the oil, honey, almond extract, and eggs in a separate bowl and stir them together well. Add the oil mixture to the oat mixture and stir together with a wooden spoon or, even better, your hands. Moisten your hands first with water to keep the dough from sticking to them. Mix everything together until there are no lumps of flour or oats remaining. Scrape the mixture into the prepared pan, then use a rubber spatula or your hands to pat the mixture evenly into the pan.

3. Bake for 35 minutes, or until golden brown around the edges. Place the pan on a wire rack to cool to room temperature. When it has cooled, run a sharp knife around the edge of the pan, then place a baking sheet over it. Invert the pan onto the sheet, then remove the pan. Peel off and discard the parchment paper or aluminum foil liner. Use a long, sharp serrated knife to cut the bars lengthwise into 4 strips, then cut each strip into 6 bars. Serve the bars right side up.

4. The bars can be stored in a covered tin at room temperature for up to 1 week. To freeze, allow them to cool completely after baking. Spread them on a baking sheet and place in the freezer for at least 3 hours. When the bars are thoroughly frozen, stack them in a plastic bag for up to 3 months. Use a waterproof marker to note the contents of the bag and the date. Defrost them in the bag at room temperature for 1 to 2 hours.

LORA SAYS: Cutting the bars bottom side up reduces crumbs and helps prevent the crust from cracking. Use a heavy, serrated knife so that you are cutting the bars, not just pushing them apart.

LORA SAYS: To toast wheat germ, spread the wheat germ in a thin layer on a baking sheet and place in a preheated 350°F oven for 10 to 15 minutes, or until lightly browned. Cool completely in the pan before using or storing.

Sam's Mint Squares

Makes: 16 squares

What you'll need:

9-inch square baking pan

sharp, heavy knife for chopping chocolate

microwave or small metal bowl and pan of simmering water, for melting chocolate

mesh sieve

hand-held electric mixer

mixing spoon

offset metal spatula

Baking time: 30 minutes

My youngest son, Sam, has loved these rich, fudgy mint squares since he was old enough to say, "I want more." Be careful when adding the green food coloring to the frosting, a little goes a long way. Remember: You're going for the delicate, pale, barely tinted look, not the deep-woods-in-summer look.

FOR PREPARING THE PAN

1 tablespoon unsalted butter or solid vegetable shortening, softened

FOR THE MINT SQUARES

3 ounces (3 squares) unsweetened chocolate, chopped

1½ sticks (12 tablespoons) unsalted butter, softened

¾ cup plus 2 tablespoons all-purpose flour

¾ teaspoon baking soda

½ teaspoon salt

½ cup granulated sugar

½ cup packed light brown sugar

2 extra-large eggs

1 teaspoon peppermint extract (see page 49)

1½ cups mint chocolate chips

FOR THE FROSTING

1 cup confectioners' sugar (if sugar is lumpy, sift first, then measure)

3 to 4 tablespoons milk

1½ teaspoons peppermint extract

2 to 3 drops green food coloring (optional)

1. Preheat the oven to 350°F with a rack in the center of the oven. Use the butter or solid vegetable shortening to butter or oil the insides of the baking pan. Set aside.

2. To make the cake, melt the unsweetened chocolate with the butter either in the microwave or in a small metal mixing bowl set over, but not touching, a pan of gently simmering water. Set it aside to cool for 10 minutes.

3. Place a mesh sieve over a small mixing bowl and add the flour, baking soda, and salt. Shake the contents into the bowl and set aside.

4. In a large mixing bowl, combine the granulated sugar, brown sugar, and eggs. With the mixer on medium speed, beat until light and fluffy, about 3 minutes. Move the beaters around the bowl and scrape down the sides of the bowl with a rubber spatula several times while mixing. Reduce the mixer speed to low, and beat in the peppermint extract and the cooled melted chocolate mixture. Add the flour mixture and the mint chocolate chips and mix together, on low speed, just until incorporated.

5. Pour and scrape the mixture in the prepared pan and smooth the top with a rubber spatula. Bake for 30 minutes, or until the top is dry and shiny. Don't use a cake tester, as the interior will be somewhat runny when the cake is done.

6. While the cake is baking, prepare the frosting. Place the confectioners' sugar in a small mixing bowl and add enough of the milk to form a paste the consistency of heavy cream. Stir in the peppermint extract and the food coloring, if you are using it. Stir well to combine, then cover the frosting until you are ready to use it.

7. When the cake is done, remove it from the oven and let it cool in the pan for 10 minutes. Scrape the frosting onto the still-warm cake and spread it evenly with an offset metal spatula. Let the frosted cake cool completely, then cut it into 16 squares.

8. The bars can be stored in a covered tin at room temperature for up to 1 week. Cushion the bars between layers of plastic wrap or wax paper to protect the frosting. To freeze, allow them to cool completely after baking, then spread them on a baking sheet and place in the freezer for at least 3 hours. When the bars are thoroughly frozen, stack them in a freezer-strength recloseable gallon-size plastic bag for up to 3 months. Use a waterproof marker to note the contents of the bag and the date. Defrost them in the bag at room temperature for 1 to 2 hours.

LORA SAYS: Baking chips are available in a wonderful assortment of flavors from white, milk, dark, and mint chocolate to espresso, peanut butter, and butterscotch.

Cappuccino Bars

Makes: 20 bars

What you'll need:

9-inch square baking pan

baking sheet for toasting pecans

sharp, heavy knife for chopping pecans

mesh sieve

hand-held electric mixer

mixing spoon

Baking time: 30 minutes

No, they don't have a frothy milk head, but these pretty bars do pack a wallop like a mild cup of java. Coffee-flavored chocolate chips can be found in gourmet and confectionery stores. A company called Cloud Nine makes heavenly espresso-flavored chocolate chips that are available in some supermarkets and upscale grocery stores. Other coffee-flavored chips can be found in the King Arthur Flour Baker's Catalogue (see page 316).

FOR PREPARING THE PAN

1 tablespoon unsalted butter or solid vegetable shortening, softened

FOR THE BARS

1 cup all-purpose flour

½ teaspoon salt

½ teaspoon baking powder

¼ teaspoon baking soda

1 stick (8 tablespoons) unsalted butter, softened

1 cup packed light brown sugar

1 extra-large egg

2 teaspoons pure vanilla extract

1 cup coffee-flavored chocolate chips

1 cup pecans, toasted and coarsely chopped (see pages 18–19)

1. Preheat the oven to 350°F with a rack in the center of the oven. Use the butter or solid vegetable shortening to butter or oil the insides of the baking pan. Set aside.

2. Place a mesh sieve over a medium mixing bowl and add the flour, salt, baking powder, and baking soda. Shake the contents into the bowl and set aside.

3. Place the butter and brown sugar in a large mixing bowl. With the mixer on medium speed, cream the butter and brown sugar until smooth and fluffy, about 2 minutes. Add the egg and vanilla, and continue to beat on medium speed. Move the beaters around the bowl and scrape down the sides of the bowl with a rubber spatula several times while mixing. The mixture will look curdled at first, but that's okay; it will become smooth as you beat longer. Add the flour mixture, and beat on low until no traces of flour remain. Use a wooden spoon or a rubber spatula to stir in the chips and nuts.

4. Scrape the batter into the prepared pan and smooth the top with a rubber spatula. Press the batter evenly into the corners; it will form a rather thin layer. Bake for 30 minutes until golden on top and the batter has pulled away slightly from the sides of the pan. Remove the pan from the oven and while still hot, cut into a 4 by 5 grid, to make 20 bars. Cool the bars completely before removing them from the pan.

5. The bars can be stored in a covered tin at room temperature for up to 1 week. To freeze, allow them to cool completely after baking, then spread them on a baking sheet and place in the freezer for at least 3 hours. When the bars are thoroughly frozen, stack them in a freezer-strength recloseable gallon-size plastic bag for up to 3 months. Use a waterproof marker to note the contents of the bag and the date. Defrost them in the bag at room temperature for 1 to 2 hours.

LORA SAYS: If you want a stronger coffee taste, add 1 rounded tablespoon instant coffee, or espresso powder or granules dissolved in 2 tablespoons water, along with the egg and vanilla.

Pecan Mini Pies

Makes: 12 mini pies

What you'll need:

12-hole regular muffin tin with ⅓-cup capacity holes

citrus zester

small, sharp knife for cutting up butter and loosening pies from tin

baking sheet for toasting pecans

mesh sieve

fork

2 table knives or pastry blender

hand-held electric mixer

whisk

baking sheet to place under muffin tin

Baking time: 35 to 40 minutes

Bet you can't eat more than one of these (at a time, that is). If you love pralines, you'll flip over these miniature pecan pies made in a muffin tin. Don't wait for Thanksgiving to indulge your craving for pecan pie.

FOR PREPARING THE PAN

2 tablespoons unsalted butter, softened

FOR THE CRUST

1½ cups all-purpose flour

⅓ cup confectioners' sugar (if sugar is lumpy, sift first, then measure)

½ teaspoon salt

1 tablespoon Lora Brody's Dough Relaxer, optional (see page 48)

Finely grated zest of 1 large lemon

1½ sticks (12 tablespoons) unsalted butter, chilled and cut into small pieces

FOR THE FILLING

1 extra-large egg

1 tablespoon unsalted butter, melted

¼ cup packed light brown sugar

¼ cup dark corn syrup

1½ cups pecan halves, toasted (see page 18)

1. Preheat the oven to 350°F with a rack in the center of the oven. Butter the holes of the muffin tin. For easy removal of the pies, butter the top surface of the tin as well. Set aside.

2. Place a mesh sieve over a mixing bowl and add the flour, confectioners' sugar, salt, and optional Dough Relaxer. Shake the contents into the bowl. Use a fork to stir in the lemon zest.

3. Scatter the butter pieces over the flour mixture. Use two regular table knives in a criss-cross motion, or a pastry blender, to cut the butter into the flour mixture until it resembles coarse crumbs. If you use a pastry blender, stop and clean between the wires with a table knife from time to time. Press and knead the dough together into a ball with your hands. It will be very crumbly at first. Divide the dough into twelve 1½- to 2-inch balls and drop one ball into each muffin hole. Flour your fingers and use them to push a ball of dough into the bottom of each hole and up the sides, slightly above the rim of the muffin hole, to form little shells. Place the muffin tin in the freezer while you prepare the filling.

4. Break the egg into a medium mixing bowl. Beat it lightly with a fork, then add the melted butter, light brown sugar, and corn syrup. With the mixer on medium speed, beat the mixture until it is light-colored and smooth, about 2 minutes. Move the beaters around the bowl, and scrape down the sides of the bowl several times with a rubber spatula while mixing. Transfer the filling mixture to a 1-cup measure with a spout and set it aside.

5. Remove the crusts from the freezer and bake for 20 minutes until lightly browned. Remove the pan from the oven and raise the oven temperature to 375°F. Divide the pecans among the crusts. Stir or whisk the filling mixture with a fork or a whisk, then pour the mixture over the nuts in each crust. Place the prepared tin on a baking sheet to catch any baking spills.

6. Bake for 15 to 20 minutes or until the filling is bubbling and hot. Remove the mini pies from the oven and allow them to cool completely in the pan. Use the tip of a small, sharp knife to release the edges, then slide the pies out of the muffin holes.

7. The mini pies can be stored in a covered tin at room temperature for up to 1 week. To freeze, allow them to cool completely after baking, then spread them on a baking sheet and place in the freezer for at least 3 hours. When the mini pies are thoroughly frozen, place them in a freezer-strength recloseable gallon-size plastic bag for up to 3 months. Use a waterproof marker to note the contents of the bag and the date. Defrost them in the bag at room temperature for 1 to 2 hours.

Layered Marbled Cheesecake Brownies

Makes: 24 brownies

What you'll need:

9 × 13-inch baking pan, 2 inches deep

sharp, heavy knife for chopping chocolate

microwave or small metal bowl and pan of simmering water, for melting chocolate with butter

whisk

hand-held electric mixer

mesh sieve

offset metal spatula (optional)

soup spoon

table knife

wire rack

Baking time: 35 to 40 minutes

ere you've got the best of both worlds: creamy cheesecake and rich, fudgy brownie. First there's a chocolate layer, then a vanilla cream cheese layer, and finally spoonfuls of chocolate batter are swirled into vanilla batter to create a marbled effect. These golden-topped, light and dark cream cheese squares are perfect for picnics or pickup desserts after a light meal. It's important to use regular cream cheese—not the whipped or low-fat kind.

FOR PREPARING THE PAN

2 tablespoons unsalted butter or solid vegetable shortening, softened

FOR THE CHOCOLATE BATTER

8 ounces bittersweet chocolate, chopped (see page 16)

1 stick (8 tablespoons) unsalted butter

4 extra-large eggs

1⅓ cups granulated sugar

1 cup all-purpose flour

1 teaspoon baking powder

½ teaspoon salt

FOR THE VANILLA BATTER

½ stick (4 tablespoons) unsalted butter, softened

⅔ cup (about 5½ ounces) cream cheese (not the whipped or reduced-fat variety), at room temperature

⅓ cup granulated sugar

2 extra-large eggs

3 tablespoons all-purpose flour

2 teaspoons pure vanilla extract

1. Preheat the oven to 350°F with a rack in the center of the oven. Use the butter or solid vegetable shortening to generously coat the inside of the baking pan. Set aside.

2. To prepare the chocolate batter, melt the chocolate with the butter either in the microwave or in a small metal mixing bowl set over, but not touching, a pan of gently simmering water. Whisk the mixture until it is smooth, then set it aside to cool for 5 minutes.

3. Place the eggs and sugar in a large mixing bowl. With the mixer on medium speed, beat the eggs and the sugar for 30 seconds to combine, then increase the speed to high and beat until light and fluffy, about 3 minutes. Scrape down the sides of the bowl with a rubber spatula several times as you work. Place a fine-mesh sieve over the bowl and put in the flour, baking powder, and salt. Shake the flour mixture over the butter mixture. Mix on low speed until just combined. Add the cooled chocolate mixture and continue to mix on low speed until combined. Pour and scrape 2 cups of the chocolate batter into a 2-cup measure and set aside. Spread the remaining chocolate batter over the bottom of the prepared pan and smooth it with a rubber spatula or an offset spatula.

4. To make the vanilla batter, place the butter and cream cheese in another large, clean mixing bowl. Clean the beaters and, with the mixer on high speed, beat the butter with the cream cheese until smooth, about 1 minute. Add the sugar and beat for another 3 minutes, scraping down the sides of the bowl with a rubber spatula as you work. Add the eggs and flour, and beat for about 1 minute until they are incorporated. Scrape the bowl well.

Reduce the mixer speed to low and beat in the vanilla. The mixture will appear curdled, but that's okay. Pour and scrape the vanilla batter over the chocolate batter in the pan. Smooth the top with a rubber or offset spatula.

5. Use a soup spoon and a rubber spatula to drop 9 dollops of the reserved chocolate batter onto the vanilla batter. Place the dollops evenly, spaced about 1½ inches apart. Draw a table knife through the layer of chocolate dollops and the vanilla layer to create a marbled design. Don't overdo it or you'll lose the effect of marbling.

6. Bake the brownies for 35 to 40 minutes, or until the vanilla batter on top is golden brown, the edges of the cake are a deep golden brown, and the surface has cracked slightly. Remove the pan from the oven and cool to room temperature on a wire rack. When the pan has cooled completely, cut the brownies into 24 bars.

7. The brownies can be stored at room temperature, covered, for up to 24 hours, or refrigerated for 3 to 4 days. They may also be frozen. To freeze, allow them to cool completely after baking, then spread them on a baking sheet and place in the freezer for at least 3 hours. When the bars are thoroughly frozen, stack them in freezer-strength recloseable gallon-size plastic bags for up to 3 months. Use a waterproof marker to note the contents of the bags and the date. Defrost them in the bags at room temperature for 1 to 2 hours.

LORA SAYS: These look beautiful served either by themselves or on a plate filled with other "pickup" desserts, such as Lemon Squares and Apricot-Almond Bars.

LORA SAYS: It's important to use bittersweet (or even extra-bittersweet chocolate if you can find it; Lindt makes an excellent bar) to give some balance to the sweetness of the cheesecake part of these brownies.

Heavenly Oatmeal Bars

Makes: about fifty-four
2 × 1-inch bars

What you'll need:

9 × 13-inch baking pan

hand-held electric mixer

mixing spoon

wire rack

small, heavy saucepan

Baking time: 16 minutes

This special recipe comes from the Jordan Pond House in Acadia National Park in Maine. If you ever have the chance to visit in the summer when the Pond House is open, enjoy afternoon tea with a plate of scones and homemade strawberry jam, which is served on the veranda or on the sweeping lawn with its view of the ocean. Finish up with a plate of these oatmeal bars, which will make you think about moving to Maine (just for the summer . . .).

FOR PREPARING THE PAN

1 tablespoon unsalted butter or solid vegetable shortening, softened

FOR THE BARS

2 sticks (16 tablespoons) unsalted butter, softened

1⅓ cups packed dark brown sugar

¾ cup light corn syrup

2 teaspoons pure vanilla extract

5⅓ cups oats, old-fashioned or quick-cooking (see page 46)

FOR THE GLAZE

1¾ cups semisweet chocolate chips

1 cup smooth peanut butter

1. Preheat the oven to 350°F with a rack in the center of the oven. Use the butter or solid shortening to coat the inside of the baking pan. Set aside.

2. In a large mixing bowl, beat the butter with the mixer on high speed until creamy. Gradually add the dark brown sugar and continue to beat until light and fluffy, about 2 minutes.

Some little nuggets of dark brown sugar may remain in the mixture, but that's okay. Move the beaters around the bowl and scrape down the sides of the bowl with a rubber spatula several times while mixing. Lower the mixer speed to medium and beat in the corn syrup and vanilla, then stir in the oats with a wooden spoon. Spread the batter in the prepared pan and bake for 16 minutes. Remove from the oven and cool in the pan on a wire rack until lukewarm.

3. While the bars are baking and cooling, make the glaze. Place the chocolate chips and peanut butter in a small saucepan and stir over low heat until the chocolate melts and the mixture is smooth. Spread the mixture over the lukewarm bars, then cool completely or refrigerate until cold. Cut into a 6 by 9 grid, to make about 54 bars.

4. The bars can be stored in a covered tin at room temperature for up to 1 week. Cushion the bars between layers of plastic wrap or wax paper to protect the frosting. To freeze, allow them to cool completely after baking, then spread them on a baking sheet and place in the freezer for at least 3 hours. When the bars are thoroughly frozen, stack them in freezer-strength recloseable gallon-size plastic bags for up to 3 months. Use a waterproof marker to note the contents of the bags and the date. Defrost them in the bags at room temperature for 1 to 2 hours.

Peanut Brittle Bars

Makes: 36 bars

What you'll need:

9 × 13-inch baking pan

small, sharp knife for cutting
butter

sharp, heavy knife for chopping
peanuts

small, heavy saucepan

mesh sieve

mixing spoon

whisk

fork

wire rack

Baking time: 40 minutes

I am hopelessly addicted to nut brittle. Peanut brittle bars have a buttery bottom crust and a crunchy, nut-laden topping held together by caramel. These set the gold standard in my house. I happen to love the combination of salty and sweet, which is why I use dry-roasted salted nuts in this recipe. This may not appeal to everyone, so of course you have the option of using unsalted nuts.

FOR PREPARING THE PAN

1 tablespoon unsalted butter or solid vegetable shortening, softened

FOR THE BARS

1½ sticks (12 tablespoons) unsalted butter, cut into 8 pieces

2 cups all-purpose flour

1 teaspoon baking soda

½ teaspoon salt

2¼ cups oats, old-fashioned or quick-cooking (see page 46)

1½ cups packed light brown sugar

⅓ cup pure maple syrup (see page 45)

1 extra-large egg, lightly beaten

2 teaspoons pure vanilla extract

FOR THE TOPPING

1½ cups (7 ounces) dry-roasted salted peanuts, coarsely chopped (see Lora Says and page 19)

¼ cup packed dark brown sugar

⅓ cup pure maple syrup

1. Preheat the oven to 350°F with a rack in the center of the oven. Use the butter or solid vegetable shortening to coat the inside of the baking pan. Set aside.

2. To prepare the bars, melt the butter in a small saucepan set over medium heat. Set aside to cool slightly.

3. Place a mesh sieve over a medium mixing bowl and add the flour, baking soda, and salt. Shake the contents into the bowl and set aside. Place the oats and light brown sugar in a large mixing bowl. Break up any lumps of brown sugar with your fingers. Add the flour mixture, then stir well with a wooden spoon. Whisk the maple syrup, egg, and vanilla with the cooled melted butter in the saucepan. Add the maple syrup and butter mixture to the oat mixture and stir with the wooden spoon to mix the ingredients thoroughly. Be sure to scrape the spoon with a rubber spatula several times while mixing. Press the mixture evenly into the prepared pan.

4. To prepare the topping, place the peanuts and dark brown sugar in a small mixing bowl. Toss them together with a fork or a whisk. Sprinkle the mixture evenly over the oat mixture in the baking pan, then drizzle on the maple syrup.

5. Bake for 35 to 40 minutes, or until the edges are lightly browned and set, and the middle is still soft when lightly pressed. Remove the pan from the oven and cool the cake in the pan on a wire rack. When it is completely cool, cut into a 4 by 9 grid, to make 36 bars.

6. The bars can be stored in a covered tin at room temperature for up to 1 week. To freeze, allow them to cool completely after baking, then spread them on a baking sheet and place in the freezer for at least 3 hours. When the bars are thoroughly frozen, stack them in a freezer-strength recloseable gallon-size plastic bag for up to 3 months. Use a waterproof marker to note the contents of the bag and the date. Defrost them in the bag at room temperature for 1 to 2 hours.

LORA SAYS: The easiest way to remove some of the excess salt from salted nuts is to place them in a strainer or sieve, stand over the sink, and toss the nuts around vigorously. If you want to go a step further, rub them with slightly damp paper towels.

Macadamia Nut–Topped Three-Chocolate Wedges

Makes: 16 wedges

What you'll need:

9-inch springform pan

scale for weighing chocolate (optional)

sharp, heavy knife for chopping chocolate and macadamia nuts

baking sheet for toasting macadamia nuts

medium, heavy saucepan

mixing spoon

mesh sieve

whisk

cake tester

wire rack

offset spatula (optional)

Baking time: 30 minutes

hree, count 'em, three kinds of chocolate! It doesn't get much better than this. Hawaii is *really* far from Boston, so I don't get to go there very often. But when I do, I load up on macadamia nuts to bring home and keep in the freezer until I'm inspired to make these buttery, chocolate-loaded wedges.

FOR PREPARING THE PAN

½ tablespoon unsalted butter or solid vegetable shortening, softened

FOR THE BOTTOM LAYER

8 ounces best-quality white chocolate, chopped (see page 16)

½ cup packed light brown sugar

1 stick (8 tablespoons) unsalted butter

1¼ cups all-purpose flour

½ teaspoon baking powder

½ teaspoon salt

2 extra-large eggs

2 teaspoons pure vanilla extract

1½ cups semisweet chocolate chips

FOR THE TOPPING

1½ cups milk chocolate chips

1½ cups (about 6½ ounces) unsalted macadamia nuts, lightly toasted and coarsely chopped (see Lora Says and pages 18–19)

1. Preheat the oven to 350°F with a rack in the center of the oven. Use the butter or solid vegetable shortening to coat the inside of the pan. Set aside.

2. Place the white chocolate, light brown sugar, and butter in a medium saucepan over medium-low heat. Stir until all the ingredients have melted; the mixture will be slightly grainy, but smooth. Set the mixture aside to cool until warm, but not hot, to the touch, about 5 minutes. Meanwhile, place a mesh sieve over a medium mixing bowl and add the flour, baking powder, and salt. Shake the contents into the bowl and set aside. When the white chocolate mixture has cooled, whisk the eggs together in a small mixing bowl, then whisk them into the white chocolate mixture. Whisk in the vanilla and stir well with a wooden spoon. Stir in the flour mixture, then add the semisweet chocolate chips and stir them in well. The batter will be quite thick. Scrape the batter into the prepared pan and smooth the top with a rubber spatula.

3. Bake for 25 to 30 minutes, or until the top is shiny and a cake tester inserted in the outer edge has some moist crumbs and the center is still rather soft. Remove the cake from the oven and sprinkle the top evenly with the milk chocolate chips. Return the pan to the oven for 1 minute, then remove it from the oven and place it on a wire rack. Spread the milk chocolate evenly over the top of the cake, using a rubber spatula or an offset metal spatula. Sprinkle the top evenly with the chopped nuts and use your fingers to press the nuts gently into the melted chocolate. Let the cake cool completely. Run a sharp knife around the edges of the cooled cake, then remove the sides of the pan. Use a long, sharp knife to cut the cake into 16 wedges.

4. The wedges can be stored in a covered tin at room temperature for up to 1 week. To freeze, allow them to cool completely after baking, then spread them on a baking sheet and place in the freezer for at least 3 hours. When the wedges are thoroughly frozen, stack them in a freezer-strength recloseable gallon-size plastic bag for up to 3 months. Use a water-proof marker to note the contents of the bag and the date. Defrost them in the bag at room temperature for 1 to 2 hours. The whole cake can also be frozen before being cut into wedges. Transfer the cooled cake from the springform pan base to a cardboard cake round and place in the freezer for at least 3 hours. When the cake is thoroughly frozen, gently transfer the cake into a freezer-strength recloseable gallon-size plastic bag and freeze for up to 3 months. Use a waterproof marker to note the contents of the bag and the date. Defrost in the bag at room temperature for 1 to 2 hours.

LORA SAYS: To toast macadamia nuts, spread on a baking sheet in a single layer and place in a preheated 350°F oven. Toast for 8 to 10 minutes. Shake the pan several times during the toasting process. Watch carefully, as these nuts burn easily. Don't let them get more than a medium golden brown. Macadamia nuts have a very high oil content, so be careful when you take them out of the pan—they will be very hot.

LORA SAYS: The easiest way to remove some of the excess salt from salted nuts is to place them in a strainer or sieve, stand over the sink, and toss the nuts around vigorously. If you want to go a step further, rub them with slightly damp paper towels.

Hermits

Makes: 30 bars

What you'll need:

9 × 13-inch baking pan

baking sheet for toasting walnuts (optional)

sharp, heavy knife for chopping walnuts (optional)

mesh sieve

hand-held electric mixer

mixing spoon

wire rack

Baking time: 25 minutes

Hermits are the quintessential New England cookie, with their chewy edges and moist insides, but their appeal is universal—a classic combination of cinnamon, nutmeg, cloves, and allspice.

FOR PREPARING THE PAN

1 tablespoon unsalted butter or solid vegetable shortening, softened

2 tablespoons all-purpose flour

FOR THE BARS

¾ cup all-purpose flour

1½ teaspoons baking powder

1 teaspoon ground cinnamon

½ teaspoon ground nutmeg

¼ teaspoon ground cloves

¼ teaspoon ground allspice

1½ cups golden or dark raisins

2 sticks (16 tablespoons) unsalted butter, softened

⅔ cup packed light brown sugar

2 extra-large eggs

½ cup regular molasses (see page 45)

⅔ cup walnuts, toasted and coarsely chopped, optional (see pages 18–19)

1. Preheat the oven to 325°F with a rack in the center of the oven. Use the butter or solid vegetable shortening to coat the inside of the pan. Dust the coated pan with the flour, then knock out the excess. Set aside.

2. Place a mesh sieve over a medium mixing bowl and add the flour, baking powder, cinnamon, nutmeg, cloves, and allspice. Shake the contents into the bowl. Stir in the raisins and toss them in the flour mixture, then set aside.

3. Place the butter and light brown sugar in a large mixing bowl. With the mixer on high speed, cream the butter and sugar together until light and fluffy, about 2 minutes. Reduce the mixer speed to medium and add the eggs, one at a time, waiting until the first is incorporated before adding the second. Move the beaters around the bowl, and scrape down the sides of the bowl with a rubber spatula several times while mixing. Reduce the mixer speed to low and beat in the molasses. The mixture will appear curdled, but that's okay. Use a wooden spoon to stir in the flour mixture and the nuts, if you are using them.

4. Pour and scrape the batter evenly into the prepared pan and smooth the top with a rubber spatula. Bake for 20 to 25 minutes, or until the top looks dry but the center is very soft when pressed lightly with your fingers. Remove the pan from the oven and cool the cake in the pan on a wire rack. When it is completely cool, cut into 30 bars.

5. The bars can be stored in a covered tin at room temperature for up to 1 week. To freeze, allow them to cool completely after baking, then spread them on a baking sheet and place in the freezer for at least 3 hours. When the bars are thoroughly frozen, stack them in a freezer-strength recloseable gallon-size plastic bag for up to 3 months. Use a waterproof marker to note the contents of the bag and the date. Thaw them in the bag at room temperature for 1 to 2 hours.

LORA SAYS: Tossing the raisins with flour helps to keep them from clumping together when the batter is mixed and from sinking to the bottom of the pan during baking.

LORA SAYS: Ground spices lose their potency and flavor within a few months after opening the jar or can. You can maximize their shelf life by storing them in tinted jars with lids tightly closed, in a cool, dry place—not in clear jars on top of your stove.

LORA SAYS: Some people like their hermits chewy and some like them on the dry side. The baking time determines how they turn out: 18 to 20 minutes for chewy, 25 to 27 minutes for less chewy.

Cookies

Cookies

The older I get, the more I appreciate cookies. They are the perfect thing when you want just a little bit of dessert, not the whole ball game. You can keep them in the freezer and eat them one at a time without having to defrost them all (many of them can even be eaten frozen). You can arrange them on a plate and come off looking like Martha-you-know-who. There are other great things about cookies; they are universally loved. I know some people who would turn down a piece of cheesecake, but never refuse a chocolate chip cookie. You get to practice making them until you get the "keepers" as well as eating the "outtakes" without any guilt. They look cute—they are the Beanie Babies of the dessert world—and they are universally recognized. Every culture has some version of the cookie. You can't say that about a chocolate layer cake.

Once you get the hang of it, cookies are really fun to make. Fortunately the hang of it comes pretty quickly, since all those "outtakes" add up to one large piece of cheesecake.

How the Cookie Crumbles
What Should I Do If . . .

The bottoms burned? The cookies may have cooked too long: Keep a careful eye on the baking time. Set the timer for 3 to 4 minutes less than called for in the recipe, and check for doneness at that point. The oven temperatures may have been too high. Lower the temperature by 10 to 15 degrees. The rack may have been positioned too low in the oven; make sure that the rack is in the center position unless otherwise specified in the recipe. The baking sheet may have been too large for the oven, which kept the heat from circulating around the pan; use a baking sheet that doesn't fill the entire rack. Make sure that at least 1½ inches remain between the baking sheet and the oven walls. It could be that the baking sheet was not heavy enough; cheap, thin bakeware can warp in the oven and does not conduct heat evenly or well. It may be time to upgrade to better-quality bakeware that will last a lifetime. Look over the section on equipment.

The cookies stick to the baking sheet? The baking sheet may not have been prepared properly; be sure to follow the directions for lining it properly, and for greasing the lining material, if necessary. Remove the cookies from the baking sheet immediately if specified in the recipe.

When making cookies with a high butter content, I encourage you to use either a silicone pan liner, which needs no coating; parchment paper, which in some cases will need to be a coated with butter or solid vegetable shortening; or aluminum foil coated with butter or solid vegetable shortening. Use the materials called for in the recipe. Avoid nonstick spray, as the spray can give the cookies an off or rancid flavor. In addition, it tends to leave stains on the baking pan that are very hard to wash off. Butter-flavored spray, in my opinion, adds only the taste of fake butter, so I'd avoid it.

The cookies spread? The dough may have been too warm; refrigerate or freeze the formed cookies to make sure that the shortening is solid when they go into the oven. There may be too much sugar; decrease the amount by 2 tablespoons. Maybe the oven wasn't preheated correctly; cookies need to go into a hot oven to keep their shape. Cookies made with vegetable shortening or margarine will spread less than cookies made with butter. Do not reuse hot baking sheets; let them cool off before adding the next round of cookie dough. The heat will cause the cookies to spread before they have set up in the oven. A quick way to cool a baking sheet is to turn it over and run cold water over it. The baking surface will stay dry, but because the sheet is metal, it will become cool quickly.

They run into each other? Balls of dough were possibly placed too close together on the baking sheet. Leave more room between them.

They aren't all the same size? Invest in a miniature ice cream scoop that holds about 2 tablespoons of cookie dough. Give it a light coating of vegetable spray, then use it to measure out same-size balls of dough.

The cookies are dry and hard? There may have been too much flour in the dough. Reduce the amount of flour by ¼ cup next time. The oven temperature might have been too low and the cookies overbaked as a result.

They are puffed and soft and I wanted them flat and chewy? Cookies made with baking powder will rise in proportion to the amount of leavening used and the weight of the ingredients. The more baking powder, the puffier they will be. Eggs will also make cookies puffy, as will using margarine or solid vegetable shortening. Slightly underbaked cookies will fall during cooling and will therefore be flatter. Cookies made with granulated sugar will be crispier than those made with brown sugar, honey, and/or molasses. To instantly flatten cookies, remove the baking sheet from the oven when they are baked and then immediately slam the sheet down on a counter. Do this a couple of times to get the air out of the cookies. Don't try this with delicate or fragile cookies, however, as they will fall apart.

How to Make Your Own Slice-and-Bake Cookies

Any stiff cookie dough can be made ahead, then formed into a sausage-shaped roll, wrapped in plastic, and frozen for 6 months until ready to slice and bake. Or bake half the cookies when you first make the dough, then freeze the rest for another time.

Cut two 18-inch lengths of plastic wrap and place them one on top of the other to make a double layer. With one long side of plastic wrap facing you, use a rigid rubber spatula to form a line of dough down the center of the wrap. Leave at least 2 inches of plastic wrap at either end of the line. Pull one long edge of plastic wrap over the dough, then roll it away from you to form a 2½-inch-wide sausagelike cylinder, wrapping the ends and edges of the plastic wrap around to seal the roll completely. The amount of dough in the recipe will determine how long the roll is. It may be easier to make two rolls. If you plan to freeze the dough for longer than 2 weeks, wrap a double layer of aluminum foil over the plastic. Label the package with a waterproof marker and put it in the freezer.

To bake: Preheat the oven to the temperature given in the recipe. Unwrap the frozen dough and place it on a cutting board. Use a heavy chef's knife to cut the dough into ⅓-inch to ½-inch-wide slices and place them on a baking sheet lined with a silicone pan liner, parchment paper, or aluminum foil. Space them as instructed in the recipe. If you use aluminum foil to line the baking sheet, apply a light coating of softened butter or solid vegetable shortening.

Because the dough is frozen, add about 2 minutes to the baking time in the recipe.

Almond Ice Box Sugar Cookies

Makes: about 28 cookies

What you'll need:

2 heavy-duty baking sheets

silicone pan liners, parchment paper, or aluminum foil for preparing the baking sheets

small, sharp knife for cutting marzipan

mesh sieve

hand-held electric mixer

wire rack

Baking time: 28 to 32 minutes (14 to 16 minutes per sheet)

If you like the flavor of almonds you'll find it in these cookies. The flavor comes from almond extract, whole almonds garnishing the top, and the addition of marzipan (a paste made from ground almonds and sugar). You can find marzipan in the baking aisle of your supermarket, most commonly in a 7-ounce bar. This recipe calls for half that amount. After being opened, marzipan should be wrapped airtight and can be stored in the refrigerator for up to 6 months.

FOR THE COOKIES

2⅓ cups all-purpose flour

½ teaspoon salt

2 tablespoons Lora Brody's Dough Relaxer, optional (see page 48)

2 sticks (16 tablespoons) unsalted butter, softened

¾ cup granulated sugar

2 teaspoons pure almond extract

1 extra-large egg

3½ ounces marzipan, cut into small pieces

TO COMPLETE THE COOKIES

½ cup granulated sugar

28 whole blanched almonds

1. Line the baking sheets with silicone pan liners, parchment paper, or aluminum foil. It is not necessary to butter or oil the lining material. Set aside.

2. Place a mesh sieve over a medium mixing bowl and add the flour, salt, and optional Dough Relaxer. Shake the contents into the bowl and set aside.

3. Place the butter and ¾ cup sugar in a large mixing bowl. With the mixer on high speed, beat the butter and sugar together until the mixture is light and fluffy, about 2 minutes. Add the almond extract, egg, and marzipan. Reduce the mixer speed to low and beat for about 30 seconds, then increase the speed to medium. Beat until all the ingredients are well incorporated and only small lumps of marzipan remain, 2 to 3 minutes. Move the beaters around the bowl and scrape down the sides of the bowl with a rubber spatula several times while mixing. Add the flour mixture and mix on low speed until a soft dough forms—it will not form a ball of dough. Make sure that all the dry ingredients are well incorporated.

4. Scrape up a generous tablespoon of dough and roll it quickly between the palms of your hands to form a ball approximately 1½ inches in diameter. Place it on a baking sheet to rest while you continue to roll similar balls of dough until all the dough is used. You should have approximately 28 cookies.

5. Place ½ cup sugar in a small mixing bowl. Have the whole almonds ready. Roll each ball of dough in the sugar to coat it well, and place the coated balls on the baking sheets, leaving 2½ inches between each. Use your fingers to press each ball gently into a disk 1¾ inches in diameter. Place an almond in the center of each so that the top is still visible, but the sides are buried in the dough. Sprinkle each cookie with a little more sugar. Place the filled cookie sheets in the refrigerator for 1 hour or in the freezer for 30 minutes.

6. Preheat the oven to 350°F with a rack in the center of the oven. Place one pan of cookies in the oven and leave the other one in the refrigerator or freezer. Bake for 16 to 18 minutes, or until the edges are golden brown but the tops are still pale. Remove the sheet to a rack to cool and bake the second sheet of cookies. Remove the cookies from the baking sheets when they have completely cooled.

7. The cookies can be stored in a covered tin at room temperature for up to 1 week. To freeze, allow the cookies to cool completely after baking, then spread them on a baking sheet and place in the freezer for at least 3 hours. When the cookies are thoroughly frozen, stack them in freezer-strength gallon-size recloseable plastic bags for up to 3 months. Use a waterproof marker to note the contents of the bags and the date. Defrost them in the bags at room temperature for 1 to 2 hours.

This dough can be frozen for slice-and-bake cookies. See instructions on page 95.

Holiday Sugar Cookies

Makes: 5 to 6 dozen cookies

What you'll need:

mesh sieve

hand-held electric mixer

2 freezer-strength recloseable jumbo-size plastic bags

2 heavy-duty baking sheets

silicone pan liners, parchment paper, or aluminum foil

heavy-duty rolling pin

scissors

cookie cutters of your choice

offset spatula for transferring cut-out cookies to baking sheet

wire rack

Chilling time: 30 minutes to 24 hours

Baking time: 20 to 24 minutes (10 to 12 minutes per sheet)

Get out those cookie cutters and travel back to your childhood. I have a friend who invites me to make Christmas cookies at her house every year. If you have children, this is the recipe to start them baking with since it is very straightforward and the cookies don't take very long to bake. They can also be cut out in holiday shapes and decorated with colored sprinkles, available in gourmet stores and most supermarkets, or they can be frosted with the simple icing that follows.

FOR PREPARING THE BAKING SHEETS

If using aluminum foil, 1 tablespoon unsalted butter or solid vegetable shortening, softened

FOR THE COOKIES

2½ cups all-purpose flour

½ teaspoon salt

1½ sticks (12 tablespoons) unsalted butter, softened

1¼ cups granulated sugar

1 teaspoon pure vanilla extract

1 extra-large egg

1 extra-large egg yolk

Colored granulated sugar for sprinkling on cookies (optional)

1. Place a mesh sieve over a medium mixing bowl and add the flour and salt. Shake the contents into the bowl and set aside.

2. Place the butter and sugar in a large mixing bowl. With the mixer on medium-high speed, beat the butter with the sugar until it is light and fluffy, about 3 minutes. Scrape down the sides of the bowl with a rubber spatula as you work. Reduce the speed to low and mix in the vanilla. Add the egg and the egg yolk, and continue to beat on low speed until the ingredients are well combined. Move the beaters around the bowl and scrape down the sides of the bowl with a rubber spatula several times while mixing.

3. Mix in the flour until the dough forms buttery crumbs and starts to come together. Flour your hands and scoop the dough together in the bowl to form a rough ball. Divide the dough into two balls, and place each in the center of a plastic bag. Flatten each ball of dough into a disk 4 to 5 inches in diameter. Place the bags of dough in the refrigerator for at least 30 minutes, or as long as 24 hours.

4. When you are ready to roll and bake the cookies, preheat the oven to 350°F with a rack in the center of the oven. Line the cookie sheets with silicone pan liners, parchment paper, or aluminum foil. If you are using foil, apply a light coating of butter or solid vegetable shortening. Set aside.

5. Remove a bag of dough from the refrigerator, open it, and lightly dust the dough all over with flour. Reseal the bag and, starting from the center, roll the dough out evenly with a rolling pin to ⅛-inch thickness. Return the bag of rolled dough to the refrigerator and repeat the process with the remaining bag. Refrigerate that bag when it has been rolled out.

6. Working with one bag at a time, place it on a work surface and unseal it. Cut down the sides and along the bottom with scissors; remove and discard the top section of the bag. With the dough still resting on the bottom section of bag, use a 2-inch cookie cutter or a floured glass of similar size to cut the dough into shapes. Place them ½ inch apart on the prepared sheets (they will not spread during baking). Gather the dough scraps once and reroll them, then cut out additional cookies. Sprinkle them with colored sugar, if desired. Refrigerate one filled sheet while you bake the other. Bake the cookies one sheet at a time for 10 to 12 minutes, or until the cookies are golden at the edges and firm to the touch. Rotate each sheet 180 degrees halfway through the baking time. Remove the cookies from the sheets when they have baked, and transfer them to a wire rack to cool completely.

7. The cookies can be stored in a covered tin at room temperature for up to 1 week. To freeze, allow the cookies to cool completely after baking, then spread them on a baking sheet and place in the freezer for at least 3 hours. When the cookies are thoroughly frozen, stack them in freezer-strength gallon-size recloseable plastic bags for up to 3 months. Use a waterproof marker to note the contents of the bags and the date. Defrost them in the bags at room temperature for 1 to 2 hours.

This dough can be frozen for slice-and-bake cookies. See instructions on page 95.

FOR FROSTED COOKIES: Do not sprinkle the cookies with sugar before baking. After they are baked, let them cool completely before frosting. Mix together 1 cup confectioners' sugar and 2 to 3 tablespoons hot water to make a thick but creamy paste. Add a drop or two of red or green food coloring (or any color of your choice), if you wish. When using food coloring, it's better to start with a little (dip a toothpick into the bottle and then swirl into mixture and stir) and add a tiny bit more to achieve the color you want. Leave the cookies on the wire rack and, with a small spoon, apply and spread the icing on the top surfaces of the cookies. Sprinkle colored or plain granulated sugar over the icing while it is still wet, if desired. Allow the cookies to dry on the wire racks before storing.

LORA SAYS: When you chill the dough, two important things happen to make rolling easier. The fat in the dough hardens, making the dough firmer so it will hold its shape, and the gluten (protein) in the flour relaxes, allowing the dough to stretch without breaking or crumbling.

LORA SAYS: You can gather and reroll scraps of dough once or twice, but more than this will result in very tough cookies, because the rolling activates the gluten (protein) in the flour. In addition, adding more flour to the dough to keep it from sticking during each subsequent rolling will make the cookies dry and hard.

Oatmeal Raisin Cookies

Makes: 5 dozen cookies

What you'll need:

2 heavy-duty baking sheets

silicone pan liners, parchment paper, or aluminum foil for preparing the baking sheets

baking sheet for toasting walnuts (optional)

sharp, heavy knife for chopping walnuts (optional)

mesh sieve

whisk or fork

hand-held electric mixer

wire rack

Baking time: 24 to 28 minutes (12 to 14 minutes per sheet)

My friend Paul Barrett, the marketing genius at the Bertolli Olive Oil Company, shared this recipe for making absolutely perfect oatmeal raisin cookies with (you guessed it) olive oil. While you could certainly use any brand of olive oil, if you want fresh taste and light texture, both Paul and I recommend using Bertolli extra light olive oil, available in most nationwide supermarkets.

FOR PREPARING THE BAKING SHEETS

If using aluminum foil, 1½ tablespoons unsalted butter or solid vegetable shortening, softened

FOR THE COOKIES

1¾ cups all-purpose flour

1 teaspoon baking soda

½ teaspoon salt

2½ cups oats, old-fashioned or quick-cooking (see page 46)

1¼ cups packed light brown sugar

¾ cup extra light olive oil

2 extra-large eggs

2 tablespoons milk

2 teaspoons pure vanilla extract

1 cup dark or golden raisins

1 cup walnuts, toasted and chopped, optional (see pages 18–19)

1. Preheat the oven to 375°F with a rack in the center of the oven. Line the baking sheets with silicone pan liners, parchment paper, or aluminum foil. If you are using foil, apply a light coating of butter or solid vegetable shortening. Set aside.

2. Place a mesh sieve over a medium mixing bowl and add the flour, baking soda, and salt. Shake the contents into the bowl and toss in the oats using a whisk or a fork. Set aside.

3. Place the brown sugar and olive oil in a large mixing bowl. With the mixer on high speed, beat the oil and brown sugar together until they are completely blended, about 2 minutes. Reduce the speed to low and add the eggs, one at a time, making sure one is incorporated before adding the second. Move the beaters around the bowl and scrape down the sides of the bowl with a rubber spatula several times while mixing. Add the milk and vanilla, then beat on high for a minute. Scrape down the sides of the bowl. Reduce the speed to low and add the flour mixture, raisins, and nuts, if you are using them. Beat until the dry ingredients are incorporated.

4. Drop the batter on the prepared baking sheets by rounded tablespoonfuls placed 1½ inches apart. Refrigerate one filled sheet while you bake the other. Bake for 12 to 14 minutes, or until the cookies are crisp and lightly browned. Rotate each sheet 180 degrees halfway through the baking time. Remove the baking sheets from the oven and transfer the cookies to a wire rack to cool completely.

5. The cookies can be stored in a covered tin at room temperature for up to 1 week. To freeze, allow the cookies to cool completely after baking, then spread them on a baking sheet and place in the freezer for at least 3 hours. When the cookies are thoroughly frozen, stack them in freezer-strength recloseable gallon-size plastic bags for up to 3 months. Use a waterproof marker to note the contents of the bags and the date. Defrost them in the bags at room temperature for 1 to 2 hours.

Chocolate Chip Cookies

Cookies

Makes: about 30 cookies, 2½ to 3 inches in diameter

What you'll need:

2 heavy-duty baking sheets

silicone pan liners, parchment paper, or aluminum foil for preparing the baking sheets

baking sheet for toasting pecans (optional)

sharp, heavy knife for chopping pecans (optional)

mesh sieve

hand-held electric mixer

2-tablespoon ice cream scoop (optional)

wire rack

Baking time: 30 to 36 minutes (15 to 18 minutes per sheet)

My youngest son, Sam, is a self-proclaimed connoisseur of chocolate chip cookies. Fussy doesn't begin to describe how he is about their being just soft enough, having the right amount of chips, being the right size—and, most important of all—never having any nuts. Here is Sam's favorite recipe (what you do about nuts is up to you). While Sam and I prefer bittersweet chocolate chips, you have the option of using milk chocolate, white chocolate, or semisweet chocolate chips.

FOR THE COOKIES

1 cup all-purpose flour

½ cup cake flour (see page 29)

½ teaspoon baking soda

½ teaspoon salt

1 stick (8 tablespoons) unsalted butter, softened

½ cup granulated sugar

½ cup packed dark brown sugar

2 extra-large eggs

1 tablespoon pure vanilla extract

1½ cups chocolate chips (bittersweet, semisweet, milk, or white chocolate)

1½ cups pecan halves, toasted and coarsely chopped, optional (see pages 18–19)

Nonstick vegetable spray (for coating the scoop) (optional)

1. Preheat the oven to 375°F with a rack in the center of the oven. Line the baking sheets with silicone pan liners, parchment paper, or aluminum foil.

2. Place a mesh sieve over a medium mixing bowl and add the all-purpose flour, cake flour, baking soda, and salt. Shake the contents into the bowl and set aside.

3. Place the butter, granulated sugar, and dark brown sugar in a large mixing bowl. With the mixer on medium speed, cream the butter and sugars together until light and fluffy, about 3 minutes. Add the eggs, one at a time, waiting until the first is incorporated before adding the second, then beat in the vanilla. The mixture will appear slightly curdled, but will become thick and creamy as you continue beating. Move the beaters around in the bowl and scrape down the sides of the bowl with a rubber spatula several times while mixing. Add the flour mixture, beating until all traces of flour disappear. The batter will be quite thick. Use a rubber spatula to stir in the chips and the nuts, if you use them.

4. Spray the ice cream scoop with vegetable spray, if desired, to make it easier to release the dough from the scoop, or use a tablespoon measure, filled heaping full, to drop portions of batter on the baking sheets, leaving 2 inches between cookies. Refrigerate one filled sheet while you bake the other. Bake for 15 to 18 minutes, or until the cookies are golden brown around the edges and light brown on top. Rotate each sheet 180 degrees halfway through the baking time. When they have baked, remove the cookies from the oven and allow them to cool on the sheets for 2 minutes before removing them to a wire rack to cool completely.

5. The cookies can be stored in a covered tin at room temperature for up to 1 week. To freeze, allow the cookies to cool completely after baking, then spread them on a baking sheet and place in the freezer for at least 3 hours. When the cookies are thoroughly frozen, stack them in a freezer-strength recloseable gallon-size plastic bag for up to 3 months. Use a waterproof marker to note the contents of the bag and the date. Defrost them in the bag at room temperature for 1 to 2 hours.

This dough can be frozen for slice-and-bake cookies. See instructions on page 95.

LORA SAYS: For a chewier cookie, smack each baking sheet flat on the counter after removing it from the oven to deflate the dough.

LORA SAYS: This recipe uses a combination of regular all-purpose flour and lower-protein cake flour to make a softer cookie.

David's Butterscotch Cookies

Makes: about 30 cookies, 2½ to 3 inches in diameter

What you'll need:

baking sheet for toasting pecans (optional)

sharp heavy knife for chopping pecans (optional)

2 heavy-duty baking sheets

hand-held electric mixer

silicone pan liners, parchment paper, or aluminum foil for preparing the baking sheets

mesh sieve

2-tablespoon ice cream scoop (optional)

wire rack

Baking time: 30 to 36 minutes (15 to 18 minutes per sheet)

My husband, Saint-David-Sent-from-God as he is affectionately known around these parts, can take or leave many desserts. Every once in a while, however, something catches his fancy. This is true with these cookies, with their seductive buttery taste and lovely soft chunky texture. Both butterscotch baking chips and maple flavoring can be found in the baking aisle of the supermarket.

FOR THE COOKIES

1 cup all-purpose flour

½ cup cake flour (see page 29)

½ teaspoon baking soda

½ teaspoon salt

1 stick (8 tablespoons) unsalted butter, softened

½ cup granulated sugar

½ cup packed light brown sugar

2 extra-large eggs

2 teaspoons imitation maple extract (see page 32) or 2 teaspoons pure vanilla extract

1½ cups butterscotch baking chips

1½ cups pecan halves, toasted and coarsely chopped, optional (see pages 18–19)

Nonstick vegetable spray (for coating the scoop) (optional)

1. Preheat the oven to 375°F with a rack in the center of the oven. Line the baking sheets with silicone pan liners, parchment paper, or aluminum foil. It is not necessary to butter or oil the lining material. Set aside.

2. Place a mesh sieve over a medium mixing bowl and add the all-purpose flour, cake flour, baking soda, and salt. Shake the contents into the bowl and set aside.

3. Place the butter, granulated sugar, and light brown sugar in a large mixing bowl. With the mixer on medium speed, cream the butter and sugars together until light and fluffy, about 3 minutes. Add the eggs, one at a time, waiting until the first is incorporated before adding the second, then beat in the maple extract. The mixture will appear slightly curdled, but will become thick and creamy as you continue beating. Move the beaters around the bowl and scrape down the sides of the bowl with a rubber spatula several times while mixing. Add the dry ingredients, beating until all traces of flour disappear. The batter will be quite thick. Use a wooden spoon or a rubber spatula to stir in the butterscotch chips and the optional nuts.

4. Spray the ice cream scoop with nonstick vegetable spray, if desired, to make it easier to release the dough from the scoop, or use a tablespoon measure, filled heaping full, to drop portions of batter on the baking sheets, leaving 2 inches between cookies. Refrigerate one filled sheet while you bake the other. Bake for 15 to 18 minutes, or until the cookies are golden brown around the edges and light brown on top. Rotate each sheet 180 degrees halfway through the baking time. When they have baked, remove the cookies from the oven and allow them to cool on the sheets for 2 minutes before removing them to a wire rack to cool.

5. The cookies can be stored in a covered tin at room temperature for up to 1 week. To freeze, allow the cookies to cool completely after baking, then spread them on a baking sheet and place in the freezer for at least 3 hours. When the cookies are thoroughly frozen, stack them in a freezer-strength recloseable gallon-size plastic bag for up to 3 months. Use a waterproof marker to note the contents of the bag and the date. Defrost them in the bag at room temperature for 1 to 2 hours.

This dough can be frozen for slice-and-bake cookies. See instructions on page 95.

LORA SAYS: The cookie dough can be dropped onto the baking sheets in smaller, tablespoon-size portions, for smaller cookies. The recipe yield will be about 60 cookies, and they will bake in about 10 minutes.

Macadamia Nut–White Chocolate Chunk Cookies

Makes: about 30 cookies

What you'll need:

2 heavy-duty baking sheets

silicone pan liners, parchment paper, or aluminum foil for preparing the baking sheets

scale for weighing white chocolate (optional)

sharp, heavy knife for chopping white chocolate and cutting nuts

mesh sieve

hand-held electric mixer

table knife

fork

wire rack

Baking time: 20 to 24 minutes (10 to 12 minutes per sheet)

If there were a cookie associated with the lifestyles of the Rich and Famous, it would be this one. Macadamia nuts and quality white chocolate are rich both in cost and flavor. Here a little bit of batter holds together these slightly extravagant ingredients. Make them small; like all rich things, a little goes a long way. Look for best-quality white chocolate made with real cocoa butter (check the ingredients on the label) in fine supermarkets and gourmet stores. Macadamia nuts come salted and unsalted and can be found in supermarkets.

FOR THE COOKIES

1 cup plus 2 tablespoons all-purpose flour

½ teaspoon baking soda

¼ teaspoon salt (if using unsalted macadamia nuts) (see Lora Says)

1 stick (8 tablespoons) unsalted butter, softened

½ cup packed dark brown sugar

¼ cup granulated sugar

1 extra-large egg

1½ teaspoons pure vanilla extract

9 ounces white chocolate, coarsely chopped (see page 16)

1 cup macadamia nuts, each nut cut into 2 to 3 pieces (see page 19)

1. Preheat the oven to 350°F with a rack in the center of the oven. Line the baking sheets with silicone pan liners, parchment paper, or aluminum foil. Do not coat the lining material. Set aside.

2. Place a mesh sieve over a small mixing bowl and add the flour, baking soda, and salt, if you are using it. Shake the contents into the bowl and set aside.

3. Place the butter, dark brown sugar, and granulated sugar in a large mixing bowl. Use the mixer on high speed to beat the butter with the sugars until the mixture is light and fluffy, about 5 minutes. Move the beaters around the bowl and scrape down the sides of the bowl with a rubber spatula several times while mixing. Beat in the egg and the vanilla. Reduce the mixer speed to low and beat in the flour, mixing only to incorporate. Use a rubber spatula to fold in the white chocolate and the nuts.

4. Scoop up the dough in tablespoon-size portions and use a table knife to drop them onto the prepared baking sheets, leaving an inch between portions of dough. Dip a fork into cool water and use the tines to lightly flatten each ball of dough. Bake the cookies, one sheet at a time, for 10 to 12 minutes, or until the cookie tops look dry and are beginning to brown. Refrigerate one filled sheet while you bake the other. Rotate each sheet 180 degrees halfway through the baking time. When the cookies have baked, remove them from the oven and let them cool on the baking sheets for 15 minutes, then transfer them to a wire rack to cool completely.

5. The cookies can be stored in a covered tin at room temperature for up to 1 week. To freeze, allow the cookies to cool completely after baking, then spread them on a baking sheet and place in the freezer for at least 3 hours. When the cookies are thoroughly frozen, stack them in freezer-strength recloseable gallon-size plastic bags for up to 3 months. Use a waterproof marker to note the contents of the bags and the date. Defrost them in the bags at room temperature for 1 to 2 hours.

This dough can be frozen for slice-and-bake cookies. See instructions on page 95.

LORA SAYS: The easiest way to remove some of the excess salt from salted nuts is to place them in a strainer or sieve, stand over the sink, and toss the nuts around vigorously. If you want to go a step further, rub them with slightly damp paper towels.

LORA SAYS: The high oil content of macadamia nuts means they will get rancid quickly if not stored properly. If you buy them in a sealed can or jar, freeze whatever you don't use in a tightly covered container up to six months.

Shortbread

Makes: 12 wedges

What you'll need:

9-inch pie plate, regular or deep dish

small, sharp knife for cutting up butter

mesh sieve

hand-held electric mixer

wire rack

Baking time: 30 to 35 minutes

This traditional Scottish confection has few ingredients, is easy to make, and you will look like a talented cookie maker, that is, if people take the time to look at them before they wolf them down.

2½ cups all-purpose flour

¾ cup confectioners' sugar (if sugar is lumpy, sift first, then measure)

½ teaspoon salt

2 sticks (16 tablespoons) unsalted butter, chilled and cut into small pieces

Preheat the oven to 350°F with a rack in the center of the oven.

1. Place a mesh sieve over a medium mixing bowl and add the flour, confectioners' sugar, and salt. Shake the contents into the bowl. Scatter the butter pieces over the dry ingredients. With the mixer on medium speed, beat the butter with the flour mixture until the mixture forms coarse buttery crumbs. Use your hands to press the mixture together into a ball of dough.

2. Press the dough into the pie plate. Do not force the dough up the sides of the plate; it should be as flat as possible. With a sharp knife, make 6 crosswise cuts, each about ⅛ inch deep, to score the dough into 12 pie-shaped wedges. Bake the shortbread for 30 to 35 minutes, or until it is fairly firm to the touch and barely golden. Remove the shortbread from the oven and let it cool in the pan on a wire rack. While the shortbread is still hot, cut down through the score lines with a small, sharp knife to make 12 individual wedges.

3. The shortbread can be stored in a covered tin at room temperature for up to 1 week. To freeze, allow the shortbread to cool completely after baking, then spread the wedges on a baking sheet and place in the freezer for at least 3 hours. When the wedges are thoroughly frozen, stack them in a freezer-strength recloseable gallon-size plastic bag for up to 3 months. Use a waterproof marker to note the contents of the bag and the date. Defrost them in the bag at room temperature for 1 to 2 hours.

Triple Peanut Butter Cookies

Makes: 4 dozen cookies

What you'll need:

2 heavy-duty baking sheets

silicone pan liners, parchment paper, or aluminum foil for preparing the baking sheets

sharp, heavy knife for chopping peanuts

mesh sieve

hand-held electric mixer

mixing spoon

wire rack

Baking time: 24 to 28 minutes (12 to 14 minutes per sheet)

[Note: The cookies need to cool on their baking-sheet lining material in this recipe. If you have only two silicone pan liners, you will have to line a baking sheet with aluminum foil or parchment for one batch of cookies.]

These cookies contain peanuts in three forms: dry-roasted peanuts, peanut butter, and peanut butter chips (found in the baking aisle of the supermarket). You can substitute an equal amount of semisweet chocolate chips for the peanut butter chips, if you prefer. The salt in the dry-roasted peanuts gives a great counterbalance to the sweetness of the cookies.

FOR THE COOKIES

2⅔ cups all-purpose flour

½ teaspoon baking powder

½ teaspoon baking soda

½ teaspoon salt

2 tablespoons Lora Brody's Dough Relaxer, optional (see page 48)

2 sticks (16 tablespoons) unsalted butter, softened

1 cup packed dark brown sugar

1 cup granulated sugar

1¼ cups chunky peanut butter (see Lora Says)

2 extra-large eggs

1¼ cups dry-roasted salted peanuts, coarsely chopped (see page 19)

1¼ cups peanut butter chips or semisweet chocolate chips

1. Preheat the oven to 350°F with a rack set in the lower third of the oven, but not the very lowest position. Line the baking sheets with silicone pan liners, parchment paper, or aluminum foil. It is not necessary to butter or oil the lining material. Set aside.

2. Place a mesh sieve over a medium mixing bowl and add the flour, baking powder, baking soda, salt, and optional Dough Relaxer. Shake the contents into the bowl and set aside.

3. Place the butter in a large mixing bowl and use the mixer on high speed to beat until light and fluffy. Add the dark brown and granulated sugars, and beat on low speed for 30 seconds. Increase the speed to high and beat until the mixture is light and fluffy, 2 to 3 minutes. Make sure to break up any lumps of brown sugar with your fingers or a wooden spoon. Add the peanut butter and beat on medium speed until smooth, about 2 minutes. Add the eggs, one at a time, waiting until the first is incorporated before adding the second. Move the beaters around the bowl and scrape down the sides of the bowl with a rubber spatula several times while mixing. Add the peanuts and chips, and beat on low speed just until they are thoroughly incorporated.

4. Dip a tablespoon measure in water, then use it to form balls of dough 1½ inches in diameter, and place them 1½ inches apart on the prepared baking sheets. Dampen your fingers with water and press down on top of each cookie to flatten it slightly.

5. Bake the cookies one sheet at a time. Refrigerate the first filled sheet while you bake the second, and refrigerate the dough that will fill the third sheet. Bake for 12 to 14 minutes, or until the edges of the cookies are browned and the tops are a light golden brown. Rotate each sheet 180 degrees halfway through the baking time. Remove the sheets from the oven and very carefully remove the lining material with the cookies on it. The cookies are rather fragile, so be gentle. Place the liner with the cookies on it on a wire rack, and cool the cookies completely. Cool the hot baking pans and use them to finish baking the cookies.

This dough can be frozen for slice-and-bake cookies. See instructions on page 95.

6. The cookies can be stored in a covered tin at room temperature for up to 1 week. To freeze, allow the cookies to cool completely after baking, then spread them on a baking sheet and place in the freezer for at least 3 hours. When the cookies are thoroughly frozen, stack them in freezer-strength recloseable gallon-size plastic bags for up to 3 months. Use a waterproof marker to note the contents of the bags and the date. Thaw them in the bags at room temperature for 1 to 2 hours.

LORA SAYS: I've made this with both the standard commercial peanut butter, such as Skippy, and the health food kind that you grind yourself. In this recipe, the commercial peanut butter works best, as it gives a smooth texture and more pronounced taste. Don't use that opened jar of peanut butter you've had hanging around on the shelf—it's probably rancid. Taste it before you use it, and if it tastes bitter or off, throw it away and buy a fresh jar.

LORA SAYS: You can cool hot baking sheets by running them under cool water. This only works with heavy-duty sheets, as the cheap ones warp when the cold water hits the hot sheet. Invert the sheet and wet only the bottom, so you don't have to dry the sheet before reusing it.

Truly Exceptional Peanut Butter–Chocolate Chip Cookies

Makes: about 30 cookies, each 3 inches in diameter

What you'll need:

2 heavy-duty baking sheets

silicone pan liners, parchment paper, or aluminum foil for preparing the baking sheets

hand-held electric mixer

fork

wide metal spatula

wire rack

Baking time: 20 to 24 minutes (10 to 12 minutes per sheet)

Several years ago, *Gourmet* magazine ran a recipe for a peanut butter cookie made without any flour. Curious soul that I am, I whipped up a batch and found that, indeed, one can make a pretty decent peanut butter cookie without flour. One can make an exceptional version of this cookie by using chunky peanut butter and adding a healthy amount of chocolate chips. Thank you, Amy Fritch of New York City, for the inspiration and the basic recipe.

FOR PREPARING THE BAKING SHEETS

If using aluminum foil, 1½ tablespoons unsalted butter or solid vegetable shortening, softened

FOR THE COOKIES

1 cup peanut butter	1¼ teaspoons baking soda
1 cup packed light brown sugar	¾ cup semisweet chocolate chips
1 extra-large egg	

1. Preheat the oven to 350°F with a rack in the center of the oven. Line the baking sheets with silicone pan liners, parchment paper, or aluminum foil. If you are using foil, apply a light coating of butter or solid vegetable shortening. Set aside.

2. Place the peanut butter and brown sugar in a medium mixing bowl. Use the mixer on medium speed to beat them together well, about 1 minute. Scrape the sides of the bowl with a rubber spatula as you work. Add the egg and mix long enough just to combine, then sprinkle the baking soda over the top. Beat on medium speed for 1 minute until the ingredients are completely combined. Move the beaters around the bowl and scrape down the sides of the bowl with a rubber spatula several times while mixing. Reduce the mixer speed to low and add the chocolate chips.

3. Use a tablespoon measure to drop portions of dough onto the baking sheets, leaving 1½ inches between the cookies. Gently press the tops of the cookies with the tines of a fork to flatten them slightly and to form the trademark crisscross lines of these cookies. Refrigerate one filled cookie sheet while you bake the other. Bake the cookies, one sheet at a time, for 10 to 12 minutes, or until the cookies have puffed slightly and the edges are lightly browned. The cookies will be soft on the surface. Rotate each sheet 180 degrees halfway through the baking time.

4. Remove the cookies from the oven and use a wide metal spatula to transfer them carefully to a wire rack to cool completely.

5. The cookies can be stored in a covered tin at room temperature for up to 1 week. To freeze, allow the cookies to cool completely after baking, then spread them on a baking sheet and place it in the freezer for at least 3 hours. When the cookies are thoroughly frozen, stack them in freezer-strength recloseable gallon-size plastic bags for up to 3 months. Use a waterproof marker to note the contents of the bags and the date. Thaw them in the bags at room temperature for 1 to 2 hours.

LORA SAYS: This recipe works only with commercial-type processed peanut butter, the kind where the oil does not separate out.

Camp Cookies

Makes: about 3 dozen cookies

What you'll need:

2 heavy-duty baking sheets

silicone pan liners, parchment paper, or aluminum foil for preparing the baking sheets

mesh sieve

hand-held electric mixer

2-tablespoon ice cream scoop

wire rack

Baking time: 30 to 36 minutes (15 to 18 minutes per sheet)

You may be too old for camp, but you probably know someone who is (voluntarily or not) shipped off every summer to face meals of mystery meat and soft white bread. Or perhaps you've just sent your child off to college, where the food is sometimes just as unappetizing. Act on your kind thoughts. Send the kid some cookies like these. They're perfect and they won't end up as a box of broken crumbs, no matter how hard the post office tries to mangle them.

FOR PREPARING THE BAKING SHEETS

If using aluminum foil, 1½ tablespoons unsalted butter or solid vegetable shortening, softened

FOR THE COOKIES

2 cups all-purpose flour

1 teaspoon baking soda

½ teaspoon salt

½ teaspoon ground cinnamon

2 sticks (16 tablespoons) unsalted butter, softened

¾ cup peanut butter

1 cup packed dark brown sugar

2 extra-large eggs

⅓ cup milk

1 tablespoon pure vanilla extract

2 cups oats, old-fashioned or quick-cooking (see page 46)

1 cup sweetened shredded coconut

1 cup dark raisins

1 cup dry-roasted salted peanuts

Nonstick vegetable spray (for coating the scoop) (optional)

1. Preheat the oven to 350°F with a rack in the center of the oven. Line the baking sheets with silicone pan liners, parchment, paper or aluminum foil. If you are using aluminum foil, apply a light coating of butter or solid vegetable shortening. Set aside.

2. Place a mesh sieve over a medium mixing bowl and add the flour, baking soda, salt, and cinnamon. Shake the contents into the bowl and set aside.

3. Place the butter, peanut butter, and dark brown sugar in a large mixing bowl. Use the mixer on high speed to cream the mixture until it is light and fluffy, about 3 minutes. Add the eggs, one at a time, waiting until the first is incorporated before adding the second. With the mixer on medium speed, beat in the milk and vanilla. Continue to beat on medium speed while you gradually add the oats and then the flour mixture. Mix until all traces of flour disappear. With a rubber spatula fold in the coconut, raisins, and peanuts.

4. Spray the ice cream scoop with vegetable spray, if desired, to make it easier to release the dough from the scoop, or use a tablespoon measure, filled heaping full. Drop portions of dough 2 inches apart onto the prepared baking sheets. Refrigerate one filled baking sheet while you bake the other. Bake for 15 to 17 minutes, or until the cookies are golden brown and firm to the touch. Rotate each sheet 180 degrees halfway through the baking time. Remove the cookies from the oven and transfer them to wire racks to cool completely.

5. The cookies can be stored in a covered tin at room temperature for up to 1 week. To freeze, allow the cookies to cool completely after baking, then spread them on a baking sheet and place in the freezer for at least 3 hours. When the cookies are thoroughly frozen, stack them in freezer-strength recloseable gallon-size plastic bags for up to 3 months. Use a waterproof marker to note the contents of the bags and the date. Thaw them in the bags at room temperature for 1 to 2 hours.

Almond Biscotti

Makes: about 36 biscotti

What you'll need:

heavy-duty baking sheet

silicone pan liner, parchment paper, or aluminum foil for preparing the baking sheet

baking sheet for toasting almonds

mesh sieve

hand-held electric mixer

serrated knife

wire rack

Baking time: 40 minutes

Biscotti have become the cookie equivalent of bagels. You can find them in every coffee shop, and boy, are they overpriced. Wait till you see how easy and how much fun they are to make at home, because they are so versatile for any kind of flavoring imaginable. You can add nuts or leave them out or add chocolate chips, use vanilla instead of almond extract, and bake them until they are just a little crisp or until they are dunking material. This recipe for almond biscotti is a classic.

FOR PREPARING THE BAKING SHEET

If using foil, 1 tablespoon unsalted butter or solid vegetable shortening, softened

FOR THE BISCOTTI

2¼ cups all-purpose flour

1 teaspoon baking powder

½ teaspoon salt

2 extra-large eggs

1 cup granulated sugar

½ cup vegetable oil

2 teaspoons pure almond extract

1⅓ cups (5 ounces) slivered blanched almonds, toasted (see page 18)

1. Preheat the oven to 350°F with a rack in the center of the oven. Line the baking sheet with a silicone pan liner, parchment paper, or aluminum foil. If you are using aluminum foil, apply a light coating of butter or solid vegetable shortening. Set aside.

2. Place a mesh sieve over a medium mixing bowl and add the flour, baking powder, and salt. Shake the contents into the bowl and set aside.

3. Place the eggs and sugar in a large mixing bowl. With the mixer on high speed, beat the eggs with the sugar until fluffy and light, about 2 minutes. Add the vegetable oil and almond extract, and beat until the oil is incorporated and the mixture is thick and smooth, about 1 minute. Reduce the mixer speed to low and beat in the flour mixture. The dough will be quite thick. Add the nuts; it might be necessary to knead them in with your fingers.

4. Turn the dough out onto a lightly floured surface. Flour your fingers and divide the dough in half, then form each portion into a rough log. Transfer one portion of dough to one long side of the prepared baking sheet, and mold it into a smooth log 14 inches long, 2½ inches wide, and ¾ inch high. Repeat the process with the second portion of dough and place it 2 inches away from the first log.

5. Bake for 30 minutes. The logs will become light golden brown and slightly puffed. Remove the pan from the oven, but do not turn the oven off. Use a serrated knife to cut the logs carefully into ¾-inch-thick slices on a slight diagonal. Take care not to tear the silicone pan liner or parchment paper. Arrange the slices, standing upright, on the baking sheet, leaving 1 inch between cookies. Return to the oven and bake for 10 minutes more until the cut surfaces of the cookies have browned slightly and the biscotti are dry to the touch. Remove them from the oven and transfer the biscotti to a wire rack to cool completely.

6. The biscotti can be stored in a covered tin at room temperature for up to 1 week. To freeze, allow the biscotti to cool completely after baking, then spread them on a baking sheet and place in the freezer for at least 3 hours. When the biscotti are thoroughly frozen, place them in a plastic bag for up to 3 months. Use a waterproof marker to note the contents of the bag and the date. Thaw them in the bag at room temperature for 1 to 2 hours.

LORA SAYS: If your sliced biscotti won't stand up on the baking sheet for the second baking, lay them on their sides and bake for 5 minutes. Use tongs or a metal spatula to flip them over, and bake for another 5 minutes.

VARIATION: To make chocolate-dipped biscotti: Melt 8 ounces chopped, best-quality bittersweet chocolate with 6 tablespoons unsalted butter in a microwave or in a small metal mixing bowl set over, but not touching, a pan of gently simmering water. Scrape the melted chocolate mixture onto a shallow plate. Dip one long, flat side of each biscotti in the chocolate, so that it comes about halfway up the side of the cookie. Place each dipped biscotti on a wire rack, uncoated side down. Allow the chocolate to set. Store and freeze the dipped biscotti as you would plain ones.

Rugelach

Makes: 4 dozen rugelach

What you'll need:

sharp, heavy knife for chopping walnuts

mesh sieve

hand-held electric mixer

4 freezer-strength recloseable gallon-size plastic bags

heavy-duty rolling pin

fork

small, heavy saucepan

mixing spoon

2 heavy-duty baking sheets

silicone pan liners, parchment paper, or aluminum foil for preparing the baking sheets

scissors

small pastry brush

wire rack

Baking time: 48 to 54 minutes (16 to 18 minutes per sheet)

Rugelach, those delicate snail cookies filled with apricot jam, raisins, and walnuts, are wonderful. Those that taste the very best are either those made by my mother or the ones you make yourself. How about this best of both worlds? You can make your own using my mother's recipe. Cream cheese dough is typically soft and difficult to work with if you don't work fast and/or keep chilling it if it starts to soften. Don't pick a steaming hot day in a kitchen without air-conditioning to make these. Don't turn on the oven until all the cookies are formed.

FOR THE DOUGH

2 cups all-purpose flour

1 teaspoon salt

1 tablespoon Lora Brody's Dough Relaxer (optional) (see page 48)

2 sticks (16 tablespoons) unsalted butter, softened

8 ounces cream cheese (not the whipped or reduced-fat variety), room temperature (see page 33)

¼ cup granulated sugar

2 teaspoons pure vanilla extract

FOR THE FILLING

1 cup granulated sugar

½ cup packed dark brown sugar

1 teaspoon ground cinnamon

1½ cups golden raisins

1½ cups walnuts, coarsely chopped (see page 19)

One 16-ounce jar apricot
preserves

¼ cup milk

2 tablespoons granulated
sugar mixed with
1 teaspoon ground
cinnamon

1. To make the dough, place a mesh sieve over a medium mixing bowl and add the flour, salt, and optional Dough Relaxer. Shake the contents into the bowl and set aside.

2. Place the butter and cream cheese in a large mixing bowl. With the mixer on high speed, beat the butter and cream cheese together until smooth, about 2 minutes. Add the sugar and vanilla, and mix until they are combined. Move the beaters around the bowl and scrape down the sides of the bowl with a rubber spatula several times while mixing. Add the flour mixture and beat on low speed just until a soft dough is formed.

3. With a spatula scrape the dough onto a lightly floured work surface, flour your hands, and divide the dough into four parts. Dust each portion lightly with flour, and flatten each into a disk 1 inch thick and about 4 inches across. Place each disk in the center of the plastic food storage bag. If the dough is very soft at this point, refrigerate it for 15 to 20 minutes.

4. When you are ready to roll out the dough, remove a bag of dough from the refrigerator, open it, and dust both surfaces of dough lightly with flour. Return the dough to the bag, reseal the bag and, starting from the center, roll the dough out evenly with a rolling pin into a circle 9 inches in diameter. Return the bag to the refrigerator and repeat the process with the remaining three bags, refrigerating them as they are rolled.

5. Prepare the filling by combining the granulated sugar, dark brown sugar, cinnamon, raisins, and walnuts in a medium bowl. Use a fork or a whisk to mix the ingredients together. Set aside. Heat the preserves in a saucepan over low heat, stirring occasionally, until they have liquefied. Set aside.

6. Line the baking sheets with silicone pan liners, parchment paper, or aluminum foil. It is not necessary to butter or oil the lining material. Since the rugelach will cool on the pan lining material, have ready an additional piece of parchment paper or aluminum foil (or a third silicone pan liner) that is large enough to fit a baking sheet for the third round of baking.

7. Take the first rolled bag out of the refrigerator, place it on a work surface, and unseal it. Cut down the sides and along the bottom with scissors; remove and discard the top section of the bag. With the dough still resting on the bottom section of bag, use a sharp knife to cut the circle into 12 equal wedges. Make sure that you have cut all the way through the dough. You may leave the wedges close to each other; they do not have to be separated. With a small pastry brush, coat the top surface of each wedge with a thin layer of preserves, then sprinkle each wedge with a generous amount of the filling mixture. Cover the entire surface of each wedge with filling, and press it firmly into the dough. Starting at the wide end, roll up the dough and bend the ends in slightly to form a crescent. Place the rugelach 1½ inches apart on a baking sheet. Brush the tops with a little milk, then sprinkle with a little of the cinnamon sugar mixture. Repeat the cutting and filling process with the three remaining portions of dough. Fill the two baking sheets with rugelach. Place any excess rugelach on the piece of aluminum foil or parchment paper.

8. Preheat the oven to 350°F with a rack in the center of the oven. When the oven has preheated, bake the rugelach one sheet at a time and refrigerate the remaining assembled rugelach until ready to bake. Bake for 16 to 18 minutes, or until the tops are golden brown and the filling is bubbling. Carefully slide the liner material off the baking sheet, with the rugelach in place. Transfer the liner to a wire rack and let the rugelach cool for 15 minutes, then transfer them from the liner to the rack.

9. Bake the second sheet in the same way as you baked the first. While the second sheet is in the oven, turn the first baking sheet upside down and run it under cold water to cool it. Fill it with rugelach and bake. You will need to bake the rugelach in three batches.

10. The rugelach can be stored in a covered tin at room temperature for up to 1 week. To freeze, allow the rugelach to cool completely after baking, then spread them on a baking sheet and place in the freezer for at least 3 hours. When they are thoroughly frozen, stack them in plastic bags for up to 3 months. Use a waterproof marker to note the contents of the bags and the date. Defrost the rugelach in the bags at room temperature for about 30 minutes.

Snow Balls

Cookies

Makes: about 4 dozen cookies

What you'll need:

baking sheet for toasting pecans

sharp, heavy knife or food processor for chopping pecans

2 heavy-duty baking sheets

silicone pan liners, parchment paper, or aluminum foil for preparing the baking sheets

hand-held electric mixer

mesh sieve

mini ice cream scoop (optional)

small spoon for rolling baked cookies in confectioners' sugar

Baking time: 60 minutes (30 minutes per sheet)

These are the little Christmas cookies that you wait all year to eat, forgetting that they leave a trail of powdered sugar down the front of your fancy black velvet dress or Hermès tie. Pure butter, sugar, and toasted pecans (and a little bit of flour to hold the whole thing together)—the Greeks had the right idea when they invented these tasty morsels. They're called *kourambiedes*, in case you ever find yourself in Greece at Christmastime.

2 cups pecans, toasted and cooled to room temperature (see Lora Says)

2 sticks (16 tablespoons) unsalted butter, softened

¼ cup granulated sugar

1 tablespoon pure vanilla extract

2 cups all-purpose flour

½ teaspoon salt

Nonstick vegetable spray (optional)

1 cup confectioners' sugar (if sugar is lumpy, sift first, then measure)

1. Preheat the oven to 325°F with a rack in the center of the oven. Line the baking sheets with silicone pan liners, parchment paper, or aluminum foil. It is not necessary to butter or oil the lining material. Set aside.

2. Chop the toasted pecans by hand with a chef's knife or in a food processor. Whichever method you use, do not pulverize the nuts. They should be in pea-size pieces. Set aside to cool completely.

3. Place the butter and granulated sugar in a large mixing bowl and use the mixer on high speed to cream them together until the mixture is light and fluffy, about 2 minutes. Beat in

124 *Basic Baking*

the vanilla, then turn the mixer speed to low to mix in the nuts. Place a mesh sieve over the bowl and put the flour and salt in the sieve. Shake the flour and salt onto the butter mixture. Use a rubber spatula to combine all the ingredients into a soft dough.

4. Use a mini ice cream scoop or a tablespoon measure, to form walnut-size balls of dough, and place them 1½ inches apart on the prepared baking sheets. If you use an ice cream scoop, you may wish to spray it lightly with vegetable spray to make it easier to release the dough from the scoop. The cookies will not spread very much. Refrigerate one filled sheet while you bake the other. Bake for 30 minutes; rotate each pan 180 degrees halfway through the baking time. The cookies should remain quite pale.

5. Remove the cookies from the oven. Place the confectioners' sugar in a shallow bowl. Just as soon as the cookies are cool enough to handle safely, remove them from the baking sheet, several at a time, and drop them into the bowl of sugar. Use a small spoon to roll them around so that they are completely coated with sugar. Place the cookies in a single layer on a length of aluminum foil to cool completely, then roll them in sugar one more time.

6. The cookies can be stored in a covered tin at room temperature for up to 1 week. To freeze, allow the cookies to cool completely after baking and coating them with sugar, then spread them on a baking sheet and place in the freezer for at least 3 hours. When the cookies are thoroughly frozen, stack them in freezer-strength recloseable gallon-size plastic bags for up to 3 months. Use a waterproof marker to note the contents of the bags and the date. Thaw them in the bags at room temperature for 1 to 2 hours.

LORA SAYS: Toasting nuts brings out their flavor. It's important to toast them ahead of time so that the nuts will have a chance to cool completely before they are added to the batter. Adding them while they are warm will melt the fat and make the cookies hard to handle, and they will flatten and spread during baking. Toasting the pecans before you make these cookies will make all the difference in the world. That deep, mellow, rich flavor is what makes them so special.

Ginger Cookies

Makes: 12 large cookies

What you'll need:

2 heavy-duty baking sheets

silicone pan liners, parchment paper, or aluminum foil for preparing the baking sheets

mesh sieve

hand-held electric mixer

small plate or saucer

¼-cup ice cream scoop (optional)

Baking time: 24 minutes (12 minutes per sheet)

Next time you wander into Starbucks and get a hankering for one of those mega ginger cookies with the crackled tops, don't reach for your wallet to shell out $2.50. Remind yourself that you can go home and make the same cookie right in your own kitchen.

FOR PREPARING THE BAKING SHEETS

If using aluminum foil, 1½ tablespoons unsalted butter or solid vegetable shortening, softened

FOR THE COOKIES

2¼ cups all-purpose flour

2 teaspoons baking soda

¼ teaspoon salt

1 teaspoon ground cinnamon

1 teaspoon ground ginger

1½ sticks (12 tablespoons) unsalted butter, softened

1 cup packed dark brown sugar

1 extra-large egg

¼ cup regular molasses (see Lora Says)

Granulated sugar for coating the cookie dough before baking

Nonstick vegetable spray (for coating the scoop) (optional)

1. Preheat the oven to 375°F with a rack in the center of the oven. Line the baking sheets with silicone pan liners, parchment paper, or aluminum foil. If you are using foil, apply a light coating of butter or solid vegetable shortening. Set aside.

2. Place a mesh sieve over a medium mixing bowl and add the flour, baking soda, salt, cinnamon, and ginger. Shake the contents into the bowl and set aside.

3. Cream the butter and dark brown sugar in a large mixing bowl with the mixer on high speed until the mixture is light and fluffy, about 1 minute. With the mixer on medium speed, beat in the egg and molasses, then increase the speed to high and beat for about 1 minute until the mixture no longer looks curdled. Move the beaters around the bowl and scrape down the sides of the bowl with a rubber spatula several times while mixing.

4. Mix in the flour mixture on low speed, and continue mixing until there is no trace of the dry ingredients in the batter. The batter will be rather stiff. Place some granulated sugar on a small plate or saucer. Use the ice cream scoop, if desired, or a measuring cup to form ¼-cup portions of dough. You may wish to spray the scoop or measuring cup lightly with vegetable spray to make it easier to release the dough. Transfer the dough to your hands and roll each portion of dough into a rough ball, then roll each ball in the sugar. Place six sugared balls on each baking sheet, spacing them evenly, as they will spread during baking. Dampen your fingers with water and press down lightly on each cookie to flatten it a little and dampen the top. You will need to dampen your fingers for each cookie.

5. Refrigerate one filled baking sheet while baking the other. Bake for 12 minutes, or until the cookies have spread and are firm to the touch. Rotate each sheet 180 degrees halfway through the baking time. Remove the cookies from the oven and cool them on the baking sheets.

6. The cookies can be stored in a covered tin at room temperature for up to 1 week. To freeze, allow the cookies to cool completely after baking, then spread them on a cookie sheet and place in the freezer for at least 3 hours. When the cookies are thoroughly frozen, stack them in a plastic bag for up to 3 months. Use a waterproof marker to note the contents of the bag and the date. Thaw them in the bag at room temperature for 1 to 2 hours.

This dough can be frozen for slice-and-bake cookies. See instructions on page 95.

LORA SAYS: For a chewier cookie, smack each baking sheet flat on the counter after removing it from the oven to deflate the dough.

LORA SAYS: There is a big difference in taste between regular and blackstrap molasses. Regular molasses is subtle when used in the correct amount; blackstrap, if used in the amount called for in this recipe, will overpower everything with a strong, unpleasant taste. The less chemically treated unsulphured molasses is easy to find and preferable to the treated, or "sulphured," variety.

Meringue Clouds

Makes: 30 cookies

What you'll need:

2 heavy-duty baking sheets

silicone pan liners, parchment paper, or aluminum foil for preparing the baking sheets

hand-held electric mixer

¼-cup dry measuring cup

Baking time: 1 hour plus 1 hour rest in turned-off oven

There is nothing like the melt-in-your-mouth delicate sweetness of homemade meringue. The metamorphosis from crisp cookie to tender wafer as the morsel moves back into your mouth can be—if you're a cookie freak like I am—a religious experience (the fact that these are fat free is the frosting on the cake!).

Meringues are fun to make. It takes a bit of practice to get them right, but the effort is worth it and you can eat the "outtakes." Be sure to read the information about whipping egg whites and meringue on pages 12–13—it will keep those "outtakes" to a minimum. Even the most practiced bakers save making crisp meringue for dry days. If it's pouring rain outside, make any of the other cookies in this chapter and save the meringues for a cool, dry day.

FOR THE MERINGUES

4 extra-large egg whites, at room temperature

¾ cup superfine sugar (see page 49)

Pinch of cream of tartar

2 teaspoons pure vanilla extract (optional) (see Lora says)

1. Preheat the oven to 250°F with racks in the lower and upper thirds of the oven. Make sure that the racks are not at the very top or at the very bottom of the oven. Line the baking sheets with silicone pan liners, parchment paper, or aluminum foil. Do not butter or oil any of the lining materials; these cookies will peel right off after they are completely cooled. Set aside.

2. Place the egg whites and cream of tartar in a very clean medium mixing bowl. Beat with the mixer with very clean beaters on high speed for about 1½ minutes, or until the whites are foamy and almost tripled in volume. The mixer blades will leave noticeable tracks as they move through the egg whites. With the mixer still on high speed, start sprinkling on the sugar, like a light snowfall, making sure that each addition disappears before another is added. Move the beaters around the bowl as you work, and twirl the bowl in one direction from time to time. After the sugar is added, continue to beat until the whites are stiff and glossy but not dry, about 1 minute. Be sure to scrape down the sides of the bowl with a rubber spatula several times while mixing. Soft peaks will form when the beaters are lifted out of the bowl. (Be sure to turn the mixer off when testing the peaks!) If you are adding vanilla, beat it into the whites on low speed as soon as they have reached the right consistency.

3. With a ¼-cup measure, scoop scant quarter-cup portions onto the baking sheets, placing them 1 inch apart. Bake the meringues for 1 hour. Switch the sheets top to bottom halfway through the baking time; when you do that, rotate each sheet 180 degrees as well. If the meringues begin to brown, reduce the oven temperature to 225°F. At the end of the hour, turn the oven off but leave the meringues in the oven with the door closed for 1 hour longer. At the end of the hour, remove the sheets from the oven. Carefully remove the meringues, still on their baking-sheet lining material, and place on the counter to cool completely.

4. The meringues can be stored in a covered container at room temperature for up to 1 month. They cannot be frozen.

LORA SAYS: Vanilla gives wonderful flavor to these meringues, but they will not be pure white after baking if you add vanilla. You may leave it out.

LORA SAYS: Meringues bake at a very low temperature; in essence, they are not so much cooking as drying in the oven.

LORA SAYS: If your meringues become soggy, you can crisp them up by placing them on a baking sheet in a 200°F oven for about 15 minutes. If the weather—or your kitchen—is humid, however, they'll get sticky again.

Double Chocolate Meringues

Makes: 30 cookies

What you'll need:

2 heavy-duty baking sheets

silicone pan liners, parchment paper, or aluminum foil for preparing the baking sheets

hand-held electric mixer

¼-cup dry measuring cup

Baking time: 1 hour plus 1 hour rest in turned-off oven

If chocolate in one form is wonderful, then the addition of chocolate in two forms is perfection. The combination of sweet crisp meringue and meltingly mellow chocolate chips—made even more chocolaty by cocoa powder—will zoom these featherweight confections right to the top of your list of favorites.

FOR THE MERINGUES

4 extra-large egg whites, at room temperature

Pinch of cream of tartar

¾ cup superfine sugar (see page 49)

3 tablespoons unsweetened cocoa powder, not Dutch-processed (see page 15)

1 cup semisweet chocolate chips

1. Preheat the oven to 250°F with racks in the lower and upper thirds of the oven. Make sure that the racks are not at the very top or at the very bottom of the oven. Line the baking sheets with silicone pan liners, parchment paper, or aluminum foil. Do not butter or oil any of the lining materials; these cookies will peel right off after they are completely cooled. Set aside.

2. Place the egg whites and cream of tartar in a very clean medium mixing bowl. Beat with the mixer with very clean beaters on high speed for about 1½ minutes, or until the whites are foamy and almost tripled in volume. The mixer blades will leave noticeable tracks as they move through the egg whites. With the mixer still on high speed, start sprinkling on the sugar, like a light snowfall, making sure that each addition disappears before another is added. Move the beaters around the bowl as you work, and twirl the bowl in one direction from time to time. After the sugar is added, continue to beat until the whites are stiff and glossy but not dry, about 1 minute. Be sure to scrape down the sides of the bowl with a rubber spatula several times while mixing. Soft peaks will form when the beaters are lifted out of the bowl. (Be sure to turn the mixer off when testing the peaks!) As soon as the meringue has reached the right consistency, reduce the mixer speed to low and mix in the cocoa powder. Turn off the mixer and sprinkle the chocolate chips on the meringue. Use a rubber spatula to gently fold in the chips. Be very careful not to overmix; you do not want to deflate the meringue.

3. With a ¼-cup measure, scoop scant ¼-cup portions onto the baking sheets, placing them 1 inch apart. Bake the meringues for 1 hour. Switch the sheets top to bottom halfway through the baking time; when you do that, rotate each sheet 180 degrees as well. If the meringues begin to brown, reduce the oven temperature to 225°F. At the end of the hour, turn the oven off but leave the meringues in the oven with the door closed for 1 hour longer. At the end of the hour, remove the sheets from the oven. Carefully remove the meringues, still on their baking-sheet lining material, and place on the counter to cool completely.

4. The meringues can be stored in a covered container at room temperature for up to 1 month. They cannot be frozen.

Cakes

· ·

The other day I gave a private cooking lesson to two young women, college freshmen. When asked what they would like to make, they both shrugged and said in surprise, "Whatever."

"How about a chocolate cake? Would you like to learn that?" I asked.

Incredulously one of them asked. "You can do that?"

"What, make a chocolate cake?"

"No, teach us how to make one, like, from scratch?"

"Why do you find that so difficult to believe?" I asked.

"Because no one *makes* cake, I mean it's like something you buy . . ."

Later, as we ate the cake that they had made, I asked them why they thought no one made homemade cake anymore.

"Did you think it was hard to do?" I asked.

"No," said one, "but I guess I always assumed it was hard; why else would people use mixes?" Then she said, "You know, it's the same amount of dishes to wash, and this tastes way, way better."

"And it wasn't as hard as you thought, right?" I asked.

"No," said the other, "not nearly. Actually, it was fun."

"Good, so you'll be making chocolate cake from scratch from now on, right?"

They looked at each other, then at me and replied, "Whatever."

Cake Walk
What Should I Do If . . .

It's stuck in the pan? The pan wasn't prepared properly. Besides using good-quality, heavy-duty pans, pan preparation is probably the most important step in cake making. Always apply a generous coating of butter or solid vegetable shortening to the bottom and sides of the pan(s), then line the pans with parchment paper. You can use precut 9-inch liners, or you can trace the pans on a length of parchment paper from a roll, and cut circles to fit the bottom of the pan(s). Do not use aluminum foil to line the pan(s); use wax paper only as a last resort. Coat the liner(s) with butter or solid vegetable shortening too, then dust with flour and knock out the excess. Precut parchment paper liners in many sizes are available in gourmet supply shops and many hardware stores.

To remove the cake from the pan, run the tip of a sharp knife around the edge to release it, place a wire rack over the top, then invert the pan onto the rack. If the cake does not release from the pan, rap the bottom smartly with your knuckles. If this doesn't work, jiggle the pan to try to loosen it—chances are the bottom is sticking. If you simply can't get the cake out in one piece or without leaving some of the bottom behind, don't worry.

It's burned on the bottom? The pans were placed too far down in the oven. Next time use the center rack. Use heavy-duty cake pans; inexpensive, thin pans are poor and uneven conductors of heat.

The layers are so skinny? Did you remember to add the baking powder or baking soda? Did you allow the batter to sit too long before baking? Did you use the correct-size pan? A pan that is too large will result in a skimpy layer.

The cake has a domed top? The batter may have been overbeaten; next time, go easier on the mixing. The oven temperature may have been too high; check the recipe and the oven thermostat. The pan may have been too small for the amount of batter, or the outside got set before the center, and the center continued to rise. The best solution is to use a gadget called Magi-Cake Strips®, which wrap around the outside of the pan during baking. These are available in gourmet stores and by mail order (see page 315).

The cake sinks in the middle? The cake was underbaked. Use a cake tester to make sure the interior is cooked. It should come out clean and dry.

The cake falls apart and all I have is crumbs? Double-check that the correct amount of sugar, shortening, and liquid was used. Make sure to mix the batter just until all the dry ingredients are incorporated.

It's got big holes? Too much mixing. Make sure that all the ingredients are at room temperature, and then you won't have to mix so much.

It's too tough? Too much mixing. The wrong kind of flour may have been used. Never use bread (high gluten) flour for making cakes. If the recipe calls for cake flour, use cake flour.

It's too dry? Check to make sure that you added the right amount of liquid and that you didn't measure the flour incorrectly. Check the baking time and your thermostat. It's possible that the cake overbaked or was baked in too hot an oven.

It's raw in the middle? Check the baking time and the oven thermostat, and use a cake tester.

It's soggy on the bottom? The cake remained in the pan too long during cooling, so that moisture condensed and was trapped under the layer. Remove the cake from the pan and allow it to cool on a wire cake rack, according to the recipe directions.

All the chocolate chips/raisins/nuts sank to the bottom? The batter wasn't thick enough; check the amount of flour and liquid. The batter may have been mixed too much after the chips/raisins/nuts were added. Instead of mixing them in, fold them in gently just before pouring the batter into the prepared pan.

I want to store a frosted cake? There are two storage options for a frosted cake. The most convenient by far is a deep, round covered plastic storage container for round cakes—layered or not—and a covered rectangular container for rectangular cakes and cupcakes. The containers accommodate cakes that must be stored in the refrigerator or kept at room temperature, and make transporting a cake very easy. Rubbermaid makes a 22-cup, round container that accommodates any single- or double-layer round cake in this book, as well as a 33-cup rectangular container that holds a 9 by 13-inch cake or any baked good that is smaller. If you don't have a storage container, you can cover the cake with plastic wrap. To ensure that the plastic wrap does not stick to the frosting, plant about ten toothpicks in the cake surface, leaving about one inch of wood exposed. Cut a piece or pieces of plastic wrap large enough to cover the whole cake. (For a high, round cake you may have to cut two identical pieces and place them on the cake so that they cross in the middle. A 9 by 13-inch cake will need two pieces that overlap down the center of the cake.) Drape the plastic wrap over the picks, and tuck it loosely under the cake plate.

Chocolate Miracle Cake

Makes: one 9-inch square cake; 8 servings

What you'll need:

9-inch square baking pan, 2 inches deep

sharp, heavy knife for chopping chocolate

microwave or small metal bowl and pan of simmering water for melting chocolate

mixing spoon

hand-held electric mixer

mesh sieve

small saucepan for boiling water

Baking time: 40 to 45 minutes

The miracle here is that something that looks this messy going into the oven will come out transformed into an absolutely irresistible, rich, puddinglike dessert that comes with its own sauce. You start by making a simple stiff batter, dust it with a sugar-and-cocoa mixture, and finally add boiling water. Sounds like something from a box? Just resist the urge to mix the layers together before baking, but do give in to the urge to serve this warm from the oven with a scoop of ice cream.

FOR PREPARING THE PAN

½ tablespoon unsalted butter, softened

FOR THE BOTTOM LAYER

2 ounces (2 squares) unsweetened chocolate, chopped (see page 16)

1 stick (8 tablespoons) unsalted butter, softened

¾ cup granulated sugar

1 cup all-purpose flour

1½ teaspoons baking powder

½ teaspoon salt

½ cup milk

1 teaspoon pure vanilla extract

½ cup plus 2 tablespoons granulated sugar

½ cup packed dark brown sugar

3 rounded tablespoons unsweetened cocoa powder, not Dutch-processed (see page 15)

1½ cups boiling water

1 teaspoon pure vanilla extract

1. Preheat the oven to 350°F with a rack in the center of the oven. Butter the baking pan. Set aside.

2. To prepare the bottom layer, melt the chocolate either in the microwave or in a small metal mixing bowl set over, but not touching, a pan of gently simmering water. Stir until completely melted and smooth. Let cool slightly.

3. Combine the butter and sugar in a large mixing bowl. Using the mixer on high speed, beat the mixture until it is light and fluffy, 4 to 5 minutes. Scrape down the sides of the bowl with a rubber spatula several times while mixing. Place a mesh sieve over the bowl and add the flour, baking powder, and salt. Shake the flour mixture into the bowl, then add the milk. With the mixer on low speed, mix until well combined. The mixture will be very thick. Add the melted chocolate and the vanilla, and continue to mix on low speed until combined. Use a rubber spatula to scrape the mixture into the prepared pan and then to spread the batter to the edges of the pan. The layer will be quite thin.

4. Make the topping in the same bowl—there is no need to wash it if you have scraped it very clean. Stir together the granulated sugar, the dark brown sugar and the cocoa powder. Rub the mixture with your fingers to get rid of any lumps. Sprinkle it evenly over the batter in the pan. Place the boiling water in a measuring cup with a spout and add the vanilla, then drizzle it slowly and carefully over the batter, being careful to disturb the batter as little as possible. Bake until the top is crusty and cracked in several places, and the sauce is bubbling around the edges, 40 to 45 minutes. Remove the cake from the oven and let it cool slightly, 15 to 20 minutes.

5. To serve, use a spoon to scoop up a portion of cake, then top with some of the sauce from the bottom of the pan for each serving.

6. This cake is best eaten shortly after it is baked. Leftovers can be stored, covered with plastic wrap, for up to 48 hours at room temperature. The cake cannot be frozen.

LORA SAYS: The reason you need to be careful not to get any water—even in the form of steam—into chocolate while it's being melted is that oil (in this case, cocoa butter, the fat in chocolate) and water *really* don't mix, and the chocolate will get hard and grainy and will be useless in the recipe. Learning to melt chocolate in the microwave will save time and will ensure a larger measure of success (see page 16).

LORA SAYS: This cake is not the most beautiful in the world, so cut the cake in the kitchen and bring the dessert plates to the table. A scoop of ice cream or a nice dab of whipped cream on top of each slice would earn some stars in the glamour department.

Carrot Cake with Cream Cheese Frosting

Makes: one 9 by 13-inch cake; 18 servings

What you'll need:

9 × 13-inch baking pan, 2 inches deep

parchment paper for lining the cake pan

peeler and grater for carrots

sharp, heavy knife for chopping walnuts

mesh sieve

fork for stirring

hand-held electric mixer

cake tester

wire rack

Baking time: 40 minutes

Years ago, when one could afford to go to Nantucket without selling off family valuables, we rented a ramshackle cottage down the road from Fred Rogers. My boys were four and six at the time. They were delirious at the idea of having Mr. Rogers for a neighbor. The other great thing about Nantucket that summer was our proximity to a farm stand that sold—in addition to native peaches, tomatoes, and sweet corn that was so perfect it never needed butter—squares of carrot cake with cream cheese frosting that looked like plump, white-topped, orange-bottomed pillows in their tight plastic wrapping. You had to get there before the pieces of cake were either poked to death by children trying to find the biggest ones, or the frosting had melted and stuck to the plastic. We'd eat them on our way to the beach, wiping our mouths with the backs of our hands, hoping we'd run into Mr. Rogers also eating a piece of that cake. That would truly have been a wonderful day in the neighborhood.

FOR PREPARING THE PAN

1½ tablespoons unsalted butter or solid vegetable shortening, softened

2 tablespoons all-purpose flour

FOR THE CAKE

2 cups all-purpose flour

1 teaspoon baking powder

1 teaspoon baking soda

½ teaspoon salt

2 teaspoons ground
cinnamon

1½ teaspoons ground
ginger

1 teaspoon ground
nutmeg

4 extra-large eggs

¾ cup vegetable oil

¾ cup packed dark brown
sugar

¾ cup granulated sugar

2 teaspoons pure vanilla
extract

2 cups grated peeled
carrots (about 3 large
carrots)

1½ cups (6 ounces)
walnuts, coarsely chopped

1 cup golden or dark
raisins

FOR THE FROSTING

Cream Cheese Frosting (recipe follows)

1. Preheat the oven to 350°F with a rack in the center of the oven. Cut a 9 by 13-inch rectangle of parchment paper. Coat the sides and bottoms of the pan with some of the butter or solid vegetable shortening, then place the parchment paper liner in the pan and apply butter or shortening to the liner, too. Place the flour in the pan, shake to coat the pan with flour, then knock out the excess. Set aside.

2. Place a mesh sieve over a medium mixing bowl and add the flour, baking powder, baking soda, salt, cinnamon, ginger, and nutmeg. Shake the contents into the bowl and set aside.

3. Crack the eggs into a measuring cup with a spout, stir lightly, and set aside. Place the oil, dark brown and granulated sugar, and the vanilla in a large mixing bowl. Use the mixer on medium speed to beat the ingredients together until the sugars have dissolved and the mixture is smooth except for some small lumps of dark brown sugar that might remain, about 2 minutes. Scrape down the sides of the bowl with a rubber spatula several times while mixing. Add the eggs to the mixture and beat on medium speed until they are incorporated, about 2 minutes more. Scrape the sides of the bowl well.

4. Turn the mixer to lowest speed and add the flour mixture. You will have to use a rubber spatula to mix the flour into the wet ingredients. Beat until the mixture is smooth and no traces of flour are apparent, occasionally scraping down the bowl with a rubber spatula. Add the carrots, nuts, and raisins, and stir with a rubber spatula until they are just combined, about 1 minute. Pour and scrape the batter into the prepared pan and smooth the top with a rubber spatula. Bake until a cake tester inserted into the center of the cake comes out clean and dry, about 40 minutes.

5. Remove the cake from the oven and cool it in the pan for 20 minutes, then turn it out carefully onto a wire rack, remove the parchment paper liner, and allow the cake to cool completely. Frost with Cream Cheese Frosting.

6. The baked and cooled unfrosted cake, out of its pan, can be refrigerated, wrapped in plastic wrap, for up to 3 days. It may also be frozen for up to 3 months. Wrap the cake securely in plastic wrap and place it in a freezer-strength recloseable jumbo-size plastic bag. Label the bag with a waterproof marker. Defrost the cake in its wrapping in the refrigerator or at room temperature, and then frost it.

LORA SAYS: The dark brown sugar in this cake contributes not only to its moistness, but adds a deeper, mellow taste associated with homey desserts like this one.

LORA SAYS: Be sure to use nice, fresh, firm, bright-colored carrots for this cake. They taste sweeter and are moister than carrots that have sat around awhile.

Cream Cheese Frosting

Cakes

Makes: 3 generous cups

What you'll need:

hand-held electric mixer;

flexible metal spatula

1 pound cream cheese (not the whipped or reduced-fat variety) at room temperature

¾ stick (6 tablespoons) unsalted butter, softened

1½ cups confectioners' sugar (if sugar is lumpy, sift first, then measure)

1½ teaspoons pure vanilla extract

1. Combine the cream cheese and butter in a large mixing bowl. With the mixer set on medium high, beat the cream cheese and butter until smooth, about 1 minute. Reduce mixer speed to low, add the confectioners' sugar, and continue to beat until smooth. Beat in the vanilla until it is thoroughly incorporated.

2. To frost the cake, use a flexible metal spatula to spread a thin layer of frosting on the four sides of the cake, then apply the remainder to the top. Use the spatula to distribute the frosting evenly and to create a swirled effect, if desired.

3. The frosting may be refrigerated, covered, for up to 1 week. Bring it to room temperature before frosting the cake.

4. The frosted cake can be covered with plastic wrap and stored in the refrigerator for up to 1 week. To avoid having the plastic wrap come in direct contact with the frosting, push about 10 toothpicks halfway into the cake at even intervals around the top. Drape a sheet of plastic wrap over the toothpicks and loosely down the sides of the cake.

LORA SAYS: If you are going to transport this cake to a picnic or other informal affair, it would make sense to frost the cake in the pan after it has cooled. Cool the baked cake out of its pan on a wire rack. Rinse out the baking pan, dry it well, and invert it over the cooled cake on its cooling rack so that the pan encloses the cake. Hold the cake pan and rack together and flip the whole thing over so that the cake is back inside the pan. Use a flexible spatula to spread the top of the cake with frosting. Unless you are pretty heavy-handed with the frosting, there will be some left over, since you aren't frosting the sides of the cake.

Classic Yellow Layer Cake with Milk Chocolate Frosting

Makes: one 9-inch 2-layer cake; 8 to 10 servings

What you'll need:

two 9-inch round cake pans, 2 inches deep

parchment paper for lining the pans

small, sharp knife for cutting up butter

mesh sieve

whisk

2 table knives or a pastry blender

hand-held electric mixer

cake tester

2 wire racks and one plastic wrap–covered baking sheet

Baking time: 30 minutes

For a moment you'll feel like Betty Crocker herself as you swirl thick milk chocolate frosting over the top of this moist, light layer cake. Poor Betty. I'll bet she never got to sit down with a slice, look winsomely at the camera, and say, "Got milk?" If you want to make someone's birthday a fantasy-become-reality, this is the cake to make. If you want to push the envelope, serve it with a scoop of ice cream. This cake and the technique for mixing the batter with an electric mixer are based on a recipe that appeared in *Cook's Illustrated* May/June 1995.

FOR PREPARING THE PANS

1½ tablespoons unsalted butter or solid vegetable shortening, softened

2 tablespoons all-purpose flour

FOR THE CAKE

2¼ cups all-purpose flour

1½ cups granulated sugar

½ teaspoon salt

2½ teaspoons baking powder

1 tablespoon Lora Brody's Dough Relaxer, optional (see page 48)

¾ cup milk

4 extra-large eggs

1 tablespoon pure vanilla extract

2 sticks (16 tablespoons) unsalted butter, chilled and cut into 8 pieces

Milk Chocolate Frosting (recipe follows)

1. Preheat the oven to 350°F with a rack in the center of the oven. Have ready two 9-inch circles of parchment paper. Coat the sides and bottoms of the pans with some of the butter or shortening, then place a parchment paper liner in each pan and apply butter or shortening to the liners, too. Place 1 tablespoon flour in each pan, shake to coat the pan with flour, then knock out the excess. Set aside.

2. Place a mesh sieve over a large mixing bowl and add the flour, sugar, salt, baking powder, and optional Dough Relaxer. Shake the contents into the bowl and set aside. Pour the milk into a 2-cup measure with a spout. Break the eggs into a cup and add the vanilla. Whisk to combine the ingredients well. Set aside.

3. Scatter the butter pieces over the flour mixture. Use two table knives in a crisscross motion, or a pastry blender, to cut the butter into the flour until the lumps are about the size of peas. (The pieces will not be uniform; none should be larger than peas.) If you are using a pastry blender, stop and scrape the blades from time to time. Add half the milk mixture. With the mixer on low speed, beat for 5 to 10 seconds, then increase the speed to high and beat for 1 minute. Move the beaters around the bowl and scrape down the sides of the bowl with a rubber spatula several times while mixing. Add the remaining milk mixture and beat until the batter looks like whipped cream and the ingredients are well incorporated, about 1 minute. Scrape the batter into the prepared pans and smooth the tops with a rubber spatula.

4. Place the pans at least 2 inches apart on the oven rack and 2 inches from the oven walls. If the oven is too narrow to accommodate the pans on one rack, use two racks positioned as close to the center as possible. Stagger the pans on the two racks; do not place one directly above or below the other. Bake until a cake tester inserted in the center of the cake comes out clean and dry, about 30 minutes. Remove the layers from the oven and cool in the pans on a rack for 10 minutes. Invert each layer onto a plastic wrap–covered baking sheet. Remove the cake pans and peel off the parchment paper liners, then reinvert each layer onto a rack to cool. When the layers have completely cooled, frost them with Milk Chocolate Frosting.

5. The baked and cooled unfrosted layers can be refrigerated, wrapped in plastic wrap, for up to 3 days. They may also be frozen for up to 3 months. Wrap each cooled layer securely in plastic wrap and place each in a freezer-strength recloseable gallon-size plastic bag. Label the bags with a waterproof marker. Defrost the layers in their wrapping in the refrigerator or at room temperature.

LORA SAYS: Baking powder and baking soda, and salt and sugar, are pairs of ingredients that look dangerously alike, and neither can in any way be substituted for the other. To make sure that you are not grabbing the wrong ingredient, use different canisters (in both size and color) to store salt and sugar, and learn to associate baking soda with a box (usually yellow-orange in color) and baking powder with a small, round container.

A sure-fire way to avoid this kind of mistake is to measure out each of the dry ingredients, and to put away each container as soon as you have finished measuring its contents. Line up the filled measuring cups and spoons on the counter in the order in which they are called for in the recipe.

Milk Chocolate Frosting

Makes: about 4 cups, plenty for two 9-inch layers

What you'll need:

sharp, heavy knife for chopping chocolate

scale to weigh chocolate (optional)

1-quart saucepan

whisk

bowl of ice and water, for cooling chocolate and cream (optional)

hand-held electric mixer

flexible metal spatula for frosting

Use best-quality milk chocolate, such as Lindt or Tobler, when you make this frosting. It is so good that you'll want to forget the cake and eat it right out of the bowl. Because you have to use this frosting soon after it is made, read the directions for frosting a layer cake (see page 22) before making the frosting.

1 cup heavy cream

10 ounces best-quality milk chocolate, coarsely chopped

1 tablespoon instant coffee granules (optional)

1 stick (8 tablespoons) unsalted butter, softened

2 cups confectioners' sugar (if sugar is lumpy, sift first, then measure)

1. Place the heavy cream in the saucepan and bring it to a gentle simmer over moderate heat. It is better if the cream is too cool than to have it too hot. Remove the pan from the heat and add the chocolate and the coffee granules, if using. Whisk until the chocolate melts, then continue to whisk until the mixture is shiny and completely free of lumps.

2. Cool the chocolate mixture completely. If you want to hurry the cooling process, set the saucepan in a bowl of ice with a little water added. To cool it even more quickly, transfer the chocolate mixture to a bowl, and set that bowl in the bowl of ice and water (just make sure not a drop of water gets into the chocolate mixture). Stir it frequently with a rubber spatula as it cools. The chocolate will get sludgy, which means the mixture is cooling. Keep scraping chocolate from the sides of the bowl. The chocolate needs to be stiff enough to stand up by itself; it should have the consistency of a soft Tootsie Roll.

3. When the chocolate has cooled, put the butter in a large mixing bowl. With the mixer on high speed, cream the butter until fluffy. Add the confectioners' sugar and beat on high speed until the mixture looks like coarse crumbs. Add the cooled chocolate to the bowl with the sugar and butter, and continue to beat on high speed. The mixture will be grainy at first. Scrape down the sides of the bowl with a rubber spatula several times while mixing. It is important to beat it only until it looks like heavy whipped cream. The beaters will leave tracks as they move through the mixture, which will be a light mocha color. This will take about 3 minutes. If it is beaten too long, the mixture will heat up and fall apart. You must use the frosting immediately.

4. Once frosted, the cake may be covered with plastic wrap or placed in a round cake carrier, and kept at room temperature for 6 to 8 hours. It may also be refrigerated for up to 24 hours. To avoid having plastic wrap come in direct contact with the frosting, push about 10 toothpicks halfway into the cake at even intervals around the top. Drape a sheet or sheets of plastic wrap over the toothpicks and loosely down the sides of the cake.

LORA SAYS: The temptation is to "play" with frosting, making dips and swirls long after the stage where the cake looks completely presentable. At some point the frosting will break down and begin to look lousy. Here are two things to remember: No one expects your cake to look as if a professional made it and almost every cosmetic flaw can be covered with a generous layer of confectioners' sugar, cocoa powder, or shredded coconut.

Snow White Layer Cake with Coconut Frosting

Makes: one 9-inch layer cake; 12 servings

What you'll need:

two 9-inch cake pans, 2 inches deep

parchment paper for lining the cake pans

whisk

mesh sieve

hand-held electric mixer

cake tester

2 wire racks

small, sharp knife for loosening cakes from pans

plastic wrap–covered baking sheet

Baking time: 35 minutes

This recipe is an adaptation of one that appeared in a book created by the editors of *Cook's Illustrated*, called *How to Make an American Layer Cake*. Usually butter and sugar are creamed together first, but here the butter is mixed right into the dry ingredients, much like pie dough, resulting in a deliciously tender but sturdy cake that won't crumble when you spread on the frosting.

FOR PREPARING THE PANS

1½ tablespoons unsalted butter, softened
2 tablespoons all-purpose flour

FOR THE CAKE

1 cup milk, at room temperature

5 extra-large egg whites (save the yolks to make crème brûlée) (see page 12)

2¼ cups cake flour (see page 29)

1¾ cups granulated sugar

4 teaspoons baking powder

1 teaspoon salt

1½ sticks (12 tablespoons) unsalted butter, softened

FOR THE FROSTING

Coconut Frosting (recipe follows)

1. Preheat the oven to 350°F with a rack in the center of the oven. Have ready two 9-inch circles of parchment paper. Coat the sides and bottoms of the pans with some butter, then place a parchment paper liner in each pan and apply butter to the liners, too. Place 1 tablespoon flour in each pan, shake to coat the pan with flour, then knock out the excess. Set aside.

2. Pour the milk and egg whites into a 2-cup measuring cup and whisk well. Set aside.

3. Place a mesh sieve over a deep mixing bowl and add the cake flour, sugar, baking powder, and salt. Shake the contents into the bowl. Add the butter and, using the mixer on low speed, combine the butter with the dry ingredients. Increase the speed to medium and mix until the mixture has formed coarse crumbs, about 1 minute.

4. Pour in 1½ cups of the milk and egg white mixture, and continue beating on medium speed until the batter is smooth and the beaters leave a trail when dragged through the batter. Scrape down the sides of the bowl with a rubber spatula from time to time as you work. Add the remaining milk mixture and beat for 30 seconds more. Pour and scrape the batter into the prepared pans. Smooth the tops with a rubber spatula.

5. Place the pans at least 2 inches apart and 2 inches from the oven walls. If the oven is too narrow to accommodate the pans on one rack, use two racks positioned as close to the center as possible. Stagger the pans on the two racks; do not place one directly above or below the other. Bake until the cakes have pulled away slightly from the sides of the pans and the tops are a light golden brown, about 35 minutes. The cake should spring back when pressed lightly with your fingers, and a cake tester inserted in the center of the cakes should come out clean and dry.

6. Remove the layers from the oven and cool in the pans on wire racks for 5 minutes. Run a small, sharp knife around the inside of each pan. Invert each layer onto a plastic wrap–covered baking sheet and remove the pan. Peel off and discard the parchment paper liner. Place a wire rack on the exposed surface, then invert each cake again on the rack so that it is right side up. Let the layers cool completely before frosting with Coconut Frosting.

7. The baked and cooled unfrosted layers can be refrigerated, wrapped in plastic wrap, for up to 3 days. They may also be frozen for up to 3 months. Wrap each cooled layer securely in plastic wrap and place each in a plastic bag. Label the bags with a waterproof marker. Defrost the layers in their wrapping in the refrigerator or at room temperature.

Coconut Frosting

Makes: 5½ cups frosting, enough for two 9-inch layers

What you'll need:

small, heavy skillet or microwave for toasting coconut

1-quart saucepan

candy thermometer

whisk or mixing spoon

hand-held electric mixer

flexible metal spatula for frosting

This frosting tends to deflate after 6 hours, so plan to eat the cake the same day you frost it.

1⅓ cups granulated sugar

⅓ cup water

3 extra-large egg whites, at room temperature

⅛ teaspoon cream of tartar

⅛ teaspoon salt

2 teaspoons pure vanilla extract

1 cup unsweetened shredded coconut, toasted (see Lora Says)

1. Place the sugar and water in the saucepan over medium heat. Clip a candy thermometer to the side of the pan, positioning it so that the probe is touching the liquid but is not touching the bottom of the pan. Stir the sugar and water with a whisk or a wooden spoon until the sugar is completely dissolved. The mixture will be opaque. Remove the pan from the heat while you prepare the egg whites.

2. Place the egg whites, cream of tartar, and salt in a deep mixing bowl. With the mixer on high speed, beat the egg whites until they are foamy, about 1 minute. Turn off the mixer and let the egg whites sit while you cook the sugar syrup.

3. Return the sugar and water to high heat and bring to a boil. Cook the sugar and water at a rapid boil until the temperature registers 238°F on the candy thermometer. Remove the pan from the heat. Return the mixer to high speed and hold the mixer with one hand and the saucepan in the other. Pour the sugar syrup into the egg whites in a slow, steady, thin stream, beating continuously. Be very careful when you do this, as a burn with hot sugar syrup is very painful. When all the syrup has been added, continue to beat, rotating the bowl and scraping down the sides frequently, until the mixture forms glossy, stiff peaks and has completely cooled. It will look like commercial marshmallow fluff. Add the vanilla and beat just to incorporate.

4. Follow directions for frosting a layer cake on page 22. Sprinkle on the toasted coconut. Once frosted, the cake may be covered with plastic wrap or placed in a round cake carrier and kept at room temperature for no more than 6 hours. To avoid having plastic wrap come in direct contact with the frosting, push about 10 toothpicks halfway into the cake at even intervals around the top. Drape a sheet or sheets of plastic wrap over the toothpicks and loosely down the sides of the cake.

VARIATION: Before frosting the cake, spread a thin layer of raspberry or strawberry jam on the top of the first (bottom) layer, then frost as directed in the recipe.

LORA SAYS: The pockets of air beaten into the egg white frosting will deflate more quickly in the dampness of the refrigerator. It's better to store this cake at room temperature and eat it soon after it is frosted.

LORA SAYS: To toast coconut, place a small, heavy skillet over medium heat. When it is hot, put in the unsweetened shreds and turn the heat to low. Cook the coconut, shaking the skillet occasionally, until it turns light golden brown, about 2 minutes. It can also be toasted in the microwave. Place the coconut in one layer on a microwave-safe plate and microwave on high for 1 minute. Toss the coconut on the plate and microwave for another minute on high. If it is not toasted by the end of the second minute, toss again and return to the microwave for another 30 seconds. Toasting coconut brings out the flavor and adds a delicious yet delicate crunch to the texture.

Devil's Food Layer Cake
with Fudge Frosting

Makes: one 9-inch 2-layer cake; 12 servings

What you'll need:

two 9-inch round cake pans, 2 inches deep

parchment paper for lining the pans

mesh sieve

hand-held electric mixer

cake tester

2 wire racks

plastic wrap–covered baking sheet

Baking time: 25 minutes

Who can resist the deepest, darkest, moistest chocolate cake layers separated by thick, creamy, excuse-me-while-I-scoop-up-a-taste-with-my-finger fudge frosting? Not me! And, most likely, not you!

FOR PREPARING THE PANS

1½ tablespoons unsalted butter or solid vegetable shortening, softened
2 tablespoons all-purpose flour

FOR THE CAKE

2 cups cake flour (see page 29)

½ cup unsweetened cocoa powder, not Dutch-processed (see page 15)

1 teaspoon baking powder

½ teaspoon baking soda

½ teaspoon salt

1½ sticks (12 tablespoons) unsalted butter, softened

2 cups granulated sugar

3 extra-large eggs

¾ cup strong brewed coffee (regular or decaffeinated), cold or at room temperature

½ cup sour cream

FOR THE FROSTING

World's Richest Fudge Frosting (recipe follows)

1. Preheat the oven to 350°F with a rack in the center of the oven. Have ready two 9-inch circles of parchment paper. Coat the sides and bottoms of the pans with some of the butter or solid vegetable shortening, then place a parchment paper liner in each pan and apply butter or shortening to the liners, too. Place 1 tablespoon flour in each pan, shake to coat the pan with flour, then knock out the excess. Set aside.

2. Place a mesh sieve over a medium mixing bowl and add the cake flour, cocoa powder, baking powder, baking soda, and salt. Shake the contents into the bowl and set aside.

3. In a large mixing bowl, cream the butter with the sugar using the mixer on high speed. Beat until the mixture is fluffy, about 3 minutes. Add the eggs, one at a time, on moderate speed, mixing well to incorporate each egg before another is added. The mixture will be light and fluffy, like yellow whipped cream. Move the beaters around the bowl and scrape down the sides of the bowl with a rubber spatula several times while mixing. Add the coffee and sour cream. Beat on moderate speed, moving the beaters around the bowl as you work. The mixture will appear curdled, but that's okay.

4. Beat in the flour mixture on medium speed, beating just until all traces of flour disappear. Scrape down the sides of the bowl. Pour and scrape the batter into the prepared pans, and smooth the tops with a rubber spatula. Place the pans at least 2 inches apart on the oven rack, and 3 inches from the oven walls. If the oven is too narrow to accommodate the pans on one rack, use two racks positioned as close to the center as possible. Stagger the pans on the two racks; do not place one directly above or below the other. Bake for 25 to 30 minutes, or until a cake tester inserted in the center of the layers comes out clean and dry. Remove the cakes from the oven and cool them in the pan for 10 minutes. Place a plastic wrap–covered baking sheet over the top of one layer and invert the layer onto the sheet. Remove the parchment paper liner. Place a wire rack over the exposed surface of the cake and invert it again, so that it is right side up on the rack. Repeat the process with the second layer. Allow the layers to cool completely before frosting with fudge frosting.

5. The baked and cooled unfrosted layers can be refrigerated, wrapped in plastic wrap, for up to 3 days. They may also be frozen for up to 3 months. Wrap each cooled layer securely in plastic wrap and place each in a freezer-strength recloseable gallon-size plastic bag. Label the bags with a waterproof marker. Defrost the layers in their wrapping in the refrigerator or at room temperature.

VARIATION: The batter may also be baked in a 9 by 13-inch baking pan. Prepare the pan as directed, and bake for 45 to 50 minutes, or until a cake tester inserted in the center of the cake comes out clean. Remove the cake from the oven and let it cool in the pan. When it is cool, cover it with plastic wrap and place a baking sheet on the pan, over the plastic wrap. Invert the cake onto the baking sheet. Place a second baking sheet on the cake and flip it onto the second sheet. Remove the plastic wrap. Frost with Fudge Frosting, cut the cake into 18 squares, and place them on a serving plate lined with a paper doily.

LORA SAYS: Baking soda starts acting as soon as it is combined with liquid, so don't waste time getting this cake into the oven.

LORA SAYS: Cake flour, which is lower in protein than all-purpose flour, is used in this recipe to produce the lighter texture associated with devil's food cake.

World's Richest Fudge Frosting

Cakes

Makes: enough to frost one 2-layer cake, one 9 × 13-inch cake, or 24 cupcakes

What you'll need:

scale for weighing chocolate (optional)

sharp, heavy knife for chopping chocolate

microwave or small metal bowl and pan of simmering water for melting chocolate

hand-held electric mixer

flexible metal spatula for frosting

Think swirls, think twirls, think hold the cake!—this frosting is great right from the bowl. The recipe makes a generous amount with enough left over for any bowl licking you care to do.

8 ounces semisweet or bittersweet chocolate, chopped (see page 16)

1 stick (8 tablespoons) unsalted butter, softened

1 cup sour cream

2 cups confectioners' sugar (if sugar is lumpy, sift first, then measure)

1. Melt the chocolate either in the microwave or in a small metal mixing bowl set over, but not touching, a pan of gently simmering water. Set aside to cool.

2. Combine the butter and sour cream in a medium mixing bowl and use the mixer on medium speed to mix the two together. Add the chocolate and mix until incorporated. Add the confectioners' sugar and beat on low for 30 seconds, then on high for 1 minute, until the mixture is light and fluffy. Follow directions for frosting a layer cake on page 22.

3. Once frosted, the cake may be covered with plastic wrap or placed in a round cake carrier and refrigerated for up to 3 days. To avoid having the plastic wrap come in direct contact with the frosting, push about 10 toothpicks halfway into the cake at even intervals around the top. Drape a sheet or sheets of plastic wrap over the toothpicks and loosely down the sides of the cake.

Flourless Chocolate Cake

Makes: one 9-inch round cake; 12 servings

What you'll need:

9-inch round cake pan, 2 inches deep

parchment paper for lining the pan

half-sheet pan or roasting pan that will hold at least 1 inch of water

sharp, heavy knife for breaking up chocolate and butter

medium saucepan

mixing spoon

whisk

hand-held electric mixer

Baking time: 30 minutes

It seems like every restaurant in the world features a flourless chocolate cake on the menu. When you see how easy it is to make one at home, you'll be amazed.

You can serve this cake warm or at room temperature. The addition of Raspberry Sauce and White Chocolate Cream will make you even more beloved by your chocolate-adoring family and friends. Keep this cake in mind for a Passover seder.

FOR PREPARING THE PAN

1½ tablespoons unsalted butter or solid vegetable shortening, softened

FOR THE CAKE

1⅓ cups superfine sugar (see page 49)

½ cup water

8 ounces (8 squares) unsweetened chocolate, broken into small pieces (see page 16)

4 ounces bittersweet chocolate, broken into small pieces

2 sticks (16 tablespoons) unsalted butter, cut into 10 chunks

5 extra-large eggs, at room temperature (see page 33)

1 recipe White Chocolate Cream (page 158)

1 recipe Raspberry Sauce (page 159), optional

1. Preheat the oven to 350°F with a rack in the center of the oven. Have ready a 9-inch circle of parchment paper. Coat the sides and bottoms of the pan with some of the butter or shortening, then place the parchment paper liner in the pan and apply butter or shortening to the liner, too. Set the cake pan in a half-sheet pan or a shallow roasting pan. Set aside.

2. Combine 1 cup of the sugar with the water in a medium saucepan. Cook over high heat, stirring occasionally, until the sugar dissolves and the mixture comes to a vigorous boil. Turn off the heat and immediately add the unsweetened and bittersweet chocolate to the hot syrup. Stir with a wire whisk until the chocolate pieces completely dissolve in the syrup. Stir in the butter, one chunk at a time, until each chunk is incorporated before adding the next.

3. In a medium mixing bowl, beat the eggs with the remaining sugar, using a whisk or the mixer on medium speed, until they are foamy and slightly thickened. Pour them into the chocolate, whisking or beating well to incorporate all the ingredients.

4. Pour and scrape the batter into the prepared pan and smooth the top with a rubber spatula. Place the cake pan into the half-sheet pan or roasting pan, then place both in the oven. Pour very hot water into the larger pan until it comes up about 1 inch on the cake pan. Bake the cake for exactly 30 minutes. The top will have a thin, dry crust, but the inside will be very moist. Carefully remove the cake pan from the oven. (Leave the larger pan with the water in it in the oven until it cools, to avoid spilling hot water.)

5. Immediately cover the top of the cake with a piece of plastic wrap. Invert the cake onto a flat plate or baking sheet. Peel off the parchment paper liner. Cover the exposed bottom with a light, flat plate and immediately invert again onto that plate. Remove the plastic wrap. Serve with White Chocolate Cream and Raspberry Sauce, if desired.

6. This cake is best eaten warm or at room temperature. Leftovers should be covered and refrigerated, although they will become dense and fudgy. The cake cannot be frozen.

LORA SAYS: This cake cooks in a water bath to a give the cake a delicate, thin, crisp crust.

LORA SAYS: For safety, place both the half-sheet pan or roasting pan and the cake pan in the oven before adding the hot water. When the cake is done, use oven mitts to lift the cake from the water bath, leaving the water-filled pan in the oven to cool. If it's a long way from your oven to the sink, and the water in the pan is in danger of overflowing when you carry it—even cold water makes a mess—use a bulb baster to transfer some water out to a bowl before transferring the pan to the sink.

White Chocolate Cream

Makes: about 2 cups

What you'll need:

scale for weighing chocolate
(optional)

sharp, heavy knife for chopping
chocolate

food processor or blender

small, heavy saucepan

This topping, which has the consistency of soft cream cheese, must be made at least 1 day in advance. It is best to make it with a food processor or blender, to dissolve any lumps of white chocolate.

12 ounces best-quality white chocolate, cut into small pieces (see page 16)

1 cup heavy cream

⅓ cup bourbon, or to taste (optional)

1. Place the pieces of white chocolate in the work bowl of a food processor or blender. Pour the cream into the saucepan set over medium-high heat, and heat to just below boiling. Watch carefully so that it doesn't boil over. Pour the hot cream over the chocolate and process or blend until completely smooth. Stir in the bourbon, if desired.

2. The cream will keep, covered, for a week in the refrigerator, or it can be frozen. If it has been refrigerated or frozen, heat it in a double boiler until thick but pourable. In its liquid state it makes a fabulous topping for fresh fruit, such as mangoes, nectarines, pineapple, or bananas. My favorite application by far, however, is to pour about ⅓ cup onto a dessert plate, place a wedge of flourless chocolate cake on top, and spoon a little raspberry sauce over the cake.

LORA SAYS: There is a big difference in both taste and texture between real white chocolate, which is made with cocoa butter, and ersatz white chocolate, which is known as "compound coating" and is made with coconut oil or palm kernel oil. Be sure to read the ingredients on the label.

Raspberry Sauce

Makes: about 3 cups

2½ cups fresh raspberries or thawed, frozen unsweetened raspberries

½ cup superfine sugar

¼ cup Chambord or other raspberry-flavored liqueur (optional)

Place the raspberries, sugar, and liqueur, if desired, in a blender or food processor fitted with the metal blade. Puree until smooth. If a seedless sauce is desired, pass the puree through a sieve.

Classic Pound Cake

● ●

Makes: 1 loaf cake; 8 to 10 servings

What you'll need:

loaf pan 8½ × 4½ × 2½-inch with 6-cup capacity

small, sharp knife for cutting up butter

mesh sieve

hand-held electric mixer

cake tester

wire rack

Baking time: 60 minutes

In the case of this superdense, moist, buttery loaf cake, "pound" refers to the weight of ingredients, not to the method of preparation. Originally it was made with a pound each of butter, eggs, sugar, and flour. Then the Surgeon General blew the whistle. Only kidding. These days pound cakes call for about half that amount of ingredients, plus the addition of baking powder to help it rise, so the final version isn't leaden. This recipe involves using several separate bowls, but you will see that this actually makes preparation easier. A little more dish washing will be amply rewarded by a slice of this heirloom cake.

FOR PREPARING THE PAN

1 tablespoon unsalted butter or solid vegetable shortening, softened
2 tablespoons all-purpose flour

FOR THE CAKE

2 cups all-purpose flour

1 teaspoon baking powder

½ teaspoon salt

2 sticks (16 tablespoons) unsalted butter, each stick cut into 8 pieces and softened

4 extra-large eggs

2 teaspoons pure vanilla extract

1 cup granulated sugar

1. Preheat the oven to 350°F with a rack in the center of the oven. Coat the loaf pan generously with the butter or solid vegetable shortening. Add the flour to coat the sides and bottom of the pan; knock out the excess. Set aside.

2. Place a mesh sieve over a medium mixing bowl and add the flour, baking powder, and salt. Shake the contents into the bowl and set aside.

3. Place the butter in a large mixing bowl. With the mixer on high speed, beat the butter until it looks like thick whipped cream, about 2 minutes. Stop occasionally to scrape down the sides of the bowl with a rubber spatula. Set aside.

4. Break the eggs into a medium mixing bowl, and add the vanilla. Without washing the beaters, beat the eggs on low speed. Gradually increase the speed, and add the sugar a little at a time, taking about a minute to add all the sugar. Continue to beat for 2 minutes more.

5. Add the egg mixture to the butter, scraping the bowl well. With the mixer on low speed, mix them together until the mixture is smooth and slightly dull-looking. With the mixer still on low, gradually add the flour mixture. At this point, it's best to finish incorporating dry ingredients by hand. Knock the excess batter from the beaters, then use a rubber spatula to fold the flour mixture in thoroughly. Scrape the batter into the prepared pan and smooth the top with a rubber spatula.

6. Bake for 1 hour. When the cake is done, the top will rise and crack, forming a golden trough, and a cake tester inserted into the center of the cake will come out clean and dry. Cool the cake in the pan for 15 minutes, then turn it out onto a cooling rack.

7. The baked and cooled cake can be refrigerated, wrapped in plastic wrap, for up to 1 week. It may also be frozen for up to 3 months. Wrap the cooled cake securely in plastic wrap, then place in a plastic bag. Label the bag with a waterproof marker. Defrost the cake in its wrapping in the refrigerator or at room temperature.

VARIATIONS: You can easily jazz up pound cake by mixing any number of things into the batter just before you pour it into the pan:

SUGGESTIONS:

- chocolate (recipe follows)

- Finely grated zest and strained juice of one large lemon, lime, or orange

- 2 teaspoons almond extract in place of the vanilla extract

- ⅓ cup poppy seeds and finely grated zest and juice of one large lemon

- 1 cup mini semisweet chocolate chips or 1 cup mint chocolate chips

- 1 cup coffee-flavored chocolate chips, coarsely chopped (*not* chocolate-covered coffee beans)

- ⅔ cup dried cranberries, blueberries, or cherries

LORA SAYS: The dry ingredients of this cake are folded in by hand rather than with an electric mixer to avoid overbeating, which will make the pound cake tough.

Chocolate Pound Cake

Makes: one 9-inch cake;
12 servings

What you'll need:

9-inch (6-cup capacity)
bundt-style pan

sharp, heavy knife for chopping
chocolate

microwave or small metal bowl
and pan of simmering water for
melting chocolate

mixing spoon

hand-held electric mixer

cake tester

wire rack

Baking time: about 1 hour

You might choose to serve this lovely, tender chocolaty cake all by itself. However, if there was ever a reason to run out and buy a couple of pints of premium coffee ice cream, this is it. Some rich, luscious hot fudge sauce wouldn't hurt, either. You can make your own from the recipe on page 308. To make a sophisticated version of a brownie sundae, cut a thick slice of cake, lay it on its side, top with warm fudge sauce, put a generous scoop of ice cream on top, and serve immediately.

FOR PREPARING THE PAN

1 tablespoon unsalted butter or solid vegetable
shortening, softened

2 tablespoons all-purpose flour

FOR THE CAKE

6 ounces (6 squares)
unsweetened chocolate,
chopped

4 sticks (1 pound) unsalted
butter, softened

1 cup granulated sugar

6 extra-large eggs, at room
temperature

2 teaspoons pure vanilla
extract

2 cups all-purpose flour

Sweetened whipped
cream (page 21) or ice
cream (optional)

1. Preheat the oven to 350°F with a rack in the center of the oven. Coat the sides and center tube of the bundt-style pan with the butter or shortening. Add the flour and shake the pan to coat the tube surface and sides. Knock out the excess flour. Set aside.

2. Melt the chocolate either in the microwave or in a small metal mixing bowl set over, but not touching, a pan of gently simmering water. Stir until it is melted and smooth. Remove it from the heat and let cool.

3. Place the butter and sugar in a large mixing bowl. With the mixer on high speed, cream the mixture until it is light and fluffy, about 5 minutes. Add the eggs, one at a time, mixing well to incorporate each egg before another is added. Move the beaters around the bowl and scrape down the sides of the bowl with a rubber spatula several times during the mixing. Beat in the vanilla, then lower the mixer speed to low and beat in the cooled chocolate. Using a rubber spatula, fold in the flour, turning the bowl and scraping the sides as you fold. Mix only until no traces of flour are visible. Pour and scrape the batter into the prepared pan and smooth the top with a rubber spatula.

4. Bake for 50 to 55 minutes, or until the edges just start to pull away from the sides of the pan and a cake tester inserted in the center of the cake comes out clean and dry. Remove the pan from the oven and place it on a wire rack to cool for 10 minutes, then unmold it onto a serving plate to cool completely.

5. To serve, slice the cake into 1½-inch wedges and serve with a dollop of sweetened whipped cream or a scoop of ice cream.

6. The baked and cooled cake can be stored at room temperature, wrapped in plastic wrap or placed in a cake carrier, for up to 5 days. It may also be frozen for up to 3 months. Wrap the cooled cake securely in plastic wrap, then place in a plastic bag. Label the bag with a waterproof marker. Defrost the cake in its wrapping in the refrigerator or at room temperature.

LORA SAYS: To make ice cream sandwiches, bake the cake in a 8½ by 4½-inch loaf pan, cut it into an even number of 1-inch-thick slices. Spread ⅓ cup softened premium ice cream over half of the slices, then top each portion with a second slice to make sandwiches. Wrap each sandwich in plastic wrap and freeze them until ready to serve.

Little Guy Cheesecake

Makes: one 9-inch cheesecake;
6 to 8 servings

What you'll need:

a food processor or hand-held
electric mixer

whisk

wire rack

Baking time: 30 minutes

This was the very first cheesecake that I learned how to make. It's easy and just about the best thing you ever tasted. There were just two problems. One was that you couldn't eat it right away. The second was that there never seemed to be enough to feed more than eight cheesecake-loving folks. While I haven't come up with a way to shorten the baking process, I can offer two options: a Little Guy Cheesecake, to feed half a dozen or so of your best friends, and the Big Boy Cheesecake (page 168), which will allow you to feed almost everyone you know. Both cheesecakes have a graham cracker crust, a baked cream cheese filling, and a sour cream topping that is added toward the end of the initial baking time. Both can be topped with fresh fruit or the more traditional canned cherries.

If you have a food processor, this is the perfect time to use it, since the action of the blade does not whip any air into the cheesecake batter. The less air whipped into the batter, the less the cheesecake will rise while it bakes, and the less it will fall and crack while it cools. If you only have a hand-held mixer, it's doubly important for the ingredients to be at room temperature, as this keeps the beating to a minimum.

FOR THE CRUST AND FILLING

One Graham Cracker Crumb Crust, baked and cooled according to the recipe on page 277 or store-bought graham cracker crust in a 9-inch pie plate

FOR THE FILLING

12 ounces best-quality cream cheese (not the whipped or reduced-fat variety), at room temperature (see page 33)

⅔ cup granulated sugar

2 teaspoons pure vanilla extract

⅓ cup heavy cream

3 extra-large eggs

FOR THE TOPPING AND GARNISH

2 cups (16 ounces) sour cream, not reduced-fat or fat-free

⅓ cup granulated sugar

2 cups (1 pint) sliced fresh strawberries, or a combination of strawberries, raspberries, and blueberries; or 1½ cups of cherry pie filling

1. Preheat the oven to 350°F with a rack in the upper third of the oven, but not the very highest position.

2. To make the filling, place the cream cheese, sugar, vanilla, heavy cream, and eggs into the bowl of a food processor fitted with the metal blade or into a very large mixing bowl. If you use a food processor, process for 1 minute, or until the batter is completely smooth, scraping down the sides of the bowl several times. If you use a hand-held mixer, beat the contents of the bowl on medium speed just until the batter is completely smooth. Scrape down the sides of the bowl several times as you work. Pour and scrape the filling into the prepared crust, smooth it with a rubber spatula, and bake for 25 minutes.

3. While the cheesecake is baking, prepare the topping. Whisk the sour cream and sugar together in a small bowl. When the cake has baked for 25 minutes, remove it from the oven, but do not turn the oven off. Drop the topping by tablespoonfuls onto the surface of the cheesecake, then use a rubber spatula to smooth it evenly over the top, to the edges. Return the cheesecake to the oven and bake for 5 minutes more. Remove the cake and cool completely on a wire rack, then refrigerate it for at least 3 hours or overnight.

4. To serve, top with strawberries, a combination of fresh berries, or cherry pie filling.

5. The cooled cheesecake, without its fruit garnish, can be refrigerated, or placed in a cake carrier, for up to 3 days. It can also be frozen, in its pie plate, for up to 3 months. Wrap it in several layers of plastic wrap, then place it in a freezer-strength recloseable jumbo-size plastic bag. Label the bag with a waterproof marker. Defrost, still wrapped, in the refrigerator overnight or at room temperature for 3 to 4 hours.

6. Once the cheesecake has been topped with fresh fruit, it can be refrigerated, covered with plastic wrap, for up to 24 hours. After 24 hours the fruit will get soft and brown. If you use canned pie filling, the cheesecake can be refrigerated, covered with plastic wrap, for up to 1 week. It cannot be frozen with its fruit garnish.

LORA SAYS: When you buy fresh berries for this cheesecake, look for firm berries that will hold their shape and stay fresh. Do not choose overripe or bruised fruit.

LORA SAYS: If you want to go one step further and put a shiny glaze on the fruit topping, empty a 6-ounce jar of currant jelly into a small saucepan. Stir over low heat, whisking constantly, until the jelly has melted and the mixture is smooth and has the consistency of unset Jell-O (moderately thick but still pourable). Use a tablespoon to spoon the glaze over the fruit, and allow it to set for 20 minutes in the refrigerator or at room temperature, uncovered.

Big Boy Cheesecake

Makes: one 9-inch cheesecake;
12 to 14 servings

What you'll need:

9-inch springform pan,
3 inches deep

heavy-duty aluminum foil

kitchen string

food processor or hand-held
electric mixer

half-sheet pan or shallow
roasting pan

whisk

wire rack

Baking time: 1 hour,
45 minutes

While the Little Guy Cheesecake, on page 165, was baked in a pie plate, its big brother is made in a springform pan and bakes in a water bath to keep the cake from drying out during the long cooking time. The outside of the pan gets wrapped in aluminum foil to prevent leaks. As with the previous recipe, using a food processor to mix the ingredients will do much to avoid the surface cracking as the cake cools.

FOR THE CRUST

1 tablespoon unsalted butter for preparing the pan

Ingredients for one Graham Cracker Crumb Crust (page 277), mixed according to the recipe, but not yet baked

FOR THE FILLING

2 pounds (32 ounces) best-quality cream cheese (not the whipped or reduced-fat variety), at room temperature (see page 33)

1 cup granulated sugar

1 tablespoon pure vanilla extract

4 extra-large eggs

½ cup heavy cream

2 cups sour cream, not
reduced-fat or fat-free

⅓ cup granulated sugar

2 cups (1 pint) sliced fresh
strawberries; a
combination of fresh
strawberries, raspberries,
and blueberries; or
1½ cups cherry pie filling

1. Preheat the oven to 400°F with a rack in the center of the oven. Tear off an 18-inch square piece of heavy-duty aluminum foil and place the springform pan in the center of it. Bring the aluminum foil up to enclose the bottom and sides of the pan. Use kitchen string, if necessary, to secure the foil by tying a length of string around the pan. Generously butter the inside of the pan. Sprinkle in the crust ingredients, then press them onto the bottom and halfway up the sides of the pan. The top edges will not be even, but that's okay. Bake the crust for 10 minutes. Remove the pan from the oven and reduce the oven temperature to 325°F.

2. Place the cream cheese, sugar, vanilla, eggs, and heavy cream in a food processor fitted with the metal blade, or in a large mixing bowl. Process for 1 minute until the filling is completely smooth, scraping down the sides of the bowl several times, or beat with a hand-held mixer on medium speed until the filling is smooth. Move the beaters around the bowl and scrape down the sides of the bowl with a rubber spatula several times while mixing. Pour and scrape the filling into the prepared crust and smooth it with a rubber spatula. Place the springform pan in the center of a half-sheet pan or a shallow roasting pan, and place both pans on the oven rack. Use a measuring cup with a spout to pour very hot water into the outer pan so that the water comes 1 inch up the sides of the springform pan.

3. Bake the cheesecake for 90 minutes, adding more water to the larger pan halfway through the cooking time, if necessary. Cover the top of the cheesecake loosely with foil if it seems to be getting too dark.

4. When the cake has baked for almost 90 minutes, prepare the topping by whisking the sour cream and sugar together in a small mixing bowl. Carefully remove the cheesecake pan from the oven and drop the topping by tablespoonfuls onto the surface of the cheesecake, then use a rubber spatula to smooth it evenly over the top, to the edges. Return the cake to the water bath and bake for 5 minutes more. Remove the cake and let it cool completely on a wire rack, then refrigerate it for at least 3 hours or overnight. (Leave the larger pan with the water in it in the oven until it cools, to avoid the risk of spilling hot water.)

5. To serve, remove the outer ring from the pan and place the cake, on its pan base, on a serving platter. Top the cheesecake with strawberries, a combination of fresh berries, or cherry pie filling. Since this is a superrich dessert, cut it in small slices. Use a long, sharp knife and run it under hot water between slices.

6. The cooled cheesecake, without its fruit garnish, can be refrigerated on its pan base and covered with plastic wrap, or placed in a cake carrier, for up to 3 days. It can also be frozen, on its pan base, for up to 3 months. Wrap it in several layers of plastic wrap, then place it in a freezer-strength recloseable jumbo-size plastic bag. Label the bag with a waterproof marker. Defrost, still wrapped, in the refrigerator overnight or at room temperature for 3 to 4 hours.

7. Once the cheesecake has been topped with fresh fruit, it can be refrigerated, covered with plastic wrap, for up to 24 hours. After 24 hours the fruit will get soft and brown. If you use canned pie filling, the cheesecake can be refrigerated, covered with plastic wrap, for up to 1 week. It cannot be frozen with its fruit garnish.

LORA SAYS: For safety, place the half-sheet pan, or roasting pan, and the springform pan in the oven before adding the hot water. When the cake is done, use oven mitts to lift the cake from the water bath, leaving the water-filled pan in the oven to cool. If it's a long way from your oven to the sink, and the water in the pan is in danger of overflowing when you carry it—even cold water makes a mess—use a bulb baster to transfer some water to a bowl before transferring the pan to the sink.

LORA SAYS: An easy way to slice cheesecake without having to deal with a messy knife is to use dental floss. Grasp the ends of an 18-inch length of floss in each hand and force it down through the cake from top to bottom. However, you'll have to slice the entire cake, since it is impossible to carve out just a piece or two using this method.

Pumpkin Cheesecake

Makes: one 9-inch cheesecake; 10 servings

What you'll need:

hand-held electric mixer and wire rack

Baking time: 30 minutes

When my dear friend Maureen Weise ran the test kitchen at Kraft and worked on developing recipes for Philadelphia cream cheese, she came up with an extraordinary answer to what to make for Thanksgiving dessert. Don't save this amazingly delicious and easy recipe just for November—it's so good you'll want to eat it any time of year.

One 9-inch Chocolate Crumb Crust, baked and cooled according to the recipe on page 279

1 pound cream cheese (not the whipped or reduced-fat variety), at room temperature (see page 33)

½ cup granulated sugar

2 extra-large eggs

½ teaspoon ground nutmeg

½ teaspoon ground cinnamon

½ teaspoon ground ginger

1 cup canned pumpkin puree (not pumpkin pie filling) (see page 49)

1. Preheat the oven to 350°F with a rack in the center of the oven.

2. Place the cream cheese and sugar in a medium mixing bowl. Use the mixer on medium speed to mix them together until smooth. Add the eggs, nutmeg, cinnamon, ginger, and pumpkin puree, and continue to mix on medium speed until well combined. Move the beaters around the bowl and scrape down the sides of the bowl with a rubber spatula several times while mixing. Pour and scrape the mixture into the prepared crust and smooth the top with a rubber spatula. Bake for 30 minutes, or until the top surface looks dry except for a spot the size of a quarter in the very center.

3. Remove the cheesecake from the oven and cool it on a wire rack for 30 minutes. You may leave the cooled cheesecake at room temperature for up to 6 hours before serving. If you need to leave it longer than 6 hours, cover the cooled cheesecake with plastic wrap or place it in a cake carrier and refrigerate for up to 3 days. Serve right from the refrigerator or bring to room temperature, as you prefer. Use a pie server to cut the cheesecake into wedges, and serve the cake plain or garnished with whipped cream.

4. The completely cooled cheesecake can be frozen in its pie plate for up to 3 months. Wrap it in several layers of plastic wrap, then place it in a freezer-strength recloseable jumbo-size plastic bag. Label the bag with a waterproof marker. Defrost the cheesecake, still wrapped, in the refrigerator overnight or at room temperature for 3 to 4 hours.

LORA SAYS: To bring cream cheese to room temperature quickly, submerge the unopened foil package in hot water for 5 minutes. Be sure to dry the package before opening it.

LORA SAYS: Mascarpone (soft Italian cream cheese, available in the dairy or cheese section of many grocery stores and most Italian markets) flavored with maple is the perfect complement to this cake: Combine 8 ounces mascarpone, ⅓ cup pure maple syrup, and 3 tablespoons packed dark brown sugar in a small mixing bowl and whisk until smooth. Pour several tablespoons of the flavored mascarpone on the bottom of a small dessert plate, then place a wedge of cheesecake on top. Use the maple-flavored mascarpone immediately or refrigerate it for up to 1 week in a tightly sealed container.

Chocolate Cheesecake

Makes: one 9-inch cheesecake; 10 servings

What you'll need:

scale for weighing chocolate (optional)

sharp, heavy knife for chopping chocolate

microwave or small metal bowl and pan of simmering water for melting chocolate

hand-held electric mixer

wire rack

Baking time: 30 minutes

What's better than a slice of decadently rich, deep, dark chocolate cheesecake? Why, a cheesecake that you can help yourself to anytime the urge strikes you, that's what. I suppose a purist would call this a cheese pie, since it's made in a pie plate. Call it what you want— as long as there's enough for seconds.

One 9-inch Chocolate Crumb Crust, baked and cooled according to the recipe on page 279

8 ounces bittersweet chocolate, chopped (see page 16)

1 pound (16 ounces) cream cheese (not the whipped or reduced-fat variety), at room temperature (see Lora Says)

½ cup packed light brown sugar

2 extra-large eggs

1 tablespoon pure vanilla extract

1. Preheat the oven to 350°F with a rack in the center of the oven.

2. Melt the chocolate either in the microwave or in a small metal mixing bowl set over, but not touching, a pan of gently simmering water. Remove from the heat and set aside.

3. Place the cream cheese and the light brown sugar in a medium mixing bowl. Use the mixer on medium speed to mix them together until smooth. Add the eggs, vanilla extract, and melted chocolate, and continue to mix on medium speed until well combined. Move the beaters around the bowl and scrape down the sides of the bowl with a rubber spatula several times while mixing. Pour and scrape the mixture into the prepared crust and smooth the top with a rubber spatula. Bake for 30 minutes, or until the top surface looks dry except for a spot the size of a quarter in the very center.

4. Remove the cheesecake from the oven and cool it on a wire rack for 30 minutes. You may leave the cooled cheesecake at room temperature for up to 6 hours before serving. If you need to leave it longer than 6 hours, cover the cooled cheesecake with plastic wrap or place it in a cake carrier and refrigerate for up to 3 days. Serve right from the refrigerator or bring to room temperature, as you prefer.

5. The completely cooled cheesecake can be frozen in its pie plate for up to 3 months. Wrap it in several layers of plastic wrap, then place it in a freezer-strength recloseable jumbo-size plastic bag. Label the bag with a waterproof marker. Defrost the cheesecake, still wrapped, in the refrigerator overnight or at room temperature for 3 to 4 hours.

VARIATION: To make a white chocolate cheesecake, substitute 8 ounces melted white chocolate (see page 16) for the bittersweet chocolate, and substitute 6 tablespoons granulated sugar for the light brown sugar.

LORA SAYS: To bring cream cheese quickly to room temperature, submerge the unopened foil package in hot water for 5 minutes. Be sure to dry the package before opening it.

Cupcakes

· ·

Makes: 24 cupcakes

What you'll need:

two 12-hole regular muffin tins
with ⅓-cup capacity holes

paper or aluminum foil cupcake
liners

whisk

mesh sieve

hand-held electric mixer

soup ladle or ice cream scoop

cake tester

wire rack

Baking time: 25 minutes

These days the boundary between a muffin and a cup-cake is completely blurred. As muffins become sweeter and loaded with things like chocolate chips and cinnamon and sugar, you might as well eat a cupcake for breakfast. What still separates a muffin from a cupcake, though, is a rich, thick swirl of frosting on top—the more the better. This batter is the same as the one for the Snow White Layer Cake on page 147. It makes a nice, firm cupcake that will not crumble when frosted.

FOR PREPARING THE MUFFIN TINS

Nonstick vegetable spray

FOR THE CUPCAKES

1 cup milk, at room
temperature

5 extra-large egg whites

2 teaspoons pure vanilla
extract

2¼ cups cake flour
(see page 29)

1¾ cups granulated sugar

4 teaspoons baking
powder

1 teaspoon salt

1½ sticks (12 tablespoons)
unsalted butter, softened

1. Preheat the oven to 350°F with two racks positioned as close to the center of the oven as possible, leaving enough head room to accommodate the lower pan. Spray the top surface of the muffin tins with nonstick vegetable spray, and place cupcake liners in the holes of the tins. Set aside.

2. Pour the milk, egg whites, and vanilla into a 2-cup measure and whisk well to combine. Set aside.

Cakes **175**

3. Place a mesh sieve over a large, deep mixing bowl and add the flour, sugar, baking powder, and salt. Shake the contents into the bowl. Add the butter and, using the mixer on low speed, combine the butter with the dry ingredients. Increase the speed to medium and mix until the mixture has formed coarse crumbs, about 1 minute. The crumbs should be no larger than peas.

4. Pour in all but ½ cup of the milk and egg mixture into the flour and continue beating on medium speed until the batter is smooth and the beaters leave a trail when dragged through the batter. Scrape down the sides of the bowl from time to time as you work. Add the remaining milk mixture and beat for 30 seconds more.

5. Use a soup ladle or ice cream scoop to fill the cupcake liners two-thirds full. Don't worry about spills—you can clean them up later. Bake for 20 to 25 minutes, or until a cake tester inserted into the center of a cupcake comes out clean and dry, and the tops are dry and spring back when lightly pressed with your finger. The cupcakes will be flat, rather than rounded.

6. Remove the tins from the oven and immediately invert the cupcakes onto a wire rack, or use the prongs of a fork to turn the cupcakes sideways to cool in the tins, then remove them. When the cupcakes have cooled completely, frost them with Creamy Chocolate Frosting (recipe follows).

7. The unfrosted cupcakes can be frozen for up to 3 months. Place the cooled cupcakes on a baking sheet and place in the freezer for at least 3 hours. When the cupcakes are frozen solid, place them in several freezer-strength recloseable gallon-size plastic bags. Label them with a waterproof marker. Defrost them in their bags at room temperature.

LORA SAYS: For easy removal of the cupcakes, it's important to spray the top (flat) surface of the tin with nonstick vegetable spray before baking so that the batter does not stick if it rises above the rims of the holes and spreads.

LORA SAYS: Always use paper or aluminum foil cupcake liners. It's easy to prepare the tin, cleanup is simple, and the cupcakes can be removed from the tin quickly. If you don't have enough muffin tins, you can place filled aluminum foil cupcake liners on a cookie sheet. The foil will support portions of batter almost as well as a muffin tin.

Creamy Chocolate Frosting

Makes: about 2 cups

What you'll need:

scale for weighing chocolate (optional)

sharp, heavy knife for chopping chocolate

small, heavy saucepan

whisk

fine-mesh sieve (optional)

metal bowl filled with ice water

10 ounces semisweet or bittersweet chocolate, chopped (see page 16)

1 cup (8 ounces) heavy cream

1. Place the heavy cream in the saucepan set over medium-high heat and allow it to come to a simmer. Tiny bubbles will form around the edges. Be careful not to let the mixture boil, as it will quickly overflow. Lower the heat and add the chocolate. Whisk gently for 30 seconds, then remove the pan from the heat. Whisk until the mixture is completely smooth. If any lumps remain, strain the mixture through a fine-mesh sieve.

2. Place the saucepan in a metal bowl filled with ice water and continue to whisk until it starts to thicken to the consistency of sour cream. At this point, remove the pan from the ice water. Hold a cooled cupcake firmly by the paper liner and turn it over and dip the top into the frosting, rotating it in the frosting to form a swirl. It might take some practice to feel like Betty Crocker, but you can either double dip to cover the cupcake adequately or eat the "outtakes." Repeat with the remaining cupcakes. If the frosting becomes too stiff, place the pan over low heat for a minute or so, whisking constantly, until it softens enough to continue.

3. Place the frosted cupcakes on a platter and leave at room temperature for 24 hours, or place them in a cake carrier or other covered container and refrigerate for up to 2 days.

Chocolate Crunch Cupcakes

C upcakes would be perfect if you didn't have to wait for them to cool and then make some frosting to cover their tops. My idea of perfection is taking cupcakes out of the oven, letting them cool 15 minutes, and then digging in. Here, you have the best of both worlds: buttery yellow cupcakes and a chocolate streusel topping made with, among other things, chopped macadamia nuts. You can, if you wish, substitute an equal amount of chopped walnuts or pecans for the macadamia nuts.

This recipe has a long list of ingredients—don't let it put you off. The cupcakes are really easy to make.

Makes: 24 cupcakes

What you'll need:

two 12-hole regular muffin tins

paper or aluminum foil cupcake liners

small, sharp knife for cutting up butter

food processor

mesh sieve

whisk

hand-held electric mixer

¼-cup ice cream scoop (optional)

cake tester

wire rack

Baking time: 25 minutes

FOR PREPARING THE MUFFIN TINS

Nonstick vegetable spray

FOR THE TOPPING

⅔ cup granulated sugar

½ cup all-purpose flour

¼ cup unsweetened cocoa powder, not Dutch-processed (see page 15)

1 cup semisweet chocolate chips

1 cup macadamia nuts (see page 48)

3 tablespoons unsalted butter, chilled and cut into small pieces

2½ cups all-purpose flour

1 tablespoon baking powder

½ teaspoon salt

1 cup milk

3 extra-large eggs, at room temperature

2 teaspoons pure vanilla extract

2 sticks (16 tablespoons) unsalted butter, softened

2 cups granulated sugar

1. Preheat the oven to 350°F with two racks positioned as close to the center of the oven as possible, leaving enough head room to accommodate the lower pan. Spray the top surface of the muffin tins with nonstick vegetable spray, and place cupcake liners in the holes of the tins. Set aside.

2. Place all the topping ingredients in the bowl of a food processor fitted with the metal blade. Process by pulsing briefly about 20 times, or until the mixture resembles large crumbs. Set aside.

3. To make the cupcakes, place a mesh sieve over a medium mixing bowl and add the flour, baking powder, and salt. Shake the contents into the bowl and set aside.

4. Measure the milk into a 2-cup measure with a spout or medium mixing bowl, then add the eggs and vanilla. Whisk well to combine. Set aside.

5. Place the butter and sugar in a large mixing bowl. Use the mixer on low speed to cream them together for 30 seconds. Increase the speed to high and beat for 3 minutes until the mixture looks like fluffy mashed potatoes. Move the beaters around the bowl and scrape down the sides of the bowl with a rubber spatula several times while mixing. Lower the speed to medium and pour in one-third of the milk mixture. Mix that in, then add half the dry ingredients; mix only until just incorporated. Pour in half the remaining milk mixture, and mix it in. Add the remaining flour, and then the last of the milk mixture. Beat only until just incorporated; overmixing will make the cupcakes tough.

6. Use a ¼-cup measure or ice cream scoop to scoop the batter into the prepared tins. Sprinkle each cupcake with 2 tablespoons of the topping. Bake for 25 to 30 minutes. The cupcakes are done when they are puffed, the edges are golden, and a cake tester inserted into the center comes out clean and dry.

7. Remove the tins from the oven and transfer the cupcakes to a wire rack to cool—or, if you can't wait, eat them after 15 minutes of cooling.

8. Place the cupcakes on a platter and leave at room temperature for 24 hours, or place them in a cake carrier or other covered container and refrigerate for up to 2 days. They can be frozen for up to 3 months. Place the cooled cupcakes on a baking sheet and place in the freezer for at least 3 hours. When the cupcakes are frozen solid, place them in several freezer-strength recloseable gallon-size plastic bags. Label them with a waterproof marker. Defrost them in their bags at room temperature.

VARIATION: This recipe can be baked as a cake. Pour and scrape half the batter into a well-buttered 9 by 13-inch pan that is 2 inches deep, then sprinkle half the topping evenly over the surface. Pour on the remaining batter, then top with the rest of the topping. Bake at 350°F for 45 to 50 minutes, or until a cake tester inserted into the center comes out clean and dry. Cool in the pan on a wire rack before cutting into 18 servings.

LORA SAYS: Always use paper or aluminum foil liners. It's easy to prepare the pan, cleanup is simple, and the cupcakes can be removed from the tin quickly. If you don't have enough muffin tins, you can place filled aluminum foil liners on a cookie sheet. The foil will support portions of batter almost as well as a muffin tin.

Pineapple Upside-Down Cake

Makes: one 9-inch cake;
8 servings

What you'll need:

9-inch round cake pan,
2 inches deep

small, heavy skillet

mixing spoon or whisk

small, sharp knife for cutting
pineapple rings

hand-held electric mixer

mesh sieve

Baking time: 35 minutes

I t depresses me to think that there is a whole generation of Americans who have grown up without knowing
the exquisite pleasure of pineapple upside-down cake.
Even if you don't like pineapple, the maraschino cherries
will suck you in, not to mention the flavor of the warm
brown sugar. This American classic will soar close to the
top of your top-ten list of great desserts.

FOR PREPARING THE PAN

1 tablespoon unsalted butter, softened

FOR THE TOPPING

1 stick (8 tablespoons)
unsalted butter

⅔ cup packed dark brown
sugar

One 20-ounce can sliced
pineapple rings in heavy
syrup, drained

8 to 10 whole maraschino
cherries, drained, stems
removed

1 cup pecan halves
(optional)

FOR THE BATTER

3 extra-large eggs

¾ cup granulated sugar

2 teaspoons pure vanilla
extract

1 stick (8 tablespoons)
unsalted butter, melted
and slightly cooled

1 cup all-purpose flour

1 teaspoon baking powder

½ teaspoon salt

1. Preheat the oven to 350°F with a rack in the center of the oven. Use the softened butter to generously coat the bottom and sides of the cake pan. Set aside.

2. To make the topping (which, as assembled, starts off at the bottom of the pan), melt the butter in a small skillet placed over moderate heat. Add the dark brown sugar and cook, stirring constantly, until the sugar has melted. Stir or whisk vigorously until the mixture is smooth and looks a little like hot fudge. Pour the mixture into the prepared pan, tilting the pan and using a rubber spatula to spread the mixture evenly over the bottom.

3. Place the pineapple rings on the brown sugar mixture, around the edge of the pan, touching the edge of the pan and each other. You should be able to place one ring in the center as well. Be as creative as you want in cutting a remaining ring or two into small wedges to fill in between circles. Place a whole cherry in the center of each pineapple ring, and elsewhere if you wish. If you are adding pecans, scatter them over the pineapple. Set the pan aside.

4. Break the eggs into a medium mixing bowl. Add the sugar and vanilla. Beat with the mixer on high speed until the mixture is light and foamy and slightly thickened, about 3 minutes. Scrape down the sides of the bowl with a rubber spatula several times while mixing. Add the cooled butter and mix on low speed until the butter is just incorporated.

5. Place a mesh sieve over the bowl and place the flour, baking powder, and salt in the sieve. Sift the dry ingredients directly onto the batter. Use a rubber spatula to fold in the flour, scraping down the sides of the bowl as you work. Mix until you can no longer see any signs of flour; the batter will appear slightly lumpy. Pour and scrape the batter over the pineapple mixture in the pan and smooth the top.

6. Bake 35 minutes, or until the top is browned and springs back when gently pushed with your finger. Remove from the oven and allow to cool in the pan for 10 minutes before inverting onto a flat serving plate. Serve warm or at room temperature. Cut into wedges and serve, if you wish, with a scoop of vanilla ice cream or a dollop of whipped cream.

7. The baked and cooled cake can be stored, covered with plastic wrap, for up to 24 hours at room temperature or in the refrigerator for 3 days. This cake does not freeze well at all.

Song-of-the-South Date Nut Cake with Butter Rum Frosting

Makes: one 9-inch cake; 12 servings

What you'll need:

9-inch springform pan, 3 inches deep

sharp, heavy, knife for chopping walnuts

mesh sieve

scissors

nonstick vegetable spray

citrus zester

citrus reamer

hand-held electric mixer

aluminum foil for covering baking cake (optional)

small knife to release cake from sides of pan

long, serrated knife for splitting cake

2 wide metal spatulas

2 wire racks

Baking time: 50 minutes

Let me say right off the bat that I hate, loathe, and despise fruitcake. Those overly sweet doorstops with flecks of weird green fruit make me shudder. If you share my aversion but crave the taste of moist, rich cake laden with goodies, then look no further. This fabulous holiday dessert is it.

This gorgeous, generous-size cake is like a treasure chest full of hidden surprises: nuggets of sweet dried dates, bits of crunchy walnut, zesty orange peel, all topped with a lovely butter cream frosting kissed with rum. Wait till you make the unusual caramelized orange garnish—you'll feel like a professional baker!

FOR PREPARING THE PAN

1 tablespoon unsalted butter, softened

FOR THE CAKE

2½ cups all-purpose flour

1 tablespoon baking powder

½ teaspoon baking soda

½ teaspoon salt

½ teaspoon ground cinnamon

1¼ cups (8 ounces) dried dates, packed

1 cup walnuts, coarsely chopped (see page 19)

1 large orange

About 1 cup milk

1 stick (8 tablespoons) unsalted butter, softened

1 cup granulated sugar

3 extra-large eggs

2 teaspoons pure vanilla extract

Butter Rum Frosting (recipe follows)

1. Preheat the oven to 350°F with a rack in the center of the oven. Butter the pan with the butter. Set aside.

2. Place a mesh sieve over a medium mixing bowl and add the flour, baking powder, baking soda, salt, and ground cinnamon. Shake the contents into the bowl. Spray the blades of a pair of scissors with nonstick vegetable spray. Working directly over the bowl of dry ingredients, use the scissors to snip each date into 6 pieces. Toss them in the flour to coat them; this will help prevent their falling to the bottom of the cake as it bakes. Toss the walnuts in the flour also. Finely grate the zest of the orange and add that to the dry ingredients as well. Set aside.

3. Use a citrus reamer to juice the orange into a 2-cup measure with a spout, then add enough milk to make 1¼ cups (10 ounces) liquid. The liquid will curdle, but that's okay. Set aside.

4. Place the butter and sugar in a large mixing bowl. Use the mixer on high speed to cream the butter with the sugar until light and fluffy, about 3 minutes. Beat in the eggs, one at a time, waiting until one is incorporated before adding another. Continue to beat for 3 minutes until foamy and pale. Move the beaters around the bowl and scrape down the sides of the bowl several times while mixing. The mixture may appear curdled, but that's okay. Beat in the vanilla.

5. With the mixer on low, add half the dry ingredients. Mix until incorporated, then add half of the orange juice and milk mixture and beat until incorporated. Beat in the remaining dry ingredients, then finish with the rest of the liquid. Scrape down the sides of the bowl occasionally as you work.

6. Pour and scrape the batter into the prepared pan and smooth the top with a rubber spatula. Bake for 40 minutes, checking to see how the cake is browning. If it is very brown, cover loosely with aluminum foil. Continue to bake for about 10 minutes more, or until the top is nicely browned and has risen well. The top may crack, but that's okay. Remove the cake from the oven and run a knife around the edges to help release the cake. Remove the sides of the pan and let the cake cool on the pan base.

7. When the cake has cooled, use a long, serrated knife to slice the cake horizontally through the center, rotating the cake as you cut. Use two wide metal spatulas to transfer the top half to a wire rack. Invert the bottom layer onto another wire rack, remove the springform pan base, then invert it again onto a flat serving plate so that it rests cut side up.

8. When thoroughly cooled, frost with Butter Rum Frosting.

9. The baked and cooled unfrosted cake can be refrigerated, wrapped in plastic wrap, for up to 1 week. It may also be frozen for up to 3 months. Wrap the cooled cake securely in plastic wrap, then place in a freezer-strength recloseable jumbo-size plastic bag. Label the bag with a waterproof marker. Defrost the cake in its wrapping in the refrigerator or at room temperature.

Butter Rum Frosting

Makes: enough frosting for 2 generous layers

What you'll need:

hand-held electric mixer

flexible metal spatula

Making a pure buttercream frosting can be tricky; so much depends on having the butter at just the right temperature and consistency. An easy way to a sure-fire success is to add cream cheese, which is far more forgiving than just using butter. It's essential to use the bar kind of cream cheese like Philadelphia brand, not the kind that has air whipped into it. This frosting is flavored with dark rum. If you only have light rum, then use it, rather than buy a whole new bottle. Buying a "nip" (a small "airplane" bottle) is an easy alternative to a whole bottle. If you don't want to use alcohol, you can use 2 tablespoons of alcohol-free rum flavoring instead. I also suggest using orange juice or pure maple syrup in place of the rum.

1 stick (8 tablespoons) unsalted butter, softened

8 ounces cream cheese (not the whipped or reduced-fat variety), at room temperature (see page 33)

One 16-ounce box confectioners' sugar (3¾ cups) (if sugar is lumpy, sift first, then measure)

3 to 4 tablespoons dark rum (orange juice or real maple syrup may be used)

Caramelized Orange Chips (recipe follows), optional garnish

1. In a large, deep mixing bowl, beat the butter and cream cheese with the mixer on high speed. Scrape down the sides of the bowl with a rubber spatula several times while mixing. Sift in the sugar and beat on low speed until the mixture starts to form a ball, about 30 seconds. Add the rum or other flavoring of your choice, and continue to beat on high speed until smooth and fluffy.

2. If the frosting seems soft, cover and refrigerate it before frosting the cake. Be sure that the cake is thoroughly cold before frosting. See directions for how to frost a layer cake on page 22. You will probably have more than enough, so don't put it all on. If the frosting softens up as you work, put the cake and the remaining frosting in the refrigerator to set up.

3. As an optional garnish, break up some Caramelized Orange Chips and place them on top of the frosted cake. Refrigerate the cake until serving time.

4. Once it has been frosted, the cake can be refrigerated, covered with plastic wrap or placed in a cake carrier, for up to 4 days. To avoid having the plastic wrap come in direct contact with the frosting, push about 10 toothpicks halfway into the cake at even intervals around the top. Drape a sheet of plastic wrap over the toothpicks and loosely down the sides of the cake. The frosted cake cannot be frozen.

VARIATION: Sprinkle 2 additional tablespoons dark rum over the bottom layer of the cake (cut side up) before frosting.

LORA SAYS: If you're bent on saving calories, you can use reduced-fat cream cheese in the frosting, but *never* use fat-free cream cheese or whipped cream cheese.

LORA SAYS: This cake is a festive dessert to have around at holiday time; it serves a crowd, a little goes a long way since it's so rich, it stays fresh a long time, and it looks pretty.

Caramelized Orange Chips

Makes: about 1 cup chips

What you'll need:

heavy-duty baking sheet

heavy-duty aluminum foil

very sharp, serrated knife

Baking time: 15 to 20 minutes

When I first saw these in a fancy New York restaurant I just about swooned. Some poor pastry chef, I thought, must have slaved away for hours making these paper-thin circles of candied orange. They reminded me of the ethereal burned-sugar topping on crème brûlée After a little research I figured out how to make them at home in a very short time. You'll need a very sharp serrated knife—unless you have access to a mandoline, a fancy food guillotine.

1 thick-skinned seedless orange, such as a navel orange

About ½ cup granulated sugar

1. Preheat the oven to 200°F with a rack in the center of the oven. Line the baking sheet with heavy-duty aluminum foil.

2. Use the knife to slice the orange into the thinnest possible slices.

3. Sprinkle the baking sheet surface evenly with about ¼ cup sugar. Lay the orange slices on the sugar, and sprinkle the slices with another ¼ cup sugar, or enough to cover the slices generously.

4. Place the baking sheet in the oven and check the orange slices after 15 minutes to make sure that the sugar has caramelized and that the oranges have turned a deep golden brown. If not, cook another 3 to 4 minutes, checking often to make sure they don't turn black. You want them as deep brown as they can get without actually burning; otherwise they'll be hard to remove from the foil after cooling. They will not cook evenly. Don't touch them— they are dangerously hot! Cool the slices on the foil to room temperature. When they have cooled and hardened, peel them off. They may break as you lift them off the foil, but that's okay. Try not to eat all of them! Store at room temperature in an airtight container.

LORA SAYS: Make extra orange chips and serve them along with or instead of after-dinner mints. They're also great crushed up and served on hot oatmeal.

American Linzer Torte

Makes: one 9-inch torte;
8 to 10 servings

What you'll need:

9-inch springform pan,
3 inches deep

heavy-duty aluminum foil

baking sheet

food processor for grinding
almonds

citrus zester

fine-mesh sieve for straining
lemon juice

mixing spoon

hand-held electric mixer

small offset spatula (optional)

whisk

wire rack

small, sharp knife

small sieve for sifting
confectioners' sugar

Baking time: 1 hour

While this is not any more challenging than many other recipes in this book, there are a few added steps. For that reason especially read all the way through the recipe before you start (you should be doing that anyway), since you'll have to reserve some of the mixture that makes the bottom layer of the torte for use in the topping.

Classic Linzer torte is made with a butter and ground almond crust and layered with raspberry preserves. What makes this torte American is the oats, which add crunch and nutty flavor and turn it into a thick batter that can be spread rather than rolled. Some of the batter is dropped by small spoonfuls over the raspberry topping so it forms a top crust. It's important to use really top-quality raspberry preserves so that you taste fruit, not sugar. I like the kind with seeds, but you may prefer seedless.

FOR PREPARING THE PAN

1 tablespoon unsalted butter or solid vegetable shortening, softened

FOR THE CRUST

1 cup oats, old-fashioned
or quick-cooking
(see page 46)

¾ cup (3 ounces) slivered
blanched almonds, finely
ground (see page 19)

½ cup all-purpose flour

¼ teaspoon salt

1½ sticks (12 tablespoons)
unsalted butter, softened

¾ cup confectioners' sugar
(if sugar is lumpy, sift first,
then measure)

1 extra-large egg, lightly
beaten

Finely grated zest of
1 large lemon

¾ teaspoon pure almond
extract

FOR THE TOPPING

⅔ cup of the crust
mixture, above

¼ cup (1 ounce) blanched
almonds, finely ground

1 cup best-quality
raspberry preserves
(one 10- to 12-ounce jar)

2 tablespoons strained
fresh lemon juice

2 tablespoons
confectioners' sugar (if
sugar is lumpy, sift first,
then measure)

1. Preheat the oven to 350°F with a rack in the center of the oven. Use the butter or solid vegetable shortening to generously coat the bottom and sides of the springform pan. Wrap the bottom of the pan in heavy-duty aluminum foil (to prevent butter from dripping onto the bottom of the oven) and place the wrapped pan on a baking sheet. Set aside.

2. To make the crust, place the oats, ground almonds, flour, and salt in a large mixing bowl. Toss with a wooden spoon to combine the ingredients well. Set aside.

3. In a separate bowl, beat the butter and confectioners' sugar with the mixer on low speed for about 30 seconds so that the sugar does not fly out of the bowl. Raise the speed to high and beat until the mixture is light and fluffy, about 2 minutes. Beat in the egg, scraping the sides of the bowl with a rubber spatula several times as you mix. Beat in the lemon zest and almond extract. Scrape the butter mixture into the oat mixture and mix them together with a wooden spoon. Scrape the spoon well with a rubber spatula from time to time. Combine the two mixtures thoroughly. Scoop ⅔ cup of this mixture into a small bowl and set it aside. Spread the remaining mixture in the bottom of the prepared pan, using a small offset spatula or your moistened fingers. Bake for 25 minutes, or until it is a light brown.

4. While the crust is baking, prepare the topping. Mix the almonds with the reserved crust mixture, using a wooden spoon or a rubber spatula. In a separate small bowl, whisk the preserves and lemon juice together. When the crust has baked, remove the pan from the oven, but do not turn the oven off. Spread the raspberry mixture over the hot crust, using a rubber spatula or a small offset spatula to smooth it evenly. Use your fingers to drop teaspoon-size bits of the reserved almond crust mixture over the surface of the preserves.

5. Bake the cake for 30 to 35 minutes, or until the top is golden brown and the preserves are bubbling. Remove the cake from the oven and cool completely in the pan on a wire rack. When it has cooled, run a small knife around the inside of the pan to loosen the fruit filling from the sides of the pan. Carefully remove the sides of the pan. To serve, cut the torte into 8 to 10 wedges and place them on a serving plate. Sift the confectioners' sugar over the top.

6. The cooled, uncut torte can be stored at room temperature, wrapped securely in plastic wrap, for 2 days. Cut wedges can be stored at room temperature in a covered tin for 2 days. The uncut torte can be wrapped securely in plastic wrap, then in aluminum foil, and frozen for up to 3 months. Cut wedges should be spread on a baking sheet and placed in the freezer for at least 3 hours. When thoroughly frozen, stack them in a freezer-strength recloseable gallon-size plastic bag for up to 3 months. Use a waterproof marker to note the contents of all packaging and the date. Defrost in the packaging at room temperature for 1 to 2 hours.

LORA SAYS: You can buy ground almonds in gourmet stores and from catalogs such as the King Arthur Flour Baker's Catalogue (see page 316). If you have a food processor it's pretty easy to grind your own, although they will not be as finely ground as those you buy. The key to grinding almonds in a food processor is to do about a cup at a time, and not grind them to the point where the oil starts separating from the nuts and you end up with almond butter. Start with slivered rather than whole almonds, and add a tablespoon of granulated sugar for each cup of nuts. Use the pulse button for more control; it flings the nuts upward with each pulse, which aerates the mass and prevents overgrinding.

Biscuits, Scones, and Muffins

I n a way, muffins and scones are to quick breads and tea loaves what cookies are to pies and tarts; you get a sample of the whole plus the bonus of individual servings, which means that no one has to have a smaller portion than anyone else. It was hard to decide which recipes to choose from the hundreds of varieties of these two classics. Muffins, while not yet succumbing to the tragic fate of bagels (too many mix-ins), can certainly be found loaded with an awesome variety of ingredients. Scones are another matter. The Brits gasp in horror at the idea of anything but a few currants mixed into the batter, but oh, we Americans can't seem to leave well enough alone. Thus, there are recipes for scones sporting (good heavens!) such things as candied ginger and chocolate.

Whether you're a purist or fancy something, well, fancier, I'm sure you'll find lots of recipes in this chapter that will inspire you to try your hand at making something other than cereal or toast for breakfast.

Muffin Maladies and Their Cures

What Should I Do If . . .

They are tough? Creaming the butter and sugar with an electric mixer is fine, but continuing to beat with a mixer after you have added the flour and other dry ingredients will result in tough muffins. The trick is not to develop the gluten (protein) in the flour. By handling the batter very gently—mixing it with a rubber spatula, wooden spoon, or fork just until all the dry ingredients are moistened and no clumps of flour remain—you avoid heavy, overly chewy muffins as well as those large tunnel-shaped, uneven holes you sometimes find in the center of baked muffins. Muffin batter should not be smooth like cake batter.

For softer, more tender, higher-rising muffins and scones, you can add one teaspoon of Lora Brody's Dough Relaxer per cup of flour. For a free sample, visit my website at *www.lorabrody.com* or call 888-9-BAKEIT.

The tops are cracked and burned? You may have added too much baking powder—did you measure it carefully? The pan may have been too high up in the oven; try a lower rack position next time. The oven temperature may be too high; make sure that you've set the oven to the right temperature. Use an accurate oven thermometer to ensure that the oven's thermostat is correct.

The bottoms are soggy? You may not have removed the muffins from the tin in time to prevent the steam trapped in them from cooling and collecting in the bottom of the muffin holes. Cool the muffins in the muffin tin on a wire rack for 5 minutes, then remove them to the rack to continue cooling.

They are flat as pancakes? Did you remember to add the baking powder and/or baking soda? Did the batter sit around after the baking soda was introduced to the wet ingredients? Did you remember to preheat the oven? Did you underfill the muffin holes?

They taste weird? Sounds as if the baking soda either was not mixed in completely or was not neutralized with an acid. Did you remember to add the lemon juice or buttermilk?

They aren't all the same size? When you filled the muffin holes, you eyeballed it, right? Next time use a ¼-cup measure to fill the muffin holes two-thirds full.

They are stuck? The pan wasn't properly greased, or maybe it is so scratched and dented that the sides are no longer smooth. Use butter or solid vegetable shortening in the muffin holes, or line them with paper or aluminum foil cupcake liners. Be sure always to butter, oil, or spray the top surface of the muffin tin around the holes, so that if the muffins rise above the rim and spread they won't stick to the flat surface of the tin. Although I prefer to use butter for this because of its better taste, vegetable spray provides a quick and easy way to coat the top surface of the tin.

They are stale? If you don't plan to eat the muffins the day they were baked, allow them to cool completely, then store them in a plastic bag at room temperature for up to 24 hours. To store them for longer than that, the muffins should be frozen. Freeze them in heavy-duty recloseable plastic bags, and don't forget to label and date them with a waterproof marker. Defrost them in the bag, either in the refrigerator overnight or at room temperature for 1 to 2 hours. To heat them before eating, place them on a baking sheet in a preheated 300°F oven for 10 minutes. Some people like to microwave their muffins, but I think it makes them taste steamed.

The scones are tough? They may have been overmixed. Stir the dough by hand, with a fork just until the dry ingredients are incorporated.

The flavor is boring? Spice them up with grated lemon, orange, or lime zest; chopped candied ginger; chocolate chips; and/or chopped dried fruit, such as apricots, apples, pineapple, dates, or cranberries. Check to make sure that your spices for the recipe haven't lost their potency.

The scones are too big? Instead of cutting them into wedges after rolling the dough, use a 2-inch round cookie cutter to make biscuit-size scones. Bake them for 10 to 12 minutes instead of the specified baking time.

Buttermilk Biscuits

Makes: eleven 2½-inch biscuits; ten 3-inch biscuits

What you'll need:

heavy-duty baking sheet

silicone pan liner, parchment paper, or aluminum foil for preparing the baking sheet

microwave or small saucepan for melting butter

mesh sieve

2 table knives or a pastry blender

2½-inch or 3-inch round cookie cutter

fork

pastry brush

wire rack

Baking time: 20 minutes

Back when I was in junior high and boys took Shop, where they learned to burn their initials into leather knife holders and build birdhouses, girls had something called "Home Ec" (short for "economics"), where we learned to sew cobbler's aprons and cook. I can't say I've thought about making a cobbler's apron since I got out of junior high, but I often use this recipe—the very first thing I learned to bake in Home Ec.

These are wonderful served warm from the oven with butter and jam for breakfast or afternoon tea.

3½ cups all-purpose flour

1¼ teaspoons salt

1 tablespoon baking powder

½ teaspoon baking soda

¼ cup granulated sugar

1 tablespoon Lora Brody's Dough Relaxer, optional (see page 48)

⅓ cup solid vegetable shortening

¾ cup buttermilk (see page 49)

¾ cup heavy cream

1 tablespoon unsalted butter, melted

1. Preheat the oven to 425°F with a rack in the center of the oven. Line the baking sheet with a silicone pan liner, parchment paper, or aluminum foil. Set aside.

2. Place a mesh sieve over a large mixing bowl and add the flour, salt, baking powder, baking soda, sugar, and optional Dough Relaxer. Shake the contents into the bowl. Add the shortening and use two table knives in a crisscross motion, or a pastry blender, to cut the shortening into the flour mixture. The mixture should resemble coarse crumbs, and they will not be uniform in size. If you use a pastry blender, stop and clean between the wires with a table knife from time to time. Pour in the buttermilk and heavy cream, and mix with a fork just until the liquids are absorbed.

3. Turn the dough out onto a lightly floured work surface. Use your hands to knead it gently 4 or 5 times, and gather the dough into a ball that holds together. It is better to have the dough on the wet and sticky side and somewhat messy-looking than to overknead it into a perfectly smooth ball. Pat the dough into a circle that is ½ to ¾ inch thick. Use the cookie cutter to form biscuits. Place them 1 inch apart on the prepared baking sheet, then reroll the dough scraps and cut them as well. Brush the unbaked biscuits with the melted butter before baking, using a small pastry brush.

4. Bake the biscuits for 15 to 20 minutes, or until they are golden brown on top. Cool the biscuits on a wire rack for at least 5 minutes before serving. Biscuits are best eaten hot, right out of the oven. Plan to make these biscuits no more than 4 to 5 hours before they are to be eaten. They should not be frozen.

LORA SAYS: In place of liquid buttermilk in this recipe you can use 3 tablespoons buttermilk powder. There is no need to reconstitute it before using. Put the powder in the sieve with the other dry ingredients and add ¾ cup water along with the heavy cream in place of the liquid buttermilk.

LORA SAYS: It is important to use a sharp-edged cookie cutter for biscuits, in order to make a clean cut. A dull cutter will drag down and seal together the edges of the biscuit as you cut, causing a bad rise.

Strawberry Shortcake with Berry Sauce

The berries that make the best strawberry shortcake are not those perfectly stunning mega-specimens that you find in supermarkets year round. Wait until early summer when farm stands and grocery stores offer the small, sweet, locally grown berries. The flavor can't be beat—it's what real strawberry shortcake is all about. These biscuits should not be refrigerated or frozen.

Makes: 9 servings

What you'll need:

heavy-duty baking sheet

silicone pan liner, parchment paper, or aluminum foil for preparing the baking sheet

small, sharp knife for cutting up butter and hulling and quartering strawberries

mesh sieve

whisk

2 table knives or a pastry blender

3-inch round cookie cutter

pastry brush

hand-held electric mixer

fork

wire rack

large, chilled metal bowl and chilled beaters of hand-held electric mixer

Baking time: 14 minutes

FOR THE BISCUITS

3 cups all-purpose flour

5 tablespoons granulated sugar

1 tablespoon plus 1 teaspoon baking powder

Rounded ½ teaspoon salt

1 tablespoon Lora Brody's Dough Relaxer, optional

1 extra-large egg plus one extra-large yolk (save the extra white to make the glaze)

¾ cup half-and-half

1 tablespoon pure vanilla extract

1½ sticks (12 tablespoons) unsalted butter, chilled and cut into small pieces

FOR THE GLAZE

1 extra-large egg white, lightly beaten

2 tablespoons granulated sugar

FOR THE BERRIES

2 quarts fresh
strawberries, rinsed,
dried, and hulled

⅔ cup granulated sugar

FOR THE WHIPPED CREAM AND GARNISH

2 cups heavy cream,
chilled

1 tablespoon pure vanilla
extract

2 tablespoons superfine
sugar (see page 49)

9 whole fresh
strawberries, hulled

1. Preheat the oven to 425°F with a rack in the center of the oven. Line the baking sheet with a silicone pan liner, parchment paper, or aluminum foil. Set aside.

2. Place a mesh sieve over a large mixing bowl and add the flour, sugar, baking powder, and salt and optional Relaxer. Shake the contents into the bowl and set aside. In a 2-cup measure with a spout, whisk together the egg and egg yolk, half-and-half, and vanilla, and set aside.

3. Scatter the butter pieces over the flour mixture. Use two regular table knives in a criss-cross motion, or a pastry blender, to cut the butter into the flour. The mixture should resemble coarse crumbs, and they will not be uniform in size. If you use a pastry blender, stop and clean between the wires with a table knife from time to time. Pour in the egg and half-and-half mixture and mix with a fork until the liquid ingredients are just incorporated.

4. Turn the dough out onto a lightly floured work surface. Use your hands to knead it gently 4 or 5 times, and gather the dough into a ball that holds together. It is better to have the dough be somewhat messy-looking than to overknead it into a perfectly smooth ball. Pat the dough into a 10-inch circle, ¾ inch thick. Cut out circles, using the cookie cutter. Reroll the dough scraps once; you should get 9 circles. Place them 1 inch apart on the prepared baking sheet.

5. Brush the tops of the biscuits with egg white. Sprinkle 2 tablespoons sugar over the tops. Bake for 12 to 14 minutes, or until the biscuits are a light golden brown. Remove them from the oven and transfer the biscuits to a wire rack.

6. To prepare the berries, quarter them, place them in a medium mixing bowl, and toss them gently with ⅓ cup sugar. Cover the bowl. Refrigerate the berries for 3 to 4 hours, or leave them at room temperature for about 1 hour until they have released some of their juices. When you prepare the berries, place a large metal mixing bowl and the beaters of the mixer in the refrigerator or freezer to chill for 30 minutes.

7. When you are ready to assemble the shortcakes, pour the cream into the chilled mixing bowl. With the mixer on high speed, whip the cream with the chilled beaters until it begins to thicken. Add the superfine sugar and continue beating on high speed until soft peaks form, then mix in the vanilla.

8. Cut the biscuits in half and lay each bottom half, cut side up, in a shallow bowl or rimmed dish. Spoon some of the berries and their juice over the halves, then spoon on a large dollop of whipped cream. Cover with the biscuit tops, and spoon over more of the berries. Top each shortcake with a whole strawberry, placed hulled side down. Serve immediately.

Classic Scones

Makes: 12 scones

What you'll need:

heavy-duty baking sheet

silicone pan liner, parchment paper, or aluminum foil for preparing the baking sheet

mesh sieve

wooden mixing spoon

dough scraper or sharp, straight-bladed knife

whisk

pastry brush

wire rack

Baking time: 18 minutes

Doesn't it kill you to spend $2.50 for a scone in a yuppie coffee bar? Let's see . . . 5 scones a week for 50 weeks (operating on the 2-week vacation theory) equals 250 scones at $2.50 each, throwing in 25 cents for each tip, means you could be spending $687.50 per year on something you could make so much better for a fraction of the cost at home. Who knows, maybe you'll get to be a great scone maker and go into business selling cheaper, better scones. My husband, David, loves scones, and since we are still paying college tuition and budgeting ourselves, every Sunday afternoon I make a batch and put them in the freezer in individual recloseable sandwich-size plastic bags. He pulls one out to defrost the night before and enjoys a homemade breakfast treat with his coffee in the morning.

FOR THE SCONES

2 cups all-purpose flour

1 tablespoon baking powder

½ teaspoon salt

¼ cup granulated sugar

1 tablespoon Lora Brody's Dough Relaxer, optional

1⅓ cups heavy cream

FOR THE GLAZE

1 extra-large egg

1 tablespoon heavy cream

2 tablespoons coarse (baker's) sugar (see page 49) or granulated sugar, optional

1. Preheat the oven to 425°F with a rack in the center of the oven. Line the baking sheet with a silicone pan liner, parchment paper, or aluminum foil. Set aside.

2. Place a mesh sieve over a large mixing bowl and add the flour, baking powder, salt, and sugar and optional Relaxer. Shake the contents into the bowl. Dribble in the heavy cream, mixing well with a wooden spoon. The dough will be rough, with some dry areas visible. Scrape the spoon and the sides of the bowl well with a rubber spatula, then turn the dough out onto a lightly floured surface.

3. Gently knead the dough by placing the heel of your hand in the center of the dough and pushing the dough away from you. Curl your fingers over the part of the dough farthest from you and pull it toward you, folding it in half. Rotate the dough 90 degrees and repeat the kneading process ten more times, rotating the dough each time, until the dough becomes smooth. Add as little additional flour as possible to the work surface and your hands as you work. With your hands flatten the ball of dough into a circle approximately 8 inches in diameter and ¾ inch thick. Use a dough scraper or a sharp, straight-bladed knife to cut the circle in half. Cut each half-circle into 6 equal wedges. Place the wedges at least 1 inch apart on the prepared baking sheet.

4. Make the glaze by whisking the egg with 1 tablespoon heavy cream in a small mixing bowl. Brush the tops of the scones with the glaze. Sprinkle the tops with sugar, if desired.

5. Bake about 18 minutes, or until the tops and bottoms are a golden brown. Remove the pan from the oven and place it on a rack to cool.

6. The scones can be stored in a covered tin or a perforated plastic bag (see Lora Says) at room temperature for up to 2 days. They can also be frozen. Wrap individual scones in plastic wrap, then place them on a baking sheet and freeze for at least 3 hours. When they are completely frozen, place each one in an individual recloseable sandwich-size plastic bag. Label the bag with a waterproof marker to note the contents of the bag and the date. Remove a scone from the freezer the night before, and let it defrost on the kitchen counter to be eaten the next morning.

LORA SAYS: Perforated gallon-size plastic bags, perfect for storing baked and cooled scones at room temperature—not in the freezer—can be found in some supermarkets in the plastic-storage-bag aisle. They are sold as vegetable refrigerator storage bags. They are also available as vegetable storage bags from the King Arthur Flour Baker's Catalogue (see page 316). Moisture cannot get trapped inside these bags, so the scones do not get soggy during storage.

VARIATIONS

Chocolate Chip Scones: Add ¾ cup semisweet chocolate chips to the sifted flour mixture, and toss the chips with the flour. Add the cream and mix the dough as for Classic Scones. Add ⅓ cup chopped pecans, walnuts, or slivered blanched almonds with the chocolate, if desired.

Ginger Scones: Add ½ cup finely chopped candied ginger to the sifted flour mixture, and toss the pieces with the flour. Add the cream and mix the dough as for Classic Scones. Use a pair of kitchen scissors to cut the candied ginger into small pieces. For best results, spray the blades with nonstick vegetable spray first, so that the ginger won't stick to them.

Cranberry Scones: Add ½ cup dried cranberries to the sifted flour mixture, and toss them with the flour. Add the cream and mix the dough as for Classic Scones.

Apricot Oatmeal Scones

Makes: about 10 scones, 2¼ inches in diameter

What you'll need:

heavy-duty baking sheet

silicone pan liner, parchment paper, or aluminum foil for preparing the baking sheet

small, sharp knife for cutting up butter

small, heavy saucepan

mixing spoon

paper towels for draining apricots

sharp, heavy knife for chopping apricots

mesh sieve

whisk

2 table knives or a pastry blender

2½-inch round cookie cutter

wire rack

Baking time: 15 minutes

When I was once teaching a baking class in England, the students were alternately appalled and fascinated when I suggested adding ingredients other than currants to scones. Yes, it's shockingly untraditional, but, hey!—aren't rules made to be broken? Most of the students thought this American version was swell. The rest were glad we gained independence.

¾ cup dried apricots

1 cup orange juice

1¼ cups all-purpose flour

1½ teaspoons baking powder

½ teaspoon baking soda

½ teaspoon salt

½ teaspoon ground cinnamon

1 cup oats, old-fashioned or quick-cooking (see page 46)

1 tablespoon Lora Brody's Dough Relaxer, optional

⅓ cup packed light brown sugar

1 stick (8 tablespoons) unsalted butter, chilled and cut into small pieces

½ cup milk

1. Preheat the oven to 400°F with a rack in the center of the oven. Line the baking sheet with a silicone pan liner, parchment paper, or aluminum foil. Set aside.

2. Place the dried apricots in the saucepan with the orange juice. Bring the juice to a simmer over medium heat, then reduce the heat to low and simmer the apricots for 10 minutes, or until they are quite soft. Stir them occasionally. Drain the apricots; discard the orange juice. Transfer the apricots to paper towels to cool. When they are cool enough to handle, chop them coarsely (each apricot should be cut into about 6 pieces) and set aside.

3. Place a mesh sieve over a large mixing bowl and add the flour, baking powder, baking soda, salt, cinnamon and optional Relaxer. Shake the contents into the bowl. Whisk in the rolled oats and the brown sugar, breaking up the largest lumps of brown sugar. Scatter the pieces of butter over the dry ingredients. Use 2 regular table knives in a crisscross motion, or a pastry blender, to cut the butter into the flour mixture until the butter lumps are the size of peas. If you use a pastry blender, stop and clean between the wires from time to time. Dribble in the milk, and stir the dough with a rubber spatula to moisten it. Fold in the apricots, mixing only until they are distributed. Do not overwork the dough. It will be somewhat sticky. Resist the temptation to add more flour than necessary to form and cut the dough, as this will make the scones dry and hard.

4. Scrape the dough out onto a lightly floured surface and divide it in half. Flour your fingers and knead each portion of dough gently, then pat each into a rough circle 6 inches in diameter and ¾ inch thick. Use the cookie cutter to cut each portion of dough into circles. Place them 1 inch apart on the prepared baking sheet. Gather up the scraps one time and pat them into a ¾-inch thick circle and cut additional scones.

5. Bake the scones for 15 minutes until they are a light golden brown. Remove the scones from the oven and transfer them to a wire rack to cool. The scones are best served warm from the oven.

6. The scones can be stored in a covered tin or a perforated plastic bag (see Lora Says, page 203) at room temperature for up to 2 days. They can also be frozen. Wrap individual scones in plastic wrap, then place them on a baking sheet and freeze for at least 3 hours. When they are completely frozen, place each one in an individual recloseable sandwich-size plastic bag. Label the bag with a waterproof marker to note the contents of the bag and the date. Remove a scone from the freezer the night before, and let it defrost on the kitchen counter to be eaten the next morning.

Emmy's Blue Ribbon Blueberry Muffins

Makes: 12 regular muffins or 6 jumbo muffins

What you'll need:

regular 12-hole muffin tin or jumbo 6-hole muffin tin

citrus zester

mesh sieve

fork

whisk

wooden mixing spoon

instant-read thermometer

wire rack

Baking time: 18 to 20 minutes for regular muffins; 22 to 24 minutes for jumbo muffins

Just before I started writing this book a wonderful thing happened. Emmy Clausing, freelance editor, recipe developer, and recipe tester, came into my life. She calmed me down, organized me, got me on schedule, and quelled my typical oh-my-God-how-am-I-ever-going-to-finish-this-book-on-time panic. She has a certain dedication and loads of skills that I lack: She can spell, she can find terminally missing computer files, she likes zucchini bread and, most important, she refused to give up the hunt for the perfect blueberry muffin recipe. I shudder when I think of how many she tested. I was ready to sign off on at least four that she declared substandard. Lucky for us both that we are beneficiaries of Emmy's diligence, persistence, tenacity, and exceptionally high standards. These muffins have a sugary glaze that makes the tops sparkle with texture and flavor.

FOR PREPARING THE MUFFIN TIN

1½ tablespoons unsalted butter or solid vegetable shortening, softened, *or* foil or paper cupcake liners; nonstick vegetable spray

2 cups all-purpose flour	2 extra-large eggs
1 cup granulated sugar plus 1½ tablespoons for sprinkling on the muffins	½ cup milk
	1 stick (8 tablespoons) unsalted butter, melted
2 teaspoons baking powder	1 teaspoon pure vanilla extract
½ teaspoon salt	
2⅓ cups blueberries (see Lora Says)	Finely grated zest of 1 lemon

1. Preheat the oven to 400°F with a rack in the center of the oven. Coat the holes of the muffin tin with the butter or vegetable shortening. If you are using a regular 12-hole tin, you may use aluminum foil or paper cupcake liners in the holes instead. For easy removal of the baked muffins, spray the top surface of either size tin with nonstick vegetable spray. Set aside.

2. Place a mesh sieve over a large mixing bowl and add the flour, 1 cup sugar, baking powder, and salt. Shake the contents into the bowl and set aside. Place ⅔ cup blueberries in a small bowl and mash them roughly with a fork. Set aside.

3. Break the eggs into a medium mixing bowl and whisk them briefly to break them up. Whisk in the milk, melted butter, vanilla, and lemon zest. Stir in the mashed blueberries with a wooden spoon or rubber spatula. Fold this mixture into the dry ingredients with a rubber spatula and mix just to combine; there should be some flour lumps remaining. Scrape the sides of the bowl as you work. Fold in the remaining whole blueberries.

4. Scrape the batter into the prepared tin, and sprinkle the tops of the muffins with 1½ tablespoons sugar. Bake regular muffins for 18 to 20 minutes and jumbo muffins for 22 to 24 minutes, or until the muffins are a golden brown, have risen nicely, and an instant-read thermometer inserted into the center of a muffin registers 190°F. When the muffins are done, remove them from the oven and let cool for 15 minutes in the pan before removing them to a wire rack.

5. The muffins can be stored in a recloseable gallon-size plastic bag at room temperature for 24 hours. They can also be frozen for up to 3 months. Wrap individual muffins in plastic wrap, then place them on a baking sheet and freeze for at least 3 hours. When they are completely frozen, place each one in an individual recloseable sandwich-size plastic bag. Label the bag with a waterproof marker to note the contents of the bag and the date. Remove a muffin from the freezer the night before, and let it defrost on the kitchen counter to be eaten the next morning.

LORA SAYS: While I think muffins taste best eaten the day they are made, they can be stored as described in the recipe. Previously frozen muffins can be warmed in a toaster oven, or in a conventional oven at 300°F, or toasted. Microwaving muffins makes them soggy and limp.

LORA SAYS: You may use frozen unsweetened blueberries in this recipe. Remove the berries from the freezer and measure them out. Place them on a plate or other flat surface in one layer when you start the recipe, to soften them a little. It is not necessary to defrost them entirely. What makes this recipe so good is the addition of some mashed berries to the batter along with the whole berries, so the frozen berries need to be soft enough to mash. Using frozen berries will extend the baking time by 2 to 3 minutes for regular muffins, 5 to 6 minutes for jumbo muffins.

LORA SAYS: When making these muffins, reserve a few of the whole berries when it is time to add them to the batter. This way you will not run out of berries as you scoop the last portion of muffin batter into the muffin tin, because you can add the reserved berries.

Lemon Poppy Seed Muffins

Makes: 12 regular muffins or 6 jumbo muffins

What you'll need:

regular 12-hole muffin tin or jumbo 6-hole muffin tin

microwave or small saucepan for melting butter

citrus zester

fine-mesh sieve for straining lemon juice

mesh sieve

whisk

hand-held electric mixer

instant-read thermometer

small, heavy saucepan

pastry brush

mixing spoon

small metal or wooden skewer

pastry brush

wire rack

Baking time: 15 to 18 minutes for regular muffins; 22 to 24 minutes for jumbo muffins

The classic coffee bar muffin is now available in your own kitchen. The zing of lemon, the crunch of sugar and poppy seeds—not one delicate crumb of buttery muffin will be left on anyone's plate. These are so good they don't need anything spread on top.

FOR PREPARING THE MUFFIN TIN

1½ tablespoons unsalted butter or solid vegetable shortening, softened, *or* aluminum foil or paper cupcake liners; nonstick vegetable spray

FOR THE MUFFINS

1½ cups all-purpose flour

2 teaspoons baking powder

½ teaspoon baking soda

½ teaspoon salt

¼ cup plus 2 tablespoons poppy seeds

1 extra-large egg

½ cup granulated sugar

¾ cup (8 ounces) lemon yogurt, regular, low-fat, or nonfat

1 stick (8 tablespoons) unsalted butter, melted

1 teaspoon pure vanilla extract

Finely grated zest of 1 lemon

¼ cup fresh, strained lemon juice

FOR THE GLAZE

½ cup granulated sugar

Finely grated zest of 1 lemon

¼ cup fresh, strained lemon juice

1. Preheat the oven to 400°F with a rack in the center of the oven. Coat the holes of the muffin tin with the butter or solid vegetable shortening. If you are using a regular 12-hole tin, you may use aluminum foil or paper cupcake liners in the holes instead. For easy removal of the baked muffins, spray the top surface of either size tin with nonstick vegetable spray. Set aside.

2. Place a mesh sieve over a large mixing bowl and add the flour, baking powder, baking soda, and salt. Shake the contents into the bowl. Whisk in the poppy seeds and set aside.

3. Place the egg and sugar in a medium mixing bowl. With the mixer on high speed, beat them together until light and fluffy, about 2 minutes. Reduce the mixer speed to medium and beat in the yogurt, melted butter, vanilla, and the lemon zest and juice until well incorporated, about 30 seconds. Using a rubber spatula, fold the egg mixture into the flour mixture, scraping down the sides of the bowl as you work, until the ingredients are just mixed.

4. Scrape the batter into the prepared tin. Bake regular muffins for 15 to 18 minutes, and jumbo muffins for 22 to 24 minutes, until the muffins have browned and risen nicely, and an instant-read thermometer inserted into the center of a muffin registers 190°F.

5. While the muffins are baking, prepare the glaze. In the saucepan stir the sugar, lemon zest, and juice together, then place the saucepan over medium heat. Bring the mixture to a simmer, then stir the glaze until the sugar dissolves. Remove the pan from the heat. When the muffins are done, remove the tin from the oven. Use a metal or wooden skewer to poke several holes in the top of each muffin. Brush each muffin generously with the lemon glaze; use all of it. Allow the muffins to cool for 10 minutes in the tin, then remove them to a wire rack to cool completely.

6. The muffins can be stored in a recloseable plastic bag at room temperature for 24 hours. They can also be frozen for up to 3 months. Wrap individual muffins in plastic wrap, then place them on a baking sheet and freeze for at least 3 hours. When they are completely frozen, place each one in an individual sandwich-size recloseable plastic bag. Label the bag with a waterproof marker to note the contents of the bag and the date. Remove a muffin from the freezer the night before, and let it defrost on the kitchen counter to be eaten the next morning.

Strawberry-Filled Muffins

Makes: 12 regular muffins or 6 jumbo muffins

What you'll need:

regular 12-hole muffin tin or jumbo 6-hole muffin tin

mesh sieve

hand-held electric mixer

cake tester

wire rack

Baking time: 20 to 25 minutes for regular muffins; 35 to 40 minutes for jumbo muffins

I am particularly proud of this recipe because I thought it up during a long drive to some particularly boring place. To stay awake I indulged in a muffin fantasy (see what happens when you get to be middle-aged?—baked goods take over for Tom Cruise). I had tried to bake whole fresh strawberries inside muffins, but they dissolved, leaving a little red puddle. While I was waiting for the state police to write out my speeding ticket (see how excited you can get over muffins?), I had an epiphany involving frozen strawberries baked inside the batter. The double good news is that the recipe worked and I only got a warning ticket. Whew!

If you have a jumbo muffin tin you can make 6 gloriously oversized muffins; in a traditional 12-hole tin you can make a dozen real-life–sized ones.

FOR PREPARING THE MUFFIN TIN

1½ tablespoons unsalted butter or solid vegetable shortening, softened, *or* aluminum foil or paper cupcake liners; nonstick vegetable spray

FOR THE MUFFINS

2 cups all-purpose flour

1 tablespoon baking
powder

Scant ¼ teaspoon nutmeg

Scant ¼ teaspoon ground
cloves

½ teaspoon salt

2 extra-large eggs

1 cup granulated sugar

½ stick (4 tablespoons)
unsalted butter, softened

¼ cup vegetable oil

¼ cup milk

2 teaspoons pure vanilla
extract

12 small or 6 large whole
frozen unsweetened
strawberries, not defrosted
(see Lora Says)

6 tablespoons cream
cheese (not the whipped
or low-fat variety), cut into
12 pieces for regular
muffins; 6 pieces for
jumbo muffins

1. Preheat the oven to 350°F with a rack in the center of the oven. Coat the holes of the muffin tin with the butter or vegetable shortening. If you are using a regular 12-hole tin, you may use aluminum foil or paper cupcake liners in the holes instead. For easy removal of the baked muffins, spray the top surface of either size tin with nonstick vegetable spray. Set aside.

2. Place a mesh sieve over a medium mixing bowl and add the flour, baking powder, nutmeg, cloves, and salt. Shake the contents into the bowl and set aside.

3. Place the eggs and sugar in a large mixing bowl. Beat with the mixer on medium speed until mixture is light and fluffy and the beaters leave a trail when they are pulled through the mixture, about 3 minutes. Scrape the sides of the bowl with a rubber spatula beating several times while mixing. Add the butter and beat until the butter is incorporated.

4. Combine the oil, milk, and vanilla in a cup with a spout. With the mixer on low speed, add half the dry ingredients to the egg mixture, then half the oil mixture. Add the remaining dry ingredients, and then the remaining oil mixture. Beat until ingredients are just incorporated. Scrape down the sides of the bowl from time to time as you work. The batter will be rather thick. Scrape the batter into the muffin holes, filling them just under two-thirds full.

5. For regular muffins, poke 1 small frozen strawberry or ½ large strawberry into each portion of batter. For jumbo muffins, use 2 small berries or 1 large one for each muffin. The berries should not be visible. Place a piece of cream cheese on top of each portion of batter, leaving the cream cheese exposed on the top.

6. Bake regular muffins for 20 to 25 minutes, and jumbo muffins for 35 to 40 minutes, or until the muffins are golden and a cake tester inserted into the batter comes out clean. The muffins will be slightly indented where the filling is. When the muffins have baked, remove them immediately from the muffin tin and cool them on a rack. Lift the muffins out carefully so as not to disturb the filling.

7. The muffins can be stored in a recloseable plastic bag at room temperature for 24 hours. They can also be frozen for up to 3 months. Wrap individual muffins in plastic wrap, then place them on a baking sheet and freeze for at least 3 hours. When they are completely frozen, place each one in an individual sandwich-size recloseable plastic bag. Label the bag with a waterproof marker to note the contents of the bag and the date. Remove a muffin from the freezer the night before, and let it defrost on the kitchen counter to be eaten the next morning.

LORA SAYS: Look for the unsweetened whole frozen berries that are sold in 10-ounce or 12-ounce bags in the frozen food aisle of the supermarket.

LORA SAYS: The term "scant" means an amount that's just shy of what the measuring cup or spoon will hold when full; I like to think of the measure as "⅞ full."

LORA SAYS: When you beat eggs and sugar together, you not only incorporate air into the mixture, which will give lightness and height, but you also dissolve the sugar, which makes the finished product less grainy.

Pumpkin Muffins with Cream Cheese Filling

Makes: 12 regular muffins or
6 jumbo muffins

What you'll need:

regular 12-hole muffin tin or
jumbo 6-hole muffin tin

fork

mesh sieve

hand-held electric mixer

wire rack

Baking time: 20 to 22 minutes
for regular muffins; 30 to 35
minutes for jumbo muffins

Between this recipe and the preceding one, I was on a real roll (well . . . a real muffin and a figurative roll). This muffin is a very special treat that shouldn't be saved just for breakfast. It's a cross between pumpkin pie and cheesecake—not unlike "Thanksgiving meets your birthday." Some of the ingredients may be a slight challenge to track down, but I found coconut milk and canned pumpkin puree in my grocery store. Since the bulk of the coconut milk will be left over, I suggest that you make Coco Loco Bananas Foster Crumble (page 298) next.

FOR PREPARING THE MUFFIN TIN

1½ tablespoons unsalted butter or solid vegetable shortening, softened, *or* aluminum foil or paper cupcake liners; nonstick vegetable spray

FOR THE FILLING

6 tablespoons cream cheese (not the whipped or reduced-fat variety), at room temperature (see page 33)

2 tablespoons pure maple syrup (see page 45)

2 cups all-purpose flour

1 tablespoon baking
powder

Scant 1 teaspoon salt

½ teaspoon ground ginger

½ teaspoon ground
cardamom

½ teaspoon ground
cinnamon

2 extra-large eggs

½ cup packed light brown
sugar

½ cup granulated sugar

1 cup canned pumpkin
puree (not pumpkin pie
filling) (see page 49)

½ cup vegetable oil

¼ cup coconut milk (see
page 48) or regular milk

⅔ cup pecan halves (about
2 ounces)

1. Preheat the oven to 350°F with a rack in the center of the oven. Coat the holes of the muffin tin with the butter or solid vegetable shortening. If you are using a regular 12-hole tin, you may use aluminum foil or paper cupcake liners in the holes instead. For easy removal of the baked muffins, spray the top surface of either size tin with nonstick vegetable spray. Set aside.

2. Place the cream cheese in a small bowl and add the maple syrup. Use a fork to blend them together until smooth. Set aside.

3. Place a mesh sieve over a medium mixing bowl and add the flour, baking powder, salt, ginger, cardamom, and cinnamon. Shake the contents into the bowl and set aside.

4. Place the eggs and light brown and granulated sugar in a large mixing bowl. With the mixer on high speed, beat the eggs and sugars together until they are thickened and light, about 2 minutes, scraping down the bowl from time to time as you work. The mixture should be thick enough to fall back into the bowl in a thick ribbon when the beaters are shut off and raised. Beat in the pumpkin puree on low speed. With the mixer still on low speed, pour in half the oil, then add half the flour mixture. Repeat with the remaining oil and flour mixture, beating until there are no streaks of flour remaining. Scrape down the sides of the bowl as you work. Beat in the coconut milk until just combined.

5. Divide the batter among the muffin holes. If you are baking regular-size muffins, place ½ tablespoon cream cheese mixture on each portion of batter, then top each with 2 or 3 pecan halves. Press down lightly on the cream cheese and nuts. For jumbo-size muffins, place 1 tablespoon of cream cheese mixture on each portion of batter, then top each with 3 or 4 pecan halves. Bake regular muffins for 20 to 22 minutes, and jumbo muffins for 30 to 35 minutes until the muffins are golden brown and have risen nicely; a cake tester inserted in the center of a muffin should come out clean. Remove the muffins from the oven and allow them to cool in the pan for 10 minutes. Transfer them carefully to a wire rack to cool.

6. The muffins can be stored in a recloseable gallon-size plastic bag at room temperature for 24 hours. They can also be frozen for up to 3 months. Wrap individual muffins in plastic wrap, then place them on a baking sheet and freeze for at least 3 hours. When they are completely frozen, place each one in an individual recloseable sandwich-size plastic bag. Label the bag with a waterproof marker to note the contents of the bag and the date. Remove a muffin from the freezer the night before, and let it defrost on the kitchen counter to be eaten the next morning.

LORA SAYS: Leftover coconut milk, an essential ingredient in piña coladas, can be frozen in a covered plastic container. Defrost at room temperature. Be sure to stir the defrosted milk before using, as coconut milk naturally separates.

Jam Muffins

Makes: 12 regular muffins

What you'll need:

12-hole muffin tin

microwave or small saucepan for melting butter

mesh sieve

hand-held electric mixer

pastry brush

wire rack

Baking time: 20 minutes

Yum—jam baked right in the muffin! I'm a no-apologies snob, since it's clear that the better the jam, the more you taste the fruit.

For best results, use butter to grease the muffin holes, rather than vegetable spray or paper cupcake liners, as the taste of these delicate muffins is enhanced by a bit of pure sweet butter in the tin. There is no need to spread anything on these!

FOR PREPARING THE MUFFIN TIN

2 tablespoons unsalted butter, softened

FOR THE MUFFINS

1½ cups all-purpose flour

1½ teaspoons baking powder

½ teaspoon baking soda

¼ teaspoon salt

1 extra-large egg

½ cup granulated sugar

1 cup sour cream

1 stick (8 tablespoons) unsalted butter, melted

1½ teaspoons pure vanilla extract

¼ cup best-quality jam or preserves, such as raspberry, blueberry, strawberry, apricot, or peach

3 tablespoons granulated
sugar

1½ tablespoons unsalted
butter, melted

1. Preheat the oven to 400°F with a rack in the center of the oven. Coat the holes of the muffin tin with the butter. For easy removal of the baked muffins, rub the top surface of the tin around the muffin holes with butter, too.

2. Place a mesh sieve over a medium mixing bowl and add the flour, baking powder, baking soda, and salt. Shake the contents into the bowl and set aside.

3. Place the egg and sugar in a large mixing bowl. With the mixer on medium speed, beat the egg and sugar together until fluffy and light, about 2 minutes. Beat in the sour cream, melted butter, and vanilla until ingredients are just incorporated. Move the beaters around the bowl and scrape down the sides of the bowl with a rubber spatula several times while mixing. Add the flour mixture and beat on low speed until no streaks of flour remain, about 30 seconds.

4. Spoon about 1½ tablespoons batter into each prepared muffin cup. Place 1 teaspoon jam on each portion of batter and press it gently onto the batter. Spoon in the remaining batter, filling the cups evenly. Bake the muffins for 20 minutes, or until they have browned and risen. Remove the muffins from the oven and cool them in the tin for 10 minutes. Transfer them carefully to a wire rack to cool completely.

5. To make the topping, while the muffins are cooling, place the sugar in a small ramekin or bowl. When the muffins are cool enough to handle, remove them from the muffin tin. Use a pastry brush to moisten the top of each with some of the melted butter, then dip the top into the sugar. Transfer the muffins to a wire rack to cool. These muffins are best eaten right after dipping, but be careful of the hot preserves in the centers.

6. The muffins can be stored in a recloseable gallon-size plastic bag at room temperature for 24 hours. They can also be frozen for up to 3 months. Wrap individual muffins in plastic wrap, then place them on a baking sheet and freeze for at least 3 hours. When they are completely frozen, place each one in an individual recloseable sandwich-size plastic bag. Label the bag with a waterproof marker to note the contents of the bag and the date. Remove a muffin from the freezer the night before, and let it defrost on the kitchen counter to be eaten the next morning.

Cranberry-Almond-Orange Muffins

Makes: 12 regular muffins or 6 jumbo muffins

What you'll need:

regular 12-hole muffin tin or jumbo 6-hole muffin tin

sharp, heavy knife for chopping almonds

food processor for chopping fresh or frozen cranberries

baking sheet for toasting almonds

citrus zester

citrus reamer

fork

mesh sieve

hand-held electric mixer

cake tester or instant-read thermometer

wire rack

Baking time: 18 to 20 minutes for regular muffins; 22 to 24 minutes for jumbo muffins

The combination of bright, tart nuggets of dried cranberries and the zing of orange in the muffins is enhanced by the crunch of toasted almonds in the streusel topping, making this muffin a real winner. You can omit the streusel topping, if you prefer.

FOR PREPARING THE MUFFIN TIN

1½ tablespoons unsalted butter or solid vegetable shortening, softened, *or* aluminum foil or paper cupcake liners; nonstick vegetable spray

FOR THE STREUSEL

¼ cup all-purpose flour

3 tablespoons packed light brown sugar

3 tablespoons blanched almonds, chopped (see page 19)

3 tablespoons unsalted butter, softened

FOR THE MUFFINS

2 cups all-purpose flour

1½ teaspoons baking powder

1 teaspoon baking soda

½ teaspoon salt

½ teaspoon ground ginger

1 cup fresh or frozen cranberries, chopped (see Lora Says) or ¾ cup dried cranberries

½ cup blanched almonds, toasted and coarsely chopped (see pages 18–19)

1 extra-large egg

½ cup granulated sugar

¾ cup buttermilk (see page 49)

⅓ cup vegetable oil

Finely grated zest of 1 orange

½ cup strained, fresh orange juice

1. Preheat the oven to 400°F with a rack in the center of the oven. Coat the holes of the muffin tin with the butter or solid vegetable shortening. If you are using a regular 12-hole tin, you may use aluminum foil or paper cupcake liners in the holes instead. For easy removal of the baked muffins, spray the top surface of either size tin with nonstick vegetable spray. Set aside.

2. To make the streusel, combine the flour, light brown sugar, and chopped almonds in a small bowl. Add the butter and mix with a fork to form nonuniform clumps of streusel. Set aside.

3. To make the muffins, place a mesh sieve over a large mixing bowl and add the flour, baking powder, baking soda, salt, and ground ginger. Shake the contents into the bowl. Scatter the fresh, frozen, or dried cranberries and the toasted almonds over the dry ingredients and stir them with a fork to coat them with flour. This will prevent their clumping together in the baked muffins. Set aside.

4. Break the egg into a medium mixing bowl and add the sugar. Beat the egg and sugar with the mixer on high speed until mixture is light and fluffy, about 2 minutes. Add the buttermilk, oil, orange zest, and orange juice. Beat on low speed until well mixed. With a rubber spatula fold this mixture into the flour mixture until just combined.

5. Ladle the batter into the prepared muffin tin, filling each hole slightly more than halfway. Top the muffins with streusel. Bake regular muffins for 18 to 20 minutes, and jumbo muffins for 22 to 24 minutes until a cake tester inserted in the middle of a muffin comes out clean, or an instant-read thermometer inserted in the center registers 190°F. Remove the tin from the oven and let the muffins cool in the tin on a wire rack for 20 to 30 minutes. Remove the muffins to the wire rack to cool completely.

6. The muffins can be stored in a recloseable gallon-size plastic bag at room temperature for 24 hours. They can also be frozen for up to 3 months. Wrap individual muffins in plastic wrap, then place them on a baking sheet and freeze for at least 3 hours. When they are completely frozen, place each one in an individual recloseable sandwich-size plastic bag. Label the bag with a waterproof marker to note the contents of the bag and the date. Remove a muffin from the freezer the night before, and let it defrost on the kitchen counter to be eaten the next morning.

LORA SAYS: Getting streusel-topped muffins out of the muffin tin is a little trickier than regular muffins. In order not to lose too much of the topping (some will come off—you get to eat it if it doesn't hit the floor), cover the cooled tin with an oversize piece of plastic wrap, pulling the edges gently down over the sides of the tin. Cover the pan with a baking sheet and invert the whole thing. You may have to shake the pan a couple of times to release the muffins. Remove the muffin tin and turn the muffins right side up.

LORA SAYS: In place of the liquid buttermilk in this recipe you can use 3 tablespoons buttermilk powder. There is no need to reconstitute it before using. Put the powder in the sieve with the other dry ingredients and add ¾ cup water along with the orange juice.

LORA SAYS: Use the pulse function of a food processor to chop both fresh and frozen cranberries. Dried cranberries don't need to be chopped, since they are small to begin with.

Banana Walnut Muffins

Makes: 12 regular muffins or 6 jumbo muffins

What you'll need:

regular 12-hole muffin tin or jumbo 6-hole muffin tin

baking sheet for toasting walnuts

sharp, heavy knife for chopping walnuts

mesh sieve

mixing spoon

hand-held electric mixer

cake tester

wire rack

Baking time: 18 to 20 minutes for regular muffins; 22 to 24 minutes for jumbo muffins

This is the perfect recipe in which to use those over-ripe bananas that have been sitting in the fruit bowl for a week or so. If you don't have soft, ripe bananas, stick a few peeled ones in a plastic bag and put them in the freezer overnight. When they defrost, they will be nice and soft.

FOR PREPARING THE MUFFIN TIN

1½ tablespoons unsalted butter or solid vegetable shortening, softened, *or* aluminum foil or paper cupcake liners; nonstick vegetable spray

FOR THE MUFFINS

2 cups all-purpose flour

1 teaspoon baking powder

1 teaspoon baking soda

½ teaspoon salt

½ teaspoon ground cinnamon

½ teaspoon ground nutmeg

½ teaspoon ground cloves

½ teaspoon ground ginger

½ cup walnuts, toasted and coarsely chopped (see pages 18–19)

About 3 large ripe bananas (1½ cups mashed)

⅓ cup packed light brown sugar

1 extra-large egg

¼ cup vegetable oil

1. Preheat the oven to 375°F with a rack in the center of the oven. Coat the holes of the muffin tin with the butter or solid vegetable shortening. If you are using a regular 12-hole tin, you may use aluminum foil or paper cupcake liners in the holes instead. For easy removal of the baked muffins, spray the top surface of either size tin with nonstick vegetable spray. Set aside.

2. Place a mesh sieve over a large mixing bowl and add the flour, baking powder, baking soda, salt, cinnamon, nutmeg, cloves, and ginger. Shake the contents into the bowl, then toss in the toasted walnuts. Stir with the mixing spoon to coat the nuts with flour, and set aside.

3. Peel the bananas and break them into large pieces. Place them in a medium mixing bowl and mash them roughly by beating them with the mixer on medium speed for 30 seconds. Add the light brown sugar and beat on medium speed for about 1 minute until only a few lumps of banana remain. Beat in the egg and oil. Use a rubber spatula to fold the banana mixture into the flour mixture, mixing until the ingredients are just incorporated; a few specks of flour should remain. Pour and scrape the batter into the prepared muffin tin. Bake regular muffins for 18 to 20 minutes, and jumbo muffins 22 to 24 minutes, or until a cake tester inserted into the center of a muffin comes out clean and the muffins are a light golden brown on top. Remove the tin from the oven and let the muffins cool in the tin for 5 minutes, then transfer the muffins to the wire rack to cool completely.

4. The muffins can be stored in a recloseable gallon-size plastic bag at room temperature for 24 hours. They can also be frozen for up to 3 months. Wrap individual muffins in plastic wrap, then place them on a baking sheet and freeze for at least 3 hours. When they are completely frozen, place each one in an individual recloseable sandwich-size plastic bag. Label the bag with a waterproof marker to note the contents of the bag and the date. Remove a muffin from the freezer the night before, and let it defrost on the kitchen counter to be eaten the next morning.

LORA SAYS: Ground spices lose their potency and flavor within a few months after opening the jar or can. You can maximize their shelf life by storing them in tinted jars with lids tightly closed, in a cool, dry place—not in clear jars on top of your stove.

Chocolate-Cherry Muffins

Makes: 12 regular muffins or 6 jumbo muffins

What you'll need:

regular 12-hole muffin tin or 6-hole jumbo muffin tin

microwave or small saucepan for boiling water

scale for weighing chocolate (optional)

sharp, heavy knife for chopping chocolate

small sieve

microwave or small metal bowl and pan of simmering water for melting chocolate

mesh sieve

hand-held electric mixer

cake tester

wire rack

Baking time: 20 to 22 minutes for regular muffins; 25 to 30 minutes for jumbo muffins

Chocolate and cherries are a natural combination, especially when the cherries are tart and surrounded by tender chocolate cake that may look like a muffin but tastes like a reason to have seconds on dessert. Whether you eat them in the morning with coffee or for a snack, or save them for a treat after a meal, these sugar-topped confections may remind of you of every reason why you should bake your own.

FOR PREPARING THE MUFFIN TIN

1½ tablespoons unsalted butter or solid vegetable shortening, softened, *or* aluminum foil or paper cupcake liners; nonstick vegetable spray

FOR THE MUFFINS

¾ cup (about 4 ounces) dried tart cherries

½ cup boiling water

6 ounces semisweet chocolate, chopped

1½ cups all-purpose flour

1½ teaspoons baking powder

½ teaspoon baking soda

½ teaspoon salt

1 tablespoon Lora Brody's Dough Relaxer, optional (see page 48)

¾ stick (6 tablespoons) unsalted butter, softened

½ cup plus 3 tablespoons granulated sugar, divided

2 extra-large eggs

1½ teaspoons pure almond extract

1. Preheat the oven to 350°F with a rack in the center of the oven. Coat the holes of the muffin tin with the butter or solid vegetable shortening. If you are using a regular 12-hole tin, you may use aluminum foil or paper cupcake liners instead. For easy removal of the baked muffins, spray the top surface of tin with nonstick vegetable spray. Set aside.

2. Place the dried cherries in a small bowl and pour the boiling water over them. Let the cherries soak for 10 minutes. Place a sieve over another small bowl and drain the cherries, reserving the liquid in the bowl. Set aside. Meanwhile, melt the chocolate either in the microwave or in a small metal mixing bowl set over, but not touching, a pan of gently simmering water. Set it aside to cool.

3. Place a mesh sieve over a medium mixing bowl and add the flour, baking powder, baking soda, salt, and the optional Dough Relaxer. Shake the contents into the bowl and set aside.

4. Place the butter and ½ cup sugar in a large mixing bowl. With the mixer on high speed, mix the butter with the sugar until it is light and fluffy, 2 to 3 minutes. Scrape the cooled chocolate into the mixture. Reduce the mixer speed to low and mix in the chocolate, then add the eggs, one at a time, waiting until the first is incorporated before adding the second. Mix in the almond extract. Move the beaters around the bowl and scrape down the sides of the bowl with a rubber spatula several times while mixing. With the mixer still on low speed, mix in the flour mixture, then the cherry soaking liquid. Use a rubber spatula to fold in the reserved cherries.

5. Mound the batter into the muffin holes. Sprinkle the tops generously with the remaining 3 tablespoons sugar. Bake regular muffins for 20 to 22 minutes, and jumbo muffins for 25 to 30 minutes, or until a cake tester inserted into the center of a muffin comes out dry. Remove the muffins from the oven and let them cool in the pan for 10 minutes, then remove the muffins to a wire rack to cool completely.

6. The muffins can be stored in a recloseable gallon-size plastic bag at room temperature for 24 hours. They can also be frozen for up to 3 months. Wrap individual muffins in plastic wrap, then place them on a baking sheet and freeze for at least 3 hours. When they are completely frozen, place each one in an individual recloseable sandwich-size plastic bag. Label the bag with a waterproof marker to note the contents of the bag and the date. Remove a muffin from the freezer the night before, and let it thaw on the kitchen counter to be eaten the next morning.

Quick Breads, Tea Loaves, and Coffee Cakes

Quick Breads, Tea Loaves and Coffee Cakes

··

There is something intensely satisfying about these plain-looking but fancy-tasting desserts. I don't know whether it's their heft, their dense, sweet moistness, their comforting taste and texture, or their unintimidating appearance that makes me think of snowy days, warm, toasty kitchens, woven pot holders, and freshly brewed pots of coffee served with half-and-half instead of that anemic no-fat "blue" milk. They are the quintessentially old-fashioned dessert that never went out of style. Isn't it lovely that you can serve them at all three meals?

We tested so many of these recipes that, unbelievably, we weren't able to eat or give away all the results, so I sliced and froze several dozen cakes, then used some of them to make bread pudding, and some—after being buttered then grilled or toasted—to serve as the basis of ice cream desserts.

Loaf cakes make dandy gifts. You can make some up ahead of time, store them in the freezer, and pull them out several hours before you need them. Wrapped in foil and tied with a ribbon, your gift will be the one your host will remember for a long, long time. To point out that this is a homemade gift you might want to include the recipe with it.

Quick Bread and Coffee Cake Cures
What Should I Do If . . .

The cake is stuck in the pan? Make sure that your pan isn't deeply scratched or dented. Take care to apply a generous coating of softened butter or solid vegetable shortening as called for in the recipe before dusting the pan with flour.

The middle sinks? The cake may be underdone; use a cake tester to check. This can sometimes happen, however, with very heavy batters, even when the cake is completely cooked through. There isn't any remedy. If it really bothers you, either fill the middle with a confectioners' sugar glaze (pages 260–61) or slice the cake before serving.

The cake doesn't rise at all? Check to make sure that you added the baking powder and/or baking soda. Make sure that you don't let the batter sit—get it into the oven as soon as possible. Be careful that you are using the right size pan—a pan that is too large can make the cake look very flat.

The batter overflows the pan? The pan was too small.

The cake is tough? The batter was overmixed. Next time, mix until the dry ingredients are just incorporated. Take care to have the butter, eggs, and other ingredients at room temperature; this will mean less beating to make a smooth batter. Make sure that you used the right kind of flour.

The top cracks? This is from the action of the baking powder or from overmixing, which means mixing air into the batter, causing the cake to rise as the oven heat expands the air bubbles, then to fall as it cools. Try not mixing the batter so much.

The cake has a funny metallic taste? Perhaps the baking soda wasn't mixed in completely. Next time sift the dry ingredients together and use your fingers or the back of a spoon to break up any lumps of baking soda left in the sieve. Perhaps the baking soda wasn't neutralized. Remember that you need to add an acid like lemon juice, buttermilk, brown sugar, or molasses when using baking soda.

I want to make smaller-size quick breads and coffee cakes? Divide the batter among several smaller pans; reduce the baking time, testing for doneness after two-thirds of the time given in the recipe is up.

The nuts/fruit sink to the bottom of the cake? Place one-third of the batter in the pan, then layer on half the nuts or fruit, then half the remaining batter, then the rest of the nuts or fruit, then the end of the batter. Or, toss the nuts and fruit with a little flour before gently mixing them into the batter.

Cinnamon Streusel Coffee Cake

Makes: one 9-inch cake;
16 servings

What you'll need:

9-inch springform pan

sharp, heavy knife for chopping nuts

fork (optional)

mesh sieve

hand-held electric mixer

small offset spatula (optional)

mixing spoon

cake tester

wire rack

Baking time: 60 minutes

Think Sunday brunch, think school bake sale, think mother-in-law coming for tea, think the perfect Christmas gift for someone who loves good food. Think any or all of these things, then rush into the kitchen and whip up this masterpiece. Friends will call you Rembrandt, your mother-in-law will think you walk on water.

FOR PREPARING THE PAN

1 tablespoon unsalted butter or solid vegetable shortening, softened

2 tablespoons all-purpose flour

FOR THE STREUSEL TOPPING

½ cup all-purpose flour

⅛ teaspoon salt

½ teaspoon ground cinnamon

½ cup packed light brown sugar

¾ stick (6 tablespoons) unsalted butter, softened

1 teaspoon pure vanilla extract

½ cup pecans or walnuts, coarsely chopped (see page 19)

FOR THE FILLING

3 tablespoons granulated sugar

1 teaspoon ground cinnamon

FOR THE CAKE

1¾ cups all-purpose flour	1 cup granulated sugar
1 teaspoon baking powder	2 extra-large eggs
1 teaspoon baking soda	1 teaspoon pure vanilla extract
½ teaspoon salt	
3 ounces cream cheese (not the whipped or reduced-fat variety), at room temperature (see page 33)	1 teaspoon pure almond extract
	1 cup sour cream or buttermilk (see page 49)
¾ stick (6 tablespoons) unsalted butter, softened	

1. Preheat the oven to 350°F with a rack in the center of the oven. Use the butter or vegetable shortening to coat the bottom and sides of the pan. Toss in the flour, shake the pan to coat the interior lightly with flour, then knock out the excess. Set aside.

2. To make the streusel topping, combine the flour, salt, cinnamon, light brown sugar, and butter in a medium mixing bowl. Use a fork or your fingers to mash the ingredients together into a coarse-textured paste. Dribble on the vanilla, then sprinkle on the nuts. Work the vanilla and nuts into the paste and set aside.

3. In a small bowl or ramekin, mix the sugar with the cinnamon and set the filling aside.

4. To prepare the batter, place a mesh sieve over a medium mixing bowl and add the flour, baking powder, baking soda, and salt. Shake the contents into the bowl and set aside.

5. Place the cream cheese and butter in a large mixing bowl. With the mixer on high speed, beat the cream cheese and butter together until light and fluffy, about 2 minutes. Add the sugar and beat until smooth, about 1 minute. Beat in the eggs, one at a time, waiting until the first is incorporated before adding the second. Move the beaters around the bowl and scrape down the sides of the bowl with a rubber spatula several times while mixing. With the mixer still on low speed, beat in the vanilla and almond extract, then increase the speed to high and beat the mixture for 1 minute. With the mixer again on low speed, beat in half the flour mixture, then half the sour cream or buttermilk, then the remaining flour mixture, then the remaining sour cream or buttermilk. Beat until all the ingredients are incorporated.

6. Spoon slightly less than half the batter into the prepared pan, and spread it evenly in the pan with a rubber spatula or a small offset spatula. Sprinkle the cinnamon-sugar filling mixture evenly over the batter. Drop the remaining batter in spoonfuls over the batter in the pan so that the sugar-covered layer is roughly covered. You can nudge the blobs of batter a little, but don't try to spread them because they will just slide around on the cinnamon sugar. The batter will smooth out as it bakes. Break the streusel topping into marble-size pieces and drop them evenly over the top of the batter.

7. Bake the cake for 55 to 60 minutes, or until the middle feels firm when you press it with your finger, and a cake tester inserted into the center comes out clean. Remove the cake from the oven and place the pan on a wire rack to cool completely. Remove the sides of the pan and cut the cake into servings.

8. The baked and cooled coffee cake can be stored at room temperature, covered securely with plastic wrap, for up to 2 days, or refrigerated for up to 1 week. It may also be frozen for up to 3 months. Transfer the cake from the springform pan base to a cardboard cake round: Slip a long, wide metal spatula under the cake and rotate the cake to loosen it completely from the pan base, then carefully transfer the cake to the cardboard cake round. Place the cake, on the round, in a freezer-strength recloseable jumbo-size plastic bag. Label the bag with a waterproof marker and freeze. Defrost the cake, in its wrapping, overnight in the refrigerator or at room temperature for 3 to 4 hours.

LORA SAYS: If you use buttermilk instead of sour cream in this recipe, the batter will be thin enough to pour, rather than spoon, into the pan. In place of liquid buttermilk in this recipe, you can use ¼ cup buttermilk powder. Put the powder in the sieve with the other dry ingredients and add 1 cup of water alternately with the flour mixture in place of the liquid buttermilk or sour cream.

Cranberry-Cherry Coffee Cake

Makes: one 10-inch bundt-style coffee cake; 12 servings

What you'll need:

10-inch (12-cup capacity) bundt-style pan

citrus zester

medium saucepan

strainer for draining soaked fruit

mesh sieve

hand-held electric mixer

cake tester

wire rack

Baking time: 45 to 50 minutes

The bright, tart flavor of dried cranberries is offset by the delicate sweetness of the dried sweet cherries in this show-stopping cake with a hint of almond. You can use either Bing or Rainier cherries. These dried fruits are available in many supermarkets and gourmet stores.

FOR PREPARING THE PAN

2 tablespoons unsalted butter or solid vegetable shortening, softened

2 tablespoons all-purpose flour

FOR THE CAKE

2 cups orange juice

1 cup dried sweet cherries

¾ cup dried cranberries

3 cups cake flour (see page 29)

1½ teaspoons baking soda

½ teaspoon salt

1 stick (8 tablespoons) unsalted butter, softened

1½ cups granulated sugar

2 extra-large eggs, at room temperature

Finely grated zest of 1 lemon

2 teaspoons pure almond extract

1¼ cups buttermilk (see page 49)

FOR THE TOPPING

1 cup confectioners' sugar (if sugar is lumpy, sift first, then measure)

½ teaspoon ground cloves

1. Preheat the oven to 350°F with a rack in the center of the oven. Use the butter or vegetable shortening to coat the inside of the pan. Toss in the flour, shake the pan to coat the interior lightly with flour, then knock out the excess. Set aside.

2. Place the orange juice, dried cherries, and cranberries in a medium saucepan over medium heat. Bring the liquid to a simmer, then remove the pan from the heat and let it sit for 15 minutes while you prepare the other ingredients. When the fruit has softened, drain it well in a strainer, pressing lightly on the fruit to release excess liquid. Discard the soaking liquid or reserve it for another use.

3. Place a mesh sieve over a medium mixing bowl and add the cake flour, baking soda, and salt. Shake the contents into the bowl and set aside.

4. Place the butter and sugar in a large mixing bowl. With the mixer on high speed, beat the butter with the sugar until it is light and fluffy, about 2 minutes. Beat in the eggs, one at a time, waiting until the first is incorporated before adding the second. Move the beaters around the bowl and scrape down the sides of the bowl with a rubber spatula several times while mixing. Lower the mixer speed to low and beat in the lemon zest and almond extract.

5. With the mixer still on low speed, beat in one-third of the flour mixture, then pour in half the buttermilk. Add half the remaining flour mixture, then the remaining buttermilk, and finally the last of the flour. Scrape the bowl often as you work. Fold in the drained cherries and cranberries with a rubber spatula.

6. Pour and scrape the batter into the prepared pan and smooth the top with a rubber spatula. Bake the cake for 45 to 50 minutes, or until the cake is golden on top and a cake tester inserted into the center of the cake comes out clean. Transfer the cake in its pan to a wire rack and let it cool for 10 minutes. Invert the cake onto the rack and let it cool completely.

7. While the cake is cooling, stir the confectioners' sugar and cloves together in a small bowl. When you are ready to serve the cake, transfer it to a serving plate and sift the confectioners' sugar mixture over the top.

8. The baked and cooled coffee cake can be stored at room temperature, wrapped in plastic wrap, for up to 2 days, or refrigerated for up to 1 week. It may also be frozen for up to 3 months. Wrap the cooled cake securely in plastic wrap, then place in a freezer-strength recloseable gallon-size plastic bag. Label the bag with a waterproof marker and freeze. Defrost the cake, in its wrapping, overnight in the refrigerator or at room temperature for 3 to 4 hours.

LORA SAYS: In place of the liquid buttermilk in this recipe, you can use 5 tablespoons buttermilk powder. There is no need to reconstitute it before using. Place the powder in the sieve with the other dry ingredients and add 1¼ cups water alternately with the flour mixture in place of the liquid buttermilk.

LORA SAYS: When fresh sweet cherries are available in the market, this cake is wonderful made with a combination of fresh cherries and dried cranberries. You will need 10 ounces fresh Bing or Rainier cherries, which will yield about 1½ cups cherry pieces once they are pitted and chopped. Add these to the batter along with 1 cup dried cranberries. If you decide to use fresh cherries, a cherry pitter is a must. A hand-held model is available in kitchen supply stores. (It will also pit many kinds of olives.) In the fall, when fresh cherries are gone and fresh cranberries are in season, the fresh and dried combination of fruits can be reversed. In the winter and spring, dried versions of both fruits are the way to go.

Swirled Sour Cream Coffee Cake

Makes: one 10-inch bundt-style cake; 12 servings

What you'll need:

10-inch (12-cup capacity) bundt-style pan

sharp, heavy knife for chopping walnuts

mesh sieve

hand-held electric mixer

mixing spoon

table knife

cake tester

wire rack

wax paper

small sieve

Baking time: 45 minutes

Back before diets were invented, sour cream was a staple in homes across America. Bananas with sour cream, egg noodles with melted butter, sour cream, and cottage cheese. . . . Imagine a grocery store dairy shelf that had never seen a container of yogurt, and you'll understand how there was a room for all that lovely sour cream. Well, now sour cream is regarded with almost the same dread as mad cow disease. We waited long enough for eggs to be back on the "can eat" list, and I'm getting tired of waiting for sour cream to make the cut. So I'll just enjoy a slice of this heavenly coffee cake.

FOR PREPARING THE PAN

1 tablespoon unsalted butter or solid vegetable shortening, softened

2 tablespoons all-purpose flour

FOR THE SWIRL

¼ cup packed light brown sugar

½ teaspoon ground cinnamon

1 tablespoon unsweetened cocoa powder, not Dutch-processed (see page 15)

½ cup walnuts, coarsely chopped (see page 19)

FOR THE CAKE

2 cups all-purpose flour

1 teaspoon baking powder

1 teaspoon baking soda

½ teaspoon salt

1 stick (8 tablespoons) unsalted butter, softened

1 cup granulated sugar

2 extra-large eggs

2 teaspoons pure vanilla extract

1 cup sour cream (see page 49)

FOR THE TOPPING

2 tablespoons confectioners' sugar (if sugar is lumpy, sift first, then measure)

1 tablespoon unsweetened cocoa powder, not Dutch-processed (see page 15)

1. Preheat the oven to 350°F with a rack in the center of the oven. Coat the sides and center tube of the pan with the butter or vegetable shortening. Toss in the flour and shake the pan to coat the tube surface and sides. Knock out the excess flour. Set aside.

2. Mix the swirl ingredients together in a mixing bowl until combined. Set aside.

3. Place a mesh sieve over a mixing bowl and add the flour, baking powder, baking soda, and salt. Shake the contents into the bowl and set aside.

4. Place the butter and sugar in a large mixing bowl. With the mixer on high speed, beat the butter with the sugar until it is light and fluffy, about 2 minutes. Beat in the eggs, one at a time, waiting until the first is incorporated before adding the second. Move the beaters around the bowl, and scrape down the sides of the bowl with a rubber spatula several times while mixing. Lower the mixer speed to low and mix in the vanilla. With the mixer still on low speed, mix in half the flour mixture, then half the sour cream. Repeat the process, and mix until no traces of flour remain. Scrape down the sides of the bowl.

5. Spoon two-thirds of the batter into the prepared pan, dropping it in dollops on the bottom. With a rubber spatula smooth the batter evenly. Sprinkle the swirl mixture evenly over the surface of the batter. Stick a table knife through the swirl topping into the batter until you touch the bottom of the pan. Rotate the knife in a gentle circular motion until the batter starts to show through the swirl mixture. It's important to mix batter and swirl together enough so that the cake won't separate after baking when it is cut into servings. Scoop up the remaining batter and drop it in 4 evenly spaced dollops on the swirled batter. Use a rubber spatula to smooth it evenly, and push down gently to connect the last layer of batter with the swirl layer. Give the pan a firm whack on the work surface to help the swirl mixture settle into the batter.

6. Bake the cake for 45 minutes, or until the top of the cake is cracked and a cake tester inserted in the center of the cake comes out clean. Remove the cake from the oven and set the pan on a wire rack to cool completely in the pan. When it has cooled, place a serving plate over the top of the pan and invert the cake onto the plate, then remove the pan.

7. When ready to serve the cake, cut four 3-inch-wide lengths of wax paper and slip them lengthwise under the bottom edges of the cake. Leave half of each strip exposed to cover the cake plate. Allow the ends of the wax paper to overlap each other. Make the topping by combining the confectioners' sugar and the cocoa powder in a small mixing bowl. Use a small sieve to sift the mixture over the top of the cake. Remove the wax paper.

8. The baked and cooled coffee cake can be stored at room temperature, wrapped in plastic wrap, for up to 2 days, or refrigerated for up to 1 week. It may also be frozen for up to 3 months. If you are going to freeze the cake, do not dust it with the cocoa and sugar. Wrap the cooled cake securely in plastic wrap, then place in a freezer-strength recloseable gallon-size plastic bag. Label the bag with a waterproof marker and freeze. Defrost the cake, in its wrapping, overnight in the refrigerator or at room temperature for 3 to 4 hours. Dust with the cocoa powder and sugar before serving.

LORA SAYS: When flouring a tube pan, toss the dusting flour onto the tube as you rotate the pan. The flour will coat the tube and fall to the bottom of the pan. Once the tube is coated, shake the pan so that the flour falls onto the sides to coat them, just as you would flour a plain round cake pan.

Blueberry Cake

Makes: one 9-inch round cake; 12 servings

What you'll need:

9-inch springform pan

sharp, heavy knife for chopping walnuts

citrus zester

fork

mesh sieve

hand-held electric mixer

cake tester

wire rack

Baking time: 60 to 65 minutes

This homey, streusel-topped coffee cake is best made with tiny wild Maine blueberries, which are available fresh in the latter part of the summer, or frozen during the rest of the year. The big, fat cultivated ones don't have nearly the same flavor, and although they are certainly acceptable for this recipe, I prefer to eat them right out of the container.

FOR PREPARING THE PAN

1 tablespoon unsalted butter or solid vegetable shortening, softened

2 tablespoons all-purpose flour

FOR THE STREUSEL

½ cup all-purpose flour

⅓ cup packed light brown sugar

⅓ cup walnuts, chopped (see page 19)

½ stick (4 tablespoons) unsalted butter, softened

2 cups all-purpose flour

2 teaspoons baking powder

1 teaspoon baking soda

½ teaspoon salt

1 stick (8 tablespoons) unsalted butter, softened

1 cup granulated sugar

2 extra-large eggs

2 teaspoons pure vanilla extract

Finely grated zest of 1 large lemon

¾ cup sour cream

2 cups fresh blueberries, picked over to remove stems and any moldy berries, or 2 cups frozen blueberries (no need to defrost before using, but separate any clumps of berries)

1. Preheat the oven to 350°F with a rack in the center of the oven. Use the butter or vegetable shortening to coat the bottom and sides of the pan. Toss in the flour and shake the pan to coat the bottom and sides. Knock out the excess flour. Set aside.

2. Make the streusel by combining the flour, light brown sugar, and walnuts in a small mixing bowl. Toss them together with a fork, then add the butter. Mash the butter with the dry ingredients to form a paste. Set aside.

3. To make the cake, place a mesh sieve over a medium mixing bowl and add the flour, baking powder, baking soda, and salt. Shake the contents into the bowl and set aside.

4. Place the butter and sugar in a large mixing bowl. With the mixer on high speed, beat the butter with the sugar until it is light and fluffy, about 2 minutes. Add the eggs, one at a time, waiting until the first is incorporated before adding the second. Move the beaters around the bowl and scrape down the sides of the bowl with a rubber spatula several times while mixing. Lower the mixer speed to low and beat in the vanilla and lemon zest. With the mixer still on low speed, beat in half the flour mixture, then half the sour cream. Repeat the process, and mix until no traces of flour remain. The batter will be quite thick. Use a rubber spatula to fold in the blueberries.

5. Scrape the batter into the prepared pan and smooth the top with a rubber spatula. Break up the streusel topping with your fingers and drop marble-size pieces of it evenly over the top of the batter.

6. Bake the cake for 60 to 65 minutes, or until a cake tester inserted into the center of the cake comes out dry. Remove the cake from the oven and place the pan on a wire rack to cool completely. When the cake is cool, remove the sides of the pan and cut the cake into servings.

7. The baked and cooled cake can be stored at room temperature, covered securely with plastic wrap, for up to 2 days, or refrigerated for up to 1 week. It may also be frozen for up to 3 months. Transfer the cake from the springform pan base to a cardboard cake round: Slip a long, wide metal spatula under the cake and rotate the cake to loosen it completely from the pan base, then carefully transfer the cake to a cardboard cake round. Place the cake, on the round, in a freezer-strength recloseable jumbo-size plastic bag. Label the bag with a waterproof marker and freeze. Defrost the cake, in its wrapping, overnight in the refrigerator or at room temperature for 3 to 4 hours.

LORA SAYS: You may substitute the same amount of fresh or frozen raspberries for the blueberries in this recipe, or you can use a combination of both berries.

Applesauce Spice Tea Cake

Makes: one 10-inch bundt-style
cake; 12 servings

What you'll need:

10-inch (12-cup capacity)
bundt-style pan

baking sheet for toasting
walnuts

sharp, heavy knife for chopping
walnuts

citrus zester

citrus reamer

fine-mesh sieve for straining
lemon juice

mesh sieve

fork

hand-held electric mixer

cake tester

wire rack

mixing spoon

Baking time: 55 minutes

I felt we were neglecting tea drinkers with all the coffee cakes in this book, so here's one you can enjoy with a cup of Earl Grey as well as with a cup of cappuccino. The spices in this moist, nut-topped cake make for a delightful taste reminiscent of spice cake.

Whether you use store-bought applesauce or make your own from the easy recipe that follows, this lovely, moist cake will make it hard to stop after one piece. It's very important to beat the eggs and sugar until they are thick, as this, along with the baking powder, is what gets the cake to rise nicely. This cake makes a great gift—it can be made ahead, cooled, glazed, then frozen.

FOR PREPARING THE PAN

2 tablespoons unsalted butter, softened

2 tablespoons all-purpose flour

FOR THE CAKE

3⅓ cups cake flour
(see page 29)

2 teaspoons baking
powder

1½ teaspoons baking soda

1½ teaspoons ground
cinnamon

1¼ teaspoons ground
allspice

1¼ teaspoons ground
nutmeg

1 teaspoon ground ginger

½ teaspoon salt

3 extra-large eggs, at room
temperature

1⅔ cups packed dark
brown sugar

1 cup vegetable oil

1 tablespoon pure vanilla
extract

2 cups unsweetened
applesauce
(recipe follows)

1½ cups walnuts, toasted
and coarsely chopped
(see pages 18–19)

FOR THE GLAZE AND TOPPING

1 cup confectioners' sugar,
sifted

Finely grated zest of
1 lemon

¼ cup fresh, strained
lemon juice

2 to 3 tablespoons hot
water

⅓ cup walnuts, toasted
and coarsely chopped

1. Preheat the oven to 350°F with a rack in the center of the oven. Coat the sides and center tube of the pan with the butter. Toss in the flour and shake the pan to coat the tube surface and sides. Knock out the excess flour. Set aside.

2. Place a mesh sieve over a medium mixing bowl and add the cake flour, baking powder, baking soda, cinnamon, allspice, nutmeg, ginger, and salt. Shake the contents into the bowl and set aside.

3. Break the eggs into a large mixing bowl. Stir them briefly with a fork to break them up slightly, then add the dark brown sugar. With the mixer on high speed, beat the eggs with the sugar until the mixture is very thick, about 6 minutes. Move the beaters around the bowl and scrape down the sides of the bowl with a rubber spatula several times while mixing. Reduce the mixer speed to medium and beat in the oil and vanilla. Beat until the mixture is smooth, about 2 minutes. Reduce the mixer speed to low and beat in the flour mixture alternately with the applesauce, beginning and ending with the flour mixture. Fold in the walnuts with a rubber spatula. Scrape the batter into the prepared pan and smooth the top with a rubber spatula.

4. Bake for 55 minutes, or until a cake tester inserted into the center of the cake comes out clean. Transfer the pan to a wire rack to cool for 10 minutes, then invert the cake onto the rack. Remove the pan and let the cake cool completely before glazing.

5. To prepare the glaze, mix the confectioners' sugar with the lemon zest and juice in a medium mixing bowl. Stir in just enough water to make a fairly liquid glaze. Transfer the cake to a serving plate and drizzle the glaze evenly over the top of the cake, allowing it to run over the sides slightly. Add more water if the glaze is not liquid enough. Sprinkle the toasted walnuts over the top, then let the cake stand until the glaze sets, about 1 hour.

6. The baked and cooled glazed cake can be stored at room temperature, wrapped in plastic wrap, for up to 2 days, or refrigerated for up to 1 week. It may also be frozen for up to 3 months. Wrap the cooled glazed cake securely in plastic wrap, then place it in a freezer-strength recloseable jumbo-size plastic bag. Label the bag with a waterproof marker and freeze. Defrost the cake, in its wrapping, overnight in the refrigerator or at room temperature for 3 to 4 hours.

Homemade Applesauce

Makes: 4 cups

What you'll need:

large, heavy saucepan

Foley food mill, potato masher, or food processor

Cooking time: about 20 minutes

A Foley food mill, an inexpensive kitchen tool available in cookware and hardware stores, helps to make this applesauce recipe incredibly easy to make, since you don't have to peel or core the apples first. The mill purees the apples and strains out the seeds and skin at the same time. Cooking the apples with the skin on adds extra flavor and a lovely pink color to the applesauce.

3 pounds crisp, flavorful apples, such as Cortland or Gala

1 cup apple cider or apple juice

FOOD MILL METHOD: Cut the unpeeled apples in half and place them in a large, heavy saucepan. Pour in the cider or apple juice, cover the pan, and place it over medium heat. Allow the liquid to come to a gentle simmer, then cook, covered, for 15 to 20 minutes, or until the apples are soft. Adjust the heat so that the mixture continues to simmer gently. Allow the apples to cool in the pan, then run them through the food mill into a bowl.

WITHOUT A FOOD MILL: Peel and quarter the apples, then cut out the tough cores and seeds. Place the apple pieces in a saucepan. Pour in the cider or apple juice, cover the pan, and place it over medium heat. Allow the liquid to come to a gentle simmer, then cook, covered, for 15 to 20 minutes, or until the apples are soft. Adjust the heat so that the mixture continues to simmer gently. Allow the apples to cool in the pan, then mash with a potato masher or puree in a food processor for 30 to 40 seconds until smooth.

Let the applesauce cool, then refrigerate it, covered, for up to 2 weeks. It may also be frozen. Spoon the applesauce into plastic containers, cover them, label, and freeze for up to 3 months. Let the applesauce defrost in the refrigerator overnight or at room temperature for 2 hours, in the container.

Crumb Cake

Makes: one 9-inch cake; 16 servings

What you'll need:

9-inch springform pan

citrus zester

small, sharp knife for cutting up butter

mesh sieve

mixing spoon

hand-held electric mixer

food processor (optional)

wire rack

cake tester

Baking time: about 1 hour

I used to be a confirmed Drake's Cakes addict. For those of you who've never had the pleasure, a Drake's Cake is a plastic-wrapped, individual-size coffee cake with a crumbly yellow cake base upon which rests a unique crumb topping that falls onto your lap when you eat it. I had given up hope of finding a homemade version of this ethereal dessert until my genius friend, baker and writer extraordinaire, P. J. Hamel, creator of the King Arthur Flour Baker's Catalogue, humbly suggested that I try her recipe.

FOR PREPARING THE PAN

1 tablespoon unsalted butter, softened

2 tablespoons all-purpose flour

FOR THE CAKE

1½ cups all-purpose flour

1 teaspoon baking powder

⅛ teaspoon baking soda

¾ teaspoon salt

1 tablespoon Lora Brody's Dough Relaxer, optional (see page 48)

½ cup plain or vanilla yogurt, or sour cream

2 teaspoons pure vanilla extract

1 teaspoon grated lemon zest

1 stick (8 tablespoons) unsalted butter, softened

1¼ cups granulated sugar

3 extra-large eggs

3 tablespoons unsalted butter, chilled and cut into 9 pieces

¼ cup solid vegetable shortening

¾ cup all-purpose flour

½ cup packed dark brown sugar

¾ teaspoon ground cinnamon

⅛ teaspoon salt

1. Preheat the oven to 325°F with a rack in the center of the oven. Use the butter to coat the bottom and sides of the pan. Toss in the flour and shake the pan to coat the bottom and sides. Knock out the excess flour. Set aside.

2. Place a mesh sieve over a medium mixing bowl and add the flour, baking powder, baking soda, salt, and optional Dough Relaxer. Shake the contents into the bowl and set aside. In a small mixing bowl stir together the yogurt, vanilla, and the lemon zest. Set aside.

3. Place the butter and sugar in a large mixing bowl. With the mixer on high speed beat the butter with the sugar until it is light and fluffy, about 2 minutes. The mixture will appear very crumbly at first. It will not form a smooth batter. Add the eggs, one at a time, beating until one is incorporated before adding another. Move the beaters around the bowl and scrape down the sides of the bowl with a rubber spatula several times while mixing. When the eggs have been added, continue beating at medium-high speed for 5 minutes. Continue to scrape the bowl as you mix. With the mixer on low speed, add the flour mixture alternately with the yogurt mixture, beginning and ending with the flour. Scrape the batter into the prepared pan and smooth the top with a rubber spatula. Bake for 35 minutes.

4. While the cake is baking, make the streusel. Place the chilled butter, shortening, flour, dark brown sugar, cinnamon, and salt in a small mixing bowl or in the bowl of a food processor fitted with the metal blade. Use a fork to combine the ingredients until they form uneven crumbs, no larger than lima beans, or process the mixture by pulsing until it is just crumbly. Don't overmix, or you will form a ball of topping, which you don't want. Set aside.

5. When the cake has baked for 35 minutes, open the oven door and pat the center lightly; it needs to be firm enough to support the streusel topping. It should feel slightly spongy but not sticky, and your finger should not easily pierce the surface. It may be necessary to bake the cake a few minutes longer. When you are ready to put on the streusel, remove the cake from the oven to a wire rack or a heatproof work surface. Close the oven door to maintain the oven temperature at 325°F. Sprinkle the streusel topping over the surface of the cake, then return it to the oven and bake for 25 minutes more, or until a cake tester inserted into the center of the cake comes out dry. Remove the cake from the oven and let it cool in the pan on a wire rack for 15 minutes. Remove the sides of the pan and let the cake continue to cool on the rack.

6. The baked and cooled cake can be stored at room temperature, covered securely with plastic wrap, for up to 2 days, or refrigerated for up to 1 week. It may also be frozen for up to 3 months. Leave the cake on the springform pan base and wrap the cake in plastic wrap. Place it in a freezer-strength recloseable jumbo-size plastic bag. Label the bag with a waterproof marker and freeze. Defrost the cake, in its wrapping, overnight in the refrigerator or at room temperature for 3 to 4 hours.

Three Wishes Gingerbread

Makes: one 9-inch square cake; 9 servings

What you'll need:

9-inch square baking pan

microwave or small saucepan for melting butter

scissors

nonstick vegetable spray (optional)

small, sharp knife for dicing gingerroot

mesh sieve

wooden mixing spoon

hand-held electric mixer

cake tester

wire rack

Baking time: 50 to 55 minutes

The name of this recipe comes from the fact that I love ginger in any form. My wish was to get as many forms of this palate-awakening root into the cake without making anyone sorry that I'd discovered ginger in the first place. If you are partial to a little kick in your cake, then use the entire amount of fresh ginger; to temper the spiciness, use 1 to 2 teaspoonfuls.

FOR PREPARING THE PAN

1 tablespoon unsalted butter or solid vegetable shortening, softened

2 tablespoons all-purpose flour

FOR THE GINGERBREAD

2 cups all-purpose flour

1 teaspoon baking soda

½ teaspoon salt

1 teaspoon ground cinnamon

½ teaspoon ground allspice

½ teaspoon ground ginger

½ teaspoon ground cloves

1 stick (8 tablespoons) unsalted butter, melted and cooled

¼ cup vegetable oil

2 extra-large eggs

½ cup packed dark brown sugar

1 cup regular molasses (see page 45)

1 cup buttermilk (see page 49)

¼ cup candied ginger, very finely diced (see Lora Says)

1 tablespoon finely diced fresh gingerroot

1. Preheat the oven to 350°F with a rack in the center of the oven. Use the butter or vegetable shortening to coat the bottom and sides of the baking pan. Add the flour and shake the pan to coat the sides and bottom; knock out the excess. Set aside.

2. Place a mesh sieve over a medium mixing bowl and add the flour, baking soda, salt, cinnamon, allspice, ginger, and cloves. Shake the contents into the bowl and set aside.

3. In a large mixing bowl, combine the melted butter, oil, eggs, dark brown sugar, molasses, and buttermilk. Stir them together well with a wooden spoon. Add the flour mixture to the butter mixture and stir them well. With the mixer, beat the mixture on medium-high speed for 1 minute. Move the beaters around the bowl and scrape down the sides of the bowl with a rubber spatula several times while mixing. The batter will be lumpy. Scatter the candied ginger and fresh gingerroot over the top (don't add them all in a clump), then stir them in. Scrape the batter into the prepared pan and smooth the top.

4. Bake for 50 to 55 minutes, or until a cake tester inserted into the center comes out clean and the cake pulls away slightly from the sides of the pan. Cool the gingerbread in the pan on a wire rack for 20 minutes. Invert the cake onto the rack, then invert it again onto a serving plate so that it sits right side up. Cut into 9 equal pieces.

5. The baked and cooled gingerbread can be stored at room temperature, wrapped in plastic wrap, for 1 day, or refrigerated for up to 2 weeks. It may also be frozen for up to 3 months. Wrap the cooled gingerbread securely in plastic wrap, then place in a plastic bag. Label the bag with a waterproof marker and freeze. Defrost the cake, in its wrapping, overnight in the refrigerator or at room temperature for 3 to 4 hours.

LORA SAYS: In place of liquid buttermilk in this recipe, use 4 tablespoons buttermilk powder. There is no need to reconstitute it before using. Place the powder in the sieve with the dry ingredients, and add 1 cup of water to the melted butter, eggs, brown sugar, and molasses in place of the liquid buttermilk.

LORA SAYS: Use a pair of kitchen scissors to cut the candied ginger into small pieces. For best results, spray the blades with nonstick vegetable spray first, so that the ginger won't stick to them.

Honey Cake

Makes: one 9 × 13-inch cake; 18 servings

What you'll need:

9 × 13-inch baking pan

scissors or small, sharp knife to cut up dried apples

citrus zester

citrus reamer

baking sheet for toasting walnuts

sharp, heavy knife for chopping walnuts

mixing spoon

small, heavy saucepan with a lid

mesh sieve

hand-held electric mixer

aluminum foil for covering the baking cake (optional)

cake tester

wire rack

fine-mesh sieve for dusting with confectioners' sugar

Baking time: 60 minutes

Every good Jewish home baker worth his or her salt has a favorite honey cake recipe. This is my mother's, which she gave me to celebrate the birth of our first child. I told her that part of the privilege of being a grandmother was that she got to make the honey cake; she took it like a good sport. When my grandson was born, I got to make honey cake and take it to China, where it made a big splash with my daughter-in-law's family.

The secret to this moist cake is dried apples, found in most supermarkets and all health food stores. The easiest way to cut them up is with scissors before they have been rehydrated in a liquid, such as brandy or apple juice or cider. This cake has a lot of ingredients, but don't let that put you off—it's quite simple to make, and the fragrant aroma and heavenly taste are worth it.

FOR PREPARING THE PAN

1½ tablespoons unsalted butter or solid vegetable shortening, softened

2 tablespoons all-purpose flour

FOR THE CAKE

1 cup dried apples, cut into ½-inch pieces

¼ cup brandy, apple cider, or apple juice

Finely grated zest of 1 large orange

½ cup fresh, strained orange juice

3 cups all-purpose flour

2 teaspoons baking powder

1 teaspoon baking soda

½ teaspoon salt

1 teaspoon ground cinnamon

3 extra-large eggs

1 cup granulated sugar

¾ cup vegetable oil

¾ cup honey

½ cup cold, strong, brewed coffee, regular or decaffeinated

1 cup golden raisins

1 cup walnuts, toasted and coarsely chopped (see pages 18–19)

Confectioners' sugar for dusting the cake after baking

1. Preheat the oven to 350°F with a rack in the center of the oven. Use the butter or vegetable shortening to coat the sides and bottom of the baking pan. Toss in the flour and shake the pan to coat the sides and bottom; knock out the excess. Set aside.

2. Place the dried apple pieces in the saucepan with the brandy, cider, or apple juice, and the orange zest and juice. Bring the mixture to a simmer without stirring, then cover the pan and simmer for about 5 minutes until the apples have absorbed most of the liquid. Lift the lid and push the fruit into the liquid from time to time as it cooks. Remove the pan from the heat and set it aside to cool slightly.

3. Place a mesh sieve over a medium mixing bowl and add the flour, baking powder, baking soda, salt, and cinnamon. Shake the contents into the bowl and set aside.

4. Place the eggs and sugar in a large mixing bowl. With the mixer on medium-high speed, beat the eggs and sugar together until they are thick and light yellow, about 5 minutes. Move the beaters around the bowl and scrape down the sides of the bowl with a rubber spatula several times while mixing. Reduce the mixer speed to low and beat in the oil, honey, and coffee. Use a rubber spatula to mix the dry ingredients into the egg mixture, mixing only until no traces of flour remain. Stir in the apples and their soaking liquid, the raisins, and the walnuts. Pour and scrape the batter into the prepared pan. Smooth the top with a rubber spatula or an offset spatula.

5. Bake the cake for 60 minutes, rotating the pan 180 degrees halfway through the baking time. If the top starts to brown before the cake is done, cover it loosely with aluminum foil. The cake will be done when a cake tester inserted into the center comes out clean. Transfer the cake to a wire rack and let it cool completely in the pan, then cut it into 18 pieces. Place about ¼ cup confectioners' sugar in a fine-mesh sieve and shake the sugar over the top of the cake.

6. The baked and cooled cake can be stored at room temperature, wrapped in plastic wrap, for 1 day, or refrigerated for up to 2 weeks. It may also be frozen before dusting with sugar for up to 3 months. Wrap the cooled cake securely in plastic wrap, then place in a freezer-strength recloseable jumbo-size plastic bag. Label the bag with a waterproof marker and freeze. Defrost the cake, in its wrapping, at room temperature, then dust with confectioners' sugar.

LORA SAYS: This plain-looking cake is well served by sharing the plate with something else. My choice would be Mixed Fruit Compote (recipe follows).

Mixed Fruit Compote

Makes: 6 cups

What you'll need:

small, sharp knife and large, heavy saucepan

Y ou may omit the sherry and replace it with an equal amount of apple cider or orange juice, or a combination of the two, to make a total of 4½ cups liquid.

2 navel (seedless) oranges

2½ cups mixed dried fruit, such as apricots, apple rings, peaches, pears, figs, raisins, and prunes

1 cup dried cherries

½ cup dried cranberries

1½ cups medium-dry sherry

3 cups apple cider or orange juice

1 cinnamon stick

Use a small, sharp knife to remove the peel of each orange in a continuous spiral or make several long pieces. Turn the peel over and use the knife to cut or scrape out and discard as much of the white pith as possible. Trim any pith from the oranges as well, then cut them into ¼-inch slices. Place the oranges and all the remaining ingredients in a large, heavy saucepan. Bring the liquid to a simmer over medium-high heat. Reduce the heat so that the mixture barely bubbles, then cover and simmer for 5 minutes. Remove the pan from the heat and let the fruit cool in the pan. The orange peel and cinnamon stick remain in the juice just to give it flavor; do not serve them. Store the fruit and its juice in a tightly sealed container in the refrigerator for up to 1 month.

Cranberry Orange Bread

Makes: 1 large loaf

What you'll need:

loaf pan 8½ × 4 × 2½ inches, with 6-cup capacity

microwave or small saucepan for melting butter

citrus zester

citrus reamer

food processor or knife for chopping cranberries

baking sheet for toasting nuts

sharp, heavy knife for chopping nuts

mesh sieve

hand-held electric mixer

cake tester

wire rack

Baking time: 55 to 60 minutes

This bread is delicious made in the fall with fresh cranberries, but it can also be made successfully with frozen cranberries or with dried cranberries rehydrated with orange juice.

FOR PREPARING THE PAN

1 tablespoon unsalted butter or solid vegetable shortening, softened

2 tablespoons all-purpose flour

FOR THE BREAD

2 cups all-purpose flour

1½ teaspoons baking powder

¼ teaspoon baking soda

¼ teaspoon salt

¼ teaspoon ground cloves

¼ teaspoon ground cardamom

¾ stick (6 tablespoons) unsalted butter, melted

⅔ cup milk

Finely grated zest of 1 large navel orange (see Lora Says)

½ cup fresh, strained orange juice

1 extra-large egg

⅔ cup granulated sugar

1 cup fresh or frozen whole cranberries, coarsely chopped (see Lora Says)

¾ cup pecans or walnuts, toasted and coarsely chopped (see pages 18–19)

1. Preheat the oven to 350°F with a rack in the center of the oven. Use the butter or vegetable shortening to coat the inside of the pan. Toss in the flour and shake the pan to coat the inside with flour. Knock out the excess. Set aside.

2. Place a mesh sieve over a medium mixing bowl and add the flour, baking powder, baking soda, salt, cloves, and cardamom. Shake the contents into the bowl and set aside.

3. Combine the melted butter, milk, orange zest, and juice in a 2-cup measure with a spout. The mixture will curdle, but that's okay. Set aside.

4. Break the egg into a large mixing bowl and add the sugar. Use the mixer on high speed to beat the egg and sugar together until light and fluffy, about 3 minutes. Reduce the speed to low and beat in the melted butter mixture. Move the beaters around the bowl and scrape down the sides with a rubber spatula several times while mixing. With the mixer still on low speed, beat in the flour mixture. Scrape down the sides of the bowl as you work. Stir in the cranberries and nuts with a rubber spatula. Pour and scrape the batter into the prepared pan, and smooth the top with a rubber spatula.

5. Bake for 55 to 60 minutes, or until a cake tester inserted in the center of the loaf comes out clean. Transfer the pan to a rack and cool the bread in the pan for 15 minutes, then run a knife around the edges of the pan to loosen the bread. Turn the loaf out onto the rack and set right side up to cool. Allow the bread to cool completely before slicing.

6. The baked and cooled loaf can be stored at room temperature, wrapped in plastic wrap, for up to 2 days, or refrigerated for up to 1 week. It may also be frozen for up to 3 months. Wrap the cooled loaf securely in plastic wrap, then place it in a freezer-strength recloseable gallon-size plastic bag. Label the bag with a waterproof marker and freeze. Defrost the loaf in its wrappings at room temperature for 2 hours.

LORA SAYS: Substitute ¾ cup sweetened dried cranberries for the fresh or frozen cranberries.

LORA SAYS: Use the pulse function of a food processor to chop both fresh and frozen cranberries. Dried cranberries don't need to be chopped.

Banana Walnut Bread

Makes: 1 large loaf

What you'll need:

loaf pan 8½ × 4½ × 2½ inches, with 6-cup capacity

citrus zester

citrus reamer

fine-mesh sieve for straining lemon juice

fork

baking sheet for toasting nuts (optional)

sharp, heavy knife for chopping nuts (optional)

mesh sieve

hand-held electric mixer

cake tester

wire rack

Baking time: 60 minutes

'm the only one in my family who likes really ripe bananas—the kind that have hung around until they are black and spotted and limp. But there are only so many overripe bananas a girl can eat, so a great solution is to make banana bread. While very ripe bananas have the best flavor, if you don't have any but are dying to make this recipe, peel whatever bananas you have on hand, stick them in a plastic bag, and freeze them until hard. Defrost them at room temperature or in the microwave, and they'll be ripe enough to use.

FOR PREPARING THE PAN

1 tablespoon unsalted butter or solid vegetable shortening, softened

2 tablespoons all-purpose flour

FOR THE BREAD

2 cups all-purpose flour

2 teaspoons baking powder

½ teaspoon baking soda

½ teaspoon salt

Finely grated zest of 1 lemon

¼ cup fresh, strained lemon juice

½ cup milk

1 stick (8 tablespoons) unsalted butter, softened

1 cup packed light brown sugar

2 extra-large eggs

1 cup mashed banana (2 very ripe, large bananas, mashed with a fork)

1 cup walnuts or pecans, toasted and coarsely chopped, optional (see pages 18–19)

1. Preheat the oven to 350°F with a rack in the center of the oven. Use the butter or vegetable shortening to coat the inside of the pan, then toss in the flour. Shake the pan to coat the bottom and sides, then knock out the excess. Set aside.

2. Place a mesh sieve over a medium mixing bowl and add the flour, baking powder, baking soda, and salt. Shake the contents into the bowl and set aside. Combine the lemon zest and juice with the milk in a small mixing bowl. The mixture will curdle, but that's okay. Set aside.

3. Place the butter and light brown sugar in a large mixing bowl. Using the mixer on high speed, beat the butter and sugar together for 3 to 4 minutes. The mixture will look like smooth butterscotch pudding. Move the beaters around the bowl and scrape down the sides of the bowl with a rubber spatula several times while mixing. Add the eggs, one at a time, waiting until the first is incorporated before adding the second. Reduce the mixer speed to low and add the milk mixture. Beat only until it is just incorporated. Beat in the bananas and then the flour mixture, mixing just until no traces of flour remain, about 30 seconds. Use a rubber spatula to fold in the optional nuts. Pour and scrape the batter into the prepared pan, and smooth the top with a rubber spatula.

4. Bake for 1 hour, or until a cake tester inserted into the center of the loaf comes out clean and dry. Remove the loaf from the oven and invert it immediately onto a wire rack. Turn it right side up and allow it to cool completely before slicing.

5. The baked and cooled loaf can be stored at room temperature, wrapped in plastic wrap, for up to 2 days, or refrigerated for up to 1 week. It may also be frozen for up to 3 months. Wrap the cooled loaf securely in plastic wrap, then place it in a freezer-strength recloseable gallon-size plastic bag. Label the bag with a waterproof marker and freeze. Defrost the loaf in its wrappings at room temperature for 2 hours.

LORA SAYS: This is another plain-looking cake that can be dolled up by serving with a spoonful of fruit compote (page 254). Or make tea sandwiches, with thin slices of banana bread enclosing a thin filling of cream cheese.

Anise Lemon Tea Cake

Makes: 1 large loaf

What you'll need:

loaf pan 8½ × 4½ × 2½ inches, with 6-cup capacity

food processor, mortar and pestle, cutting board and heavy rolling pin, or small, heavy-duty recloseable plastic bag and heavy frying pan for crushing anise seeds

citrus zester

citrus reamer

fine mesh sieve for straining lemon juice

baking sheet for toasting almonds

food processor or sharp, heavy knife and cutting board for grinding almonds

whisk

mesh sieve

hand-held electric mixer

rubber spatula

cake tester

wire rack

baking sheet

pastry brush

Baking time: 40 to 45 minutes

This was an experiment that worked beyond my wildest expectations: The mild licorice flavor of the anise seed is complemented by the toasted almonds and the tangy lemon glaze. There almost wasn't any left after I had sampled enough to make sure I didn't have to fine-tune it.

Whole anise seeds can be found in the spice aisle of the supermarket. I like the slight crunch of crushed anise seeds, which will be most flavorful if you crush them just before making this cake; there are several ways to do this (see page 20).

FOR PREPARING THE PAN

1 tablespoon unsalted butter, softened

2 tablespoons all-purpose flour

FOR THE TEA CAKE

1 cup slivered blanched almonds

½ teaspoon crushed anise seeds

1 cup granulated sugar

1½ cups all-purpose flour

2 teaspoons baking powder

½ teaspoon baking soda

½ teaspoon salt

½ cup milk

Finely grated zest of 1 large lemon

¼ cup fresh, strained lemon juice

1 stick (8 tablespoons) unsalted butter, softened

2 extra-large eggs

FOR THE GLAZE

2 cups confectioners' sugar (if sugar is lumpy, sift first, then measure)

2 to 3 tablespoons fresh, strained lemon juice

1. Preheat the oven to 350°F with a rack in the center of the oven. Use the butter to coat the inside of the pan, then toss in the flour. Shake the pan to coat the sides and bottom, then knock out the excess. Set aside.

2. Place the almonds on a heavy-duty baking sheet and bake them in the preheated oven for 10 to 12 minutes, or until they are golden brown. Stir the nuts once, halfway through the baking time. Remove the pan from the oven, but maintain the oven temperature. Let the nuts cool in the pan for 10 minutes. Place them in the bowl of a food processor fitted with the metal blade and pulse the nuts until they are finely ground. The nuts can also be chopped by hand using a chef's knife. See page 19 for instructions. Set aside.

3. Whisk the crushed anise with the sugar in a small mixing bowl. Set aside.

4. Place a mesh sieve over a medium mixing bowl and add the flour, baking powder, baking soda, and salt. Shake the contents into the bowl and set aside. Combine the milk with the lemon zest and juice in a small measuring cup with a spout. The mixture will curdle, but that's okay. Set aside.

5. Place the butter and the anise-sugar mixture in a large mixing bowl. With the mixer on high speed, beat them together until light and fluffy, about 2 minutes. Add the eggs, one at a time, waiting until the first is completely incorporated before adding the second. Move the beaters around the bowl and scrape down the sides of the bowl with a rubber spatula several times while mixing. Reduce the mixer speed to low and add the flour mixture alternately with the milk mixture, beginning and ending with the flour. Mix just until all ingredients are combined. Use a rubber spatula to fold in the ground almonds. Scrape the batter into the prepared pan and smooth the top with a rubber spatula.

6. Bake for 40 to 45 minutes, or until a cake tester inserted into the center of the cake comes out clean. The cake will sink slightly in the center as it bakes. Remove the cake from the oven and place the pan on a wire rack. Let the cake cool in the pan for 10 minutes.

7. While it is cooling in the pan, make the glaze. Mix the confectioners' sugar and the lemon juice together in a medium bowl to make a thick paste with the consistency of heavy cream. When the cake has cooled in the pan for 10 minutes, turn it out onto the rack, then place it right side up. Place the rack on a baking sheet. Brush the glaze over the warm tea cake, allowing some to drip down the sides. Let the cake cool completely before slicing.

8. The baked and cooled glazed tea cake can be stored at room temperature, wrapped in plastic wrap, for up to 2 days, or refrigerated for up to 1 week. It may also be frozen for up to 3 months. Wrap the cooled cake securely in plastic wrap, then place it in a freezer-strength recloseable gallon-size plastic bag. Label the bag with a waterproof marker and freeze. Defrost the cake in its wrappings at room temperature for about 2 hours.

LORA SAYS: You can grind several pounds of almonds at a session. Toast and cool them before grinding, then freeze the ground nuts in a freezer-strength recloseable plastic bag. There is no need to defrost the ground almonds before using them.

Peach Kuchen

Makes: 6 servings

What you'll need:

9-inch springform pan

microwave or small saucepan
for melting butter

citrus zester

fine-mesh sieve for straining
lemon juice

small, sharp knife

mixing spoon

mesh sieve

fork

cake tester

wire rack

Baking time: 35 minutes

A kuchen is a cross between a cake and a fruit tart. Make this in midsummer when fresh peaches are juicy and flavorful. You can use nectarines (no need to peel them) in place of the peaches, or Italian plums. These are longish, deep purple plums that are easily pitted by cutting them in half the long way and slipping out the pit. I leave the skin on the peaches when I make this cake. If you wish to remove the skin, see Lora Says.

FOR PREPARING THE PAN

1 tablespoon unsalted butter or solid vegetable shortening, softened

2 tablespoons all-purpose flour

FOR THE TOPPING

½ cup packed dark brown sugar

½ teaspoon ground cinnamon

½ teaspoon ground ginger

1 large lemon

2 pounds (4 to 6 large) ripe peaches

1½ cups all-purpose flour

2 teaspoons baking powder

½ teaspoon salt

½ cup granulated sugar

2 extra-large eggs

2 tablespoons milk

1 stick (8 tablespoons) unsalted butter, melted

Whipped cream, optional (see page 21)

1. Preheat the oven to 375°F with a rack in the center of the oven. Use the butter or vegetable shortening to coat the inside of the pan. Toss in the flour and shake the pan to coat the sides and bottom. Knock out the excess. Set aside.

2. Make the topping by mixing the dark brown sugar, cinnamon, and ginger in a small mixing bowl. Set aside.

3. Remove the zest from the lemon with a zester, cut the lemon in half, and squeeze the juice through a fine-mesh sieve into a large bowl. Halve and pit the peaches leaving them unpeeled, unless the skin is extremely fuzzy, then cut them into ¾-inch-thick slices. Place the slices in the bowl containing the lemon juice and toss the peaches with the juice to coat them thoroughly. Set aside.

4. Place a mesh sieve over a large mixing bowl and add the flour, baking powder, salt, and sugar. Shake the contents into the bowl and set aside.

5. Break the eggs into a 2-cup measure with a sprout and beat them with a fork briefly to break them up. Use the fork to beat in the milk, then add the melted butter and the reserved lemon zest. Dribble this mixture into the flour mixture, stirring with the fork just to moisten the dry ingredients. Do not overmix. The batter will be rather thick. Spread the batter in the prepared pan and smooth the top with a rubber spatula.

6. Drain and reserve the liquid that has accumulated with the peaches. Arrange the peach slices in a spiral design on top of the batter in the pan, then drizzle the peach juices over the peaches. Sprinkle the topping mixture evenly over the peaches.

7. Bake the kuchen for 35 minutes, or until a cake tester inserted into the center of the batter comes out clean. Remove the pan to a wire rack and let cool for 15 minutes. Remove the sides of the pan and transfer the kuchen, on its base, to a serving plate. Serve the kuchen warm or at room temperature. Top each serving with whipped cream, if desired.

8. The kuchen is wonderful served warm, shortly after it has been baked. It should not be refrigerated after baking, but may be stored at room temperature, covered lightly with plastic wrap, for up to 48 hours. It can be reheated, covered with aluminum foil, in a 300°F oven for 15 minutes. It cannot be frozen.

LORA SAYS: To remove the skin from peaches, bring a large saucepan of water to a boil. When it boils, remove it from the heat and lower the peaches into the water. Immerse them for 2 minutes, then lift them out to a work surface with a slotted utensil. When they are cool enough to handle, slip off the skins. The skins of some types of peaches are easier to slip off after blanching than others. You'll have more success with ripe peaches. You can use a small, sharp knife or a vegetable peeler to remove any remaining skin.

LORA SAYS: When a recipe calls for both zest and juice of a lemon, lime, or orange, it's easier to use a zester to remove the zest before you cut the fruit and squeeze it. You can get more juice out by first rolling the fruit on the counter, pressing down with the flat of your hand.

Pear and Honey Clafouti

Makes: 6 to 8 servings

What you'll need:

1½-quart baking dish, quiche dish, or deep-dish pie plate

scissors

nonstick vegetable spray (optional)

citrus zester

microwave or small saucepan for melting butter

baking sheet

mixing spoon

small ladle

slotted spoon

Baking time: 25 to 30 minutes

Pronounced "clah-*foo*-tee," this French dessert has fruit on the bottom and a rich batter topping. As it bakes, the fruit bubbles up through the topping to form a jewellike mosaic. If you have a white ovenproof porcelain baking dish, this is the time to use it. Be sure to use pears that are flavorful and just slightly underripe. Giant Comice and Royal Riviera pears are great for this dish, so it's time to cozy up to your friends who receive packages from Harry and David.

FOR PREPARING THE PAN

1 tablespoon unsalted butter or solid vegetable shortening, softened

FOR THE CLAFOUTI

3 pounds slightly underripe pears (4 to 6, depending on type), cut in half lengthwise, cored, then cut in ¼-inch slices

1 cup dried pears, cut into 1-inch pieces (see Lora Says)

1 teaspoon finely grated lime zest or ¼ teaspoon lime oil

4 extra-large eggs, lightly beaten

1 cup half-and-half

⅓ cup packed dark brown sugar

2 tablespoons unsalted butter, melted

⅓ cup honey

1. Preheat the oven to 350°F with a rack in the center of the oven. Use the butter or vegetable shortening to coat the baking dish, then place the baking dish on the baking sheet; to catch spills from the baking dish.

2. Place the fresh pear slices and the dried pear pieces in a large mixing bowl. Add the lime zest, eggs, half-and-half, dark brown sugar, and melted butter. Stir gently to mix thoroughly. Ladle enough of the liquid from the fruit bowl into the baking dish to cover the bottom in a thin layer. Use a slotted spoon to transfer the fruit to the baking dish so that the dish is evenly filled with fruit. Carefully pour the liquid remaining in the bowl over the fruit, then drizzle the honey over all.

3. Bake for 25 to 30 minutes, or until the top is puffed and a golden brown. Remove the clafouti from the oven and serve it hot, warm, or at room temperature.

4. The clafouti is best eaten right out of the oven. The baked clafouti can be refrigerated, covered with plastic wrap, for up to 4 days. Reheat before serving, covered loosely with aluminum foil, in a 350°F oven. It cannot be frozen.

LORA SAYS: Use a pair of kitchen scissors to cut the dried pears into small pieces. For best results, spray the blades with nonstick vegetable spray first so that the fruit won't stick to them.

LORA SAYS: To make cleanup easier, line the baking sheet under the baking dish with aluminum foil, so that any overflow won't burn on the sheet itself.

Pies and Tarts

Pies and Tarts

· ·

What would life or dessert be without a challenge or two? Yes, pie making has the sort of reputation that leaves novice bakers eyeing the store-bought variety, or glancing wistfully at frozen pie crusts. A challenge? Yes. Surmountable? Absolutely.

Start out with the crumbles and cobblers. As simple as can be to make, these homey, relaxed desserts will have you looking at fresh blueberries, apricots, bananas, and nectarines in a whole new light. Making them will give you a sense of timing, of handling forgiving toppings and doughs and, most important of all, of tasting how incomparably exquisite are the flavors of these desserts when they are homemade.

When you've got your sea legs, so to speak, then move on to pies. My advice is to sit down and read through the piecrust recipe so that you understand and can anticipate all the steps. Reading this for the first time while you're making your first pie is a little like a virgin taking a sex manual to bed. The more prepared you are, the more pleasurable your experience will be. I hope you'll cut me some slack on the metaphor; I have in fact tasted pies that are better than . . . no, never mind, I've said enough already.

Perfect Pies
What Should I Do If . . .

My crust is tough? The dough may have been manipulated too much. Add the liquid ingredients and mix only until a rough ball forms. The flour may have had too much gluten (protein); try using half all-purpose flour and half pastry flour, which is lower in protein than regular all-purpose flour, and produces a flakier, more tender crust.

The dough is too soft to roll? Chill the ball of dough for 30 minutes before rolling.

The dough falls apart when I try to roll it? Allow it to rest in the refrigerator for 15 to 20 minutes after mixing and before rolling. Try the plastic bag technique, pages 271–72.

The dough is too hard to roll? Try adding a teaspoon of Lora Brody's Dough Relaxer for each cup of flour (page 48).

The piecrust droops when I bake it? The dough was too soft; freeze it or refrigerate it for 30 minutes before baking. Perhaps the oven wasn't preheated; piecrusts need to go into a hot oven. The heat helps the crust set up fast, before it has a chance to droop. The dough may have been stretched to fit into the pie plate. Be sure to roll the dough large enough, then lay it gently in the plate.

The crust is pale and anemic after baking? Try applying an egg wash, made of 1 egg yolk mixed with 2 tablespoons milk or cream, to the crust before baking. Make sure that you add sugar if it is called for, because it's the sugar that helps give that beautiful golden brown color to baked piecrusts.

The crust burns or browns too much? Sometimes the top crust will get very brown before the baking time is up. If this happens, make an aluminum foil tent and place it loosely over the top of the pie. Make sure that the pie isn't baking too high up in the oven, where the heat is the most intense. It should bake on the center rack or, if the pie itself is very tall, lower the rack slightly. If the bottom is burning or browning too fast, check to make sure you haven't placed the pie plate on a baking sheet that was so large that it blocked the flow of hot air in the oven, trapping it under the pie.

The bottom crust is soggy? There was too much sugar in the crust; try reducing it by 1 to 2 tablespoons. The empty crust wasn't partially baked before the filling was added and the baking completed. Partial baking is different from "prebaking" or "blind baking," which are two terms that mean that a crust is completely baked before the filling is added. Because a fully baked crust requires no further time in the oven, it is used for pudding and/or fruit fillings that are ready to eat. Either partially or fully baking a crust will help keep the bottom from getting soggy. Another technique is to apply a wash made of 1 egg white beaten with a tiny pinch of salt to the crust before prebaking. This helps seal a crust that will be partially or fully baked without a filling.

The filling is bland? Check your spices to make sure that they haven't lost their potency. With fruit pies, add finely grated citrus rind (orange, lemon, or lime) as well as a few tablespoons of strained fresh lemon or lime juice.

The fruit filling is too runny? Add a little more tapioca to the fruit mixture before baking. Perhaps the pie did not cook long enough. Try increasing the baking time by 10 minutes, but be sure to cover the top of the pie loosely with aluminum foil to keep the crust from burning.

The fruit filling overflows? It's hard to predict when a fruit-filled pie will overflow the crust and make the bottom of your oven a mess. You only need to have this happen once before you learn to place fruit-filled pies on a aluminum foil–lined baking sheet. It's important not to let the burned filling remain on the oven floor, as it will impart an unpleasant burned taste to everything else that you bake.

It's hard to cut nice, even pieces? My mother makes the world's best pies, and they never look anything like the centerfold of *Bon Appétit* or *Gourmet* magazine. Her fillings ooze out and her crusts crumble when cut (a sign of a tender piecrust, as far as I'm concerned). I gave up long ago making myself nuts about picture-perfect slices of pie, and I suggest you do the same. One thing that helps make pies easier to cut is a serrated pie server. The other thing that helps is placing a large scoop of vanilla ice cream on top of the messy piece; I promise you, no one will complain about aesthetics.

Basic Piecrust: Single Crust

Makes: one crust for a 9-inch regular or deep-dish pie plate

What you'll need:

9-inch regular (1¼ inches deep) or deep-dish (2 inches deep) pie plate

mesh sieve

2 table knives, or pastry blender, or hand-held electric mixer

fork

freezer-strength recloseable jumbo-size (2-gallon) plastic bag, 13 × 15 inches

heavy rolling pin

large baking sheet

scissors

aluminum foil

paring knife

¾ cup raw rice, or dried beans, or pie weights

My mother is an amazing pie maker, and it was easier to watch her do it than attempt it myself when I was growing up. When I was on my own, armed with her recipes, my attempts were frustrating and the results were not nearly as good as hers. The big problem was rolling out the dough without it sticking, tearing, and getting so soft it would fall apart, and the crust always seemed to be tough and would shrink from the sides of the pan. Over time I figured out a way to make a crust that behaves during rolling, isn't tough, and won't shrink. I'm passing this on to you. This looks like a lengthy recipe, but, in fact, if you do it once or twice, you'll probably never have to refer to the directions again. The biggest secret to success is to be patient enough to chill the dough as directed during the making of the crust. The addition of my Dough Relaxer is optional. It makes the crust easier to roll and gives it a more tender, flaky texture.

1¼ cups all-purpose flour

Scant teaspoon of salt

2 tablespoons granulated sugar

1 tablespoon Lora Brody's Dough Relaxer, optional (see page 48)

3 tablespoons unsalted butter, chilled and cut into ¼-inch pieces

3 tablespoons solid vegetable shortening, chilled (see page 47)

1 extra-large egg

1 tablespoon white vinegar

2 tablespoons very cold water

1. Place a mesh sieve over a medium mixing bowl and add the flour, salt, sugar, and optional Dough Relaxer. Shake the contents into the bowl.

Table knife or pastry blender method: Scatter the butter pieces and the shortening over the flour. Use 2 table knives in a crisscross motion, or a pastry blender, to cut the butter and shortening into the flour mixture until it is crumbly and there are no obvious large chunks of fat. The texture of the mixture will be uneven; most of the pieces of fat will be pea-size. If you use a pastry blender, clean between the wires with a table knife from time to time. The mixing of the flour and fat by either hand method will take about 1 minute.

2. Place the egg, vinegar, and cold water in a 1-cup measure with a spout. Mix with a fork to break up the egg and combine the ingredients well. Dribble the liquid mixture into the flour mixture, stirring gently with a fork until a crumbly ball starts to form. It will look like a mess at first, but treat it tenderly. You may think that it will never form a ball of dough, but don't be tempted to add more liquid unless absolutely necessary. Continue to mix only until the dry ingredients just hold together. Scrape any dough from the mixing fork. Dust your hands, not the dough, with flour and turn the dough out onto a lightly floured work surface. Knead the dough together briefly to form a rough ball.

Hand mixer method: Scatter the butter pieces and the shortening over the flour. With the mixer on low speed, mix the shortening with the dry ingredients until fine, irregularly shaped crumbs form, about 1½ minutes. None should be larger than a lima bean. If necessary, break up any very large pieces with your fingers, but don't handle them any more than necessary, as the shortening will melt and the dough will become soft and greasy.

3. Place the egg, vinegar, and cold water in a 1-cup measure with a spout. Mix with a fork to break up the egg and combine the ingredients well. With the mixer on lowest speed, add the liquid all at once, and mix only until the dough starts to form a ball, about 20 seconds. It will be crumbly at first, but don't be tempted to add more water. Dust your hands with flour (it is better to dust your hands than to dust the dough) and turn the dough out onto a lightly floured work surface. Pat the dough together briefly to form a rough ball.

TO FINISH MIXING THE DOUGH, EITHER METHOD: Dust the inside of the plastic bag with a little flour. Place the ball of dough in the center of the bag, then flatten it with the palm of your hand into a 6-inch disk. Seal the bag and place it in the refrigerator for 1 hour, or in the freezer for 15 minutes.

TO ROLL THE DOUGH: Remove the bag of dough from the refrigerator or freezer. Thoroughly wet a paper towel with cool water, then squeeze out the water and put the towel on a work surface. Place the plastic bag on the towel to prevent it from sliding as you roll the dough. Before you start rolling, open the bag and lightly flour both surfaces of the dough, using about 1 tablespoon of flour in all, so it looks like a light dusting of snow. You do not need to reseal the bag. Use the rolling pin to roll the dough, working from the center out and rolling the dough away from you in one direction. Turn the bag 90 degrees after each roll, and always roll in the same direction. Flip the bag over as you work, to make sure that the dough isn't sticking to the bag. The bag will look slightly wrinkled. If it is sticking, open the bag and sprinkle the dough surface with a little more flour. (Remember, however, that the more flour you add, the tougher the dough will be.) Don't worry if the dough is not symmetrical; it will be trimmed later. As you roll, keep the center of the dough the same thickness as the ends. Tug gently on the bag from time to time to straighten the bottom, so that it doesn't wrinkle and distort the dough. Roll the dough into a rough circle about 13 inches in diameter. Place the bag on a baking sheet to keep it flat and return it to the refrigerator to firm up for at least 1 hour, or freeze for 15 minutes.

TO LINE A PIE PLATE: Remove the baking sheet with the dough on it from the refrigerator or freezer. Leave the plastic bag on the baking sheet. Unseal the bag and use scissors to cut open both side seams and the bottom seam. Remove and discard the whole top layer of the bag. Invert a pie plate onto the center of the dough. Turn the whole thing upside down—baking sheet and all—then remove the baking sheet. Press gently on the piece of plastic still on the surface of the dough to ease the dough into the pie pan. Discard the plastic. Leave the excess dough hanging over the plate. Flour your fingers and crimp the dough by pinching the edge of the dough between your forefingers and thumbs all around the plate. Use a paring knife to trim off the excess dough at the rim.

The crust is ready to be partially or fully baked without a filling, or to be filled and baked.

TO PARTIALLY BAKE THE PIECRUST: Place the formed shell in the refrigerator or freezer while you preheat the oven. Preheat the oven to 425°F with a rack in the center of the oven. Line the crust with a square of aluminum foil, then cover the foil with about ¾-cup raw rice, dried beans, or specially made pie weights, which are available in cookware stores. Bake the crust for 12 to 15 minutes, then remove the pie plate from the oven. Remove the aluminum foil and weights. The bottom of the crust will look slightly damp (raw) and pale, and the edges will be somewhat pale.

TO FULLY BAKE THE PIECRUST: Place the formed shell in the refrigerator or freezer while you preheat the oven. Preheat the oven to 425°F with a rack in the center of the oven. Line the crust with a square of aluminum foil, then cover the foil with about ¾-cup raw rice, dried beans, or specially made pie weights, which are available in cookware stores. Bake the crust for 15 minutes, then remove the pie plate from the oven. Remove the aluminum foil and weights. Prick the bottom of the crust all over with a fork and bake for 7 to 12 minutes more until the bottom of the crust looks dry and cooked.

STORING THE DOUGH: Pie dough that has been mixed and formed into a disk, or has been rolled and is ready to fit into a pie plate, can be placed in its plastic bag and refrigerated for up to 2 days. Either form of the dough can also be frozen in its plastic bag for up to 3 months. Defrost in the bag at room temperature.

A formed, unbaked piecrust, in its pie plate, can be wrapped securely in plastic wrap and stored in the refrigerator for 2 days. It can also be placed in a freezer-strength recloseable jumbo-size plastic bag and frozen for up to 3 months. If you are going to partially or fully bake the crust, there is no need to defrost the crust, but it is important to make sure that the oven is completely preheated before baking.

LORA SAYS: You can, or course, make perfectly good piecrust in a food processor, but there is the risk of overworking the dough. The trick is to process the ingredients to the stage just before a ball forms, then finish by hand. The plastic blade rather than the metal one is more gentle on the dough.

LORA SAYS: If you stretch the dough while you are fitting it into the pie plate, it will shrink during baking. It's better to roll it to the size you require, giving it periods of rest— in the refrigerator, if necessary—so that it rolls without stretching.

Basic Piecrust: Double Crust

Makes: double crust pastry for 9-inch regular or deep-dish pie plate

What you'll need:

9-inch regular (1¼ inches deep) or deep-dish (2 inches deep) pie plate

mesh sieve

2 table knives, or pastry blender, or hand-held electric mixer

fork

2 freezer-strength recloseable jumbo-size (2 gallon) plastic bags, each 13 × 15 inches

heavy six rolling pin

2 large baking sheets

scissors

2½ cups all-purpose flour

1½ teaspoons salt

3 tablespoons granulated sugar

2 tablespoons Lora Brody's Dough Relaxer, optional (see page 48)

5 tablespoons unsalted butter, chilled and cut into ¼-inch pieces

⅓ cup solid vegetable shortening, chilled (see page 47)

1 extra-large egg plus 1 extra-large egg yolk

2 tablespoons white vinegar

3 tablespoons very cold water

1. Place a mesh sieve over a medium mixing bowl and add the flour, salt, sugar, and optional Dough Relaxer. Shake the contents into the bowl.

Pastry blender or table knife method: Scatter the butter pieces and the shortening over the flour. Use 2 table knives in a crisscross motion, or a pastry blender, to cut the butter and shortening into the flour mixture until it is crumbly and there are no obvious large chunks of fat. The texture of the mixture will be uneven; most of the pieces of fat will be pea-size. If you use a pastry blender, stop and clean between the wires with a table knife from time to time. The mixing of the flour and fat by either hand method will take about 1 minute.

2. Place the whole egg and egg yolk, vinegar, and the cold water in a 1-cup measure with a spout. Mix with a fork to break up the egg and combine the ingredients well. Dribble the liquid mixture into the flour mixture, stirring gently with a fork until a crumbly ball starts to form. It will look like a mess at first, but treat it tenderly. You may think that it will never form a ball of dough, but don't be tempted to add more liquid unless absolutely necessary.

Continue to mix only until the dry ingredients hold together. Scrape any dough from the mixing fork. Dust your hands with flour (it is better to dust your hands than to dust the dough) and turn the dough out onto a lightly floured work surface. Knead the dough together briefly, then use a dough scraper to cut it into two rough balls.

HAND MIXER METHOD: Scatter the butter pieces and the shortening over the flour. With the mixer on low speed, mix the shortening with the dry ingredients until fine, irregular shaped crumbs form, about 1½ minutes. None should be larger than a lima bean. If necessary, break up any very large pieces with your fingers, but don't handle it any more than necessary, as the shortening will melt and the dough will become soft and greasy.

3. Place the whole egg and egg yolk, vinegar, and the cold water in a 1-cup measure with a spout. Mix with a fork to break up the egg and combine the ingredients well. With the mixer on lowest speed, add the liquid mixture all at once, and mix only until the dough starts to form a ball, about 20 seconds. It will be crumbly at first, but don't be tempted to add more water. Dust your hands with flour (it is better to dust your hands than to dust the dough) and turn the dough out onto a lightly floured work surface. Pat the dough together into a rough ball, then use a knife or a dough scraper to cut it into two even portions.

TO FINISH MIXING THE DOUGH, EITHER METHOD: Dust the insides of the plastic bags with a little flour. Place a ball of dough in the center of each bag, then flatten each ball with the palm of your hand into a 6-inch disk. Seal the bags and place them in the refrigerator for 1 hour, or in the freezer for 15 minutes.

TO ROLL THE DOUGH: Remove one bag of dough from the refrigerator or freezer. Thoroughly wet a paper towel with cool water, then squeeze out the water and put the towel on a work surface. Place the plastic bag on the towel to prevent it from sliding as you roll the dough. Before you start rolling, open the bag and lightly flour both surfaces of the dough, using about 1 tablespoon of flour in all, so it looks like a light dusting of snow. You do not need to reseal the bag. Use the rolling pin to roll the dough, working from the center out and rolling the dough away from you in one direction. Turn the bag 90 degrees after each roll, and always roll in the same direction. Flip the bag over as you work, to make sure the dough isn't sticking to the bag. The bag will look slightly wrinkled. If it is sticking, open the bag and sprinkle the dough surface with a little more flour. (Remember, however, that the more flour you add, the tougher the dough will be.) Don't worry if the dough is not symmetrical; it will be trimmed later. As you roll, keep the center of the dough the same thickness as the ends. Tug gently on the bag from time to time to straighten the bottom, so that it doesn't wrinkle and distort the dough. Roll the dough into a rough circle about 13 inches in diameter. Place the bag on a baking sheet to keep it flat and return it to the refrigerator to firm up for 1 hour, or freeze for 15 minutes. Repeat the rolling process with the second ball of dough, and return it to the refrigerator or freezer.

TO LINE A PIE PLATE WITH HALF THE DOUBLE CRUST PASTRY: Remove one baking sheet with the dough on it from the refrigerator or freezer. Leave the plastic bag on the baking sheet. Unseal the bag and use scissors to cut open both side seams and the bottom seam. Remove and discard the whole top layer of the bag. Invert a pie plate onto the center of the dough. Turn the whole thing upside down—baking sheet and all—then remove the baking sheet. Press gently on the piece of plastic still on the surface of the dough to ease the dough into the pie pan. Discard the plastic. Leave the excess dough hanging over the plate. For instructions on covering a filled pie with the rolled-out top crust, see recipe for Classic Apple Pie, page 286.

STORING THE DOUGH: Pie dough that has been mixed and formed into a disk, or that is rolled and ready to fit into a pie plate, can be refrigerated in its plastic bag and refrigerated for up to 2 days. Either form of the dough can also be frozen in its plastic bag for up to 3 months. Defrost in the bag at room temperature.

Graham Cracker Crumb Crust

Makes: one 9-inch crust

What you'll need:

9-inch pie plate, 1¼ inches deep

microwave (optional)

fork for packaged crumbs

recloseable gallon-size plastic bag and heavy saucepan or rolling pin for crushing whole crackers

Baking time: 10 to 15 minutes

Graham cracker crusts are fast, easy, and they have a rustic look that is quite forgiving. The taste of freshly ground graham crackers is better than the packaged crumbs.

FOR PREPARING THE PIE PLATE

1 teaspoon unsalted butter, softened

2 tablespoons granulated sugar

FOR THE CRUST

1¾ cups packaged graham cracker crumbs or 11 whole graham crackers (one-third of a 1-pound box)

½ teaspoon ground cinnamon

1 stick (8 tablespoons) unsalted butter

1. Preheat the oven to 350°F with a rack in the center of the oven. Put the teaspoon of butter in the pie plate and microwave on high for 15 seconds or place the pie plate in the preheated oven for 5 minutes, or until the butter is soft. Use your fingers or a paper towel to spread the softened butter on the bottom and sides of the plate.

2. If you are using packaged crumbs, place them in a medium mixing bowl and stir in the sugar and cinnamon. Whisk together well. Melt the butter either in a small pan set over medium heat or in a microwave and pour it over the crumbs. Mix the crumbs well with a fork to distribute the butter over all the crumbs.

3. If you are using whole crackers, break them in quarters, then place them in a freezer-strength recloseable gallon-size plastic bag with the sugar and cinnamon. Squeeze out all the air, then seal the bag. With the bottom of a heavy saucepan or a rolling pin, crush or roll the crumbs to a fairly uniform fineness. Melt the butter either in a small pan set over medium heat or in a microwave. Open the bag and pour in the melted butter. Reseal the bag and use your fingers to smoosh the crumbs with the butter to evenly distribute.

4. Place the crust mixture in the prepared pie plate and press the mixture up the sides of the plate all the way to the rim. Pat the crumbs evenly over the bottom, taking care not to make the crust too thick where the sides meet the bottom surface. Bake for 10 to 15 minutes, or until lightly browned and firm.

5. Once the crust has been formed, it should be baked immediately. After baking, if you don't plan to fill it immediately, the cooled crust can be stored, wrapped in plastic wrap, at room temperature for up to 3 days. It can also be frozen. Place the wrapped crust in a freezer-strength recloseable jumbo-size plastic bag and freeze for up to 3 months. Defrost the crust in its wrapping at room temperature. Do not refrigerate a baked crust before filling, as it will become soggy.

VARIATION: A half-cup of finely chopped hazelnuts or blanched almonds, or 2 tablespoons unsweetened cocoa powder (not Dutch processed) can be added to the crumbs along with the sugar and cinnamon.

LORA SAYS: The whole crust can be made in a food processor. Break the whole graham crackers into several pieces each and place them in the bowl of the food processor fitted with the metal blade. Pulse several times to break them into small, uniform pieces, then add the sugar and pulse to mix the sugar with the crumbs. Stop the motor and pour the melted butter over the crumb mixture. Pulse until the butter is well combined with the crumbs. Press the crumb mixture into the prepared pie plate and bake the crust as instructed in the recipe.

LORA SAYS: Make extra crusts in disposable aluminum pie plates and freeze in freezer-strength recloseable jumbo-size plastic bags for later use.

Chocolate Crumb Crust

Makes: one 9-inch crust

What you'll need:

9-inch pie plate, 1¼ inches deep

microwave or small saucepan for melting butter

freezer-strength recloseable gallon-size plastic bag

heavy saucepan or rolling pin

fork (optional)

Baking time: 5 minutes

When I was in grade school, at the end of the year we would invite my teacher to lunch at our house. My mother, who is a fabulous baker, would, at my insistence, make the same dessert year after year: a frozen whipped cream concoction called Famous Chocolate Refrigerator Roll, the recipe for which can be found on the back of the Nabisco Famous Chocolate Wafers box. To this day the idea of a slice of this stuff holds the same appeal it did back then, so I keep a box of Famous Chocolate wafers on hand just in case I get the overwhelming urge. . . .

The other great reason to keep a box of these chocolate wafers on hand is if you want to make a chocolate crumb piecrust, which is the first step in making a Double Espresso Ice Cream Pie (page 284), not to mention a number of other recipes in this book.

FOR PREPARING THE PIE PLATE

1 tablespoon unsalted butter, softened

FOR THE CRUST

25 Nabisco Famous Chocolate Wafers (about half a 9-ounce package) broken in several pieces

¾ stick (6 tablespoons) unsalted butter, melted and slightly cooled

¼ cup granulated sugar

1. Preheat the oven to 450°F with a rack in the center of the oven. Coat the pie plate with the butter.

2. Place the wafer pieces in the plastic bag with the sugar. Squeeze out all the air, then seal the bag. With the bottom of a heavy saucepan or a rolling pin, crush or roll the crumbs to a fairly uniform fineness. Open the bag and pour in the melted butter. Reseal the bag and use your fingers to squeeze the ingredients together until the crumbs are coated with the butter. You can, if you wish, perform the last step by placing the crumbs and the sugar in a mixing bowl and using a fork to combine the ingredients.

3. Scrape the mixture into the prepared pie plate and use your fingers to press the crumbs evenly into the bottom and up the sides. Don't worry about making the sides perfectly even. Bake the crust for 5 to 7 minutes, or until the edges look toasted. Remove the crust from the oven and cool it completely before filling.

4. Once the crust has been formed, it should be baked immediately. After baking, if you don't plan to fill it immediately, the cooled crust can be stored in the pie plate, wrapped in plastic wrap, at room temperature for up to 3 days. It can also be frozen. Place the wrapped crust, in the pie plate, in a freezer-strength recloseable jumbo-size plastic bag and freeze for up to 3 months. Defrost the crust in its wrapping at room temperature. Do not refrigerate a baked crust before filling, as it will become soggy.

LORA SAYS: If you plan to freeze the baked crust, it's important to wrap it carefully to prevent not only freezer burn but the absorption of odors in the freezer.

Chocolate Cream Pie

Makes: one 9-inch pie;
8 servings

What you'll need:

large, chilled metal mixing bowl and chilled beaters of hand-held electric mixer

mixing spoon

hand-held electric mixer

food grater (optional)

Forget birthday cake—this is what I want when October 4th rolls around (for anyone out there who cares to bring me some chocolate cream pie on the right day). You can either make the filling from scratch or use pudding mix; if you opt for a mix, make sure to use the kind you have to cook, not the instant kind. Also, if you want to make this the right way, forget that whipped cream in the aerosol can. Make your own. The difference is like that between a diamond and cubic zirconium.

You can also choose to make a traditional piecrust or a chocolate crumb crust. I happen to like the latter, since when you refrigerate the completed pie the crust won't get as soggy. Don't forget to wait until just before serving to add the whipped cream.

P.S. I forgot to mention that October 4th is my husband David's birthday, too, so don't be bringing us just one piece of pie.

Basic Piecrust for a single crust, fully baked according to the directions, page 270; or one Chocolate Crumb Crust, baked and cooled, page 279

Two 3⅛-ounce packages chocolate pudding mix, not instant, or see recipe for homemade filling, page 283

2 cups heavy cream

3 tablespoons confectioners' sugar (if lumpy, sift first, then measure)

1 tablespoon pure vanilla extract

Chocolate shavings, optional (see Lora Says)

1. Place a large metal mixing bowl and the beaters of the mixer in the freezer or the refrigerator while you prepare the pie. Cook the pudding according to package directions. Pour and scrape the pudding into the piecrust. Let the chocolate filling cool completely, preferably at room temperature.

2. When you are ready to serve the pie, place the heavy cream in the chilled bowl and beat with the chilled beaters on high speed until the cream begins to thicken. Add the confectioners' sugar and vanilla and continue to beat until the cream is stiff. Spoon the whipped cream onto the filling and swirl it decoratively with a rubber spatula. Garnish with chocolate shavings, if desired.

3. Without the whipped cream, this pie can be covered with plastic wrap and refrigerated for up to 2 days. Once garnished with whipped cream, the pie can be refrigerated for up to 1 hour. The pie cannot be frozen.

LORA SAYS: To make chocolate shavings, use a block of bittersweet or semisweet chocolate, which can be bought in gourmet stores or upscale groceries. On the medium-size holes of a food grater, grate the chocolate directly onto the surface of the whipped cream.

LORA SAYS: For a fancier presentation, use a piping bag and a star tip to pipe the whipped cream onto the filling.

Homemade Chocolate Pudding for Pie Filling

Makes: about 3½ cups

What you'll need:

scale for weighing chocolate (optional)

sharp, heavy knife for chopping chocolate

whisk

medium saucepan

4 extra-large egg yolks

1 scant cup granulated sugar

4 tablespoons all-purpose flour

3 tablespoons cornstarch

2½ cups milk

4 ounces semisweet chocolate, coarsely chopped (see page 16)

2 ounces (2 squares) unsweetened chocolate, coarsely chopped

1 teaspoon pure vanilla extract

1. Place the egg yolks, sugar, flour, and cornstarch in a medium mixing bowl and whisk them together. Add 1 or 2 tablespoons of the milk to make a thick paste.

2. Place the remaining milk in a medium saucepan set over medium heat. Cook, whisking constantly, until small bubbles begin to form around the edge of the pan. Do not boil. Pour the hot milk in a steady stream into the egg mixture, whisking as you add it. Pour this mixture back into the saucepan and place it over medium-low heat. Whisk constantly, scraping the sides and bottom of the pan, until the mixture just starts to bubble. Cook for another 30 seconds, or until the mixture becomes thick. Remove the saucepan from the heat and add the semisweet and unsweetened chocolate and the vanilla. Whisk until the chocolate melts and the mixture is smooth. Cool the filling for 10 minutes before pouring and scraping it into the prepared piecrust.

LORA SAYS: Another easy yet deliciously satisfying filling can be made, following the package directions, with 2 packages of instant chocolate pudding made with heavy cream instead of milk. Add 2 teaspoons vanilla extract. Pour it into the pie shell as soon as you finish stirring.

Double Espresso Ice Cream Pie with Chocolate Espresso Whipped Cream

Makes: one 9-inch pie; 8 servings

What you'll need:

microwave for softening ice cream (optional)

mixing spoon or spatula

aluminum foil

large, chilled metal mixing bowl and chilled beaters of hand-held electric mixer

hand-held electric mixer

small saucepan

One of the great things about this dessert is that you can make it up to 1 week ahead, freeze it, and pull it out of the freezer to serve without defrosting it. The pie can be topped with the whipped cream before freezing (it is just as good frozen), or the cream can be added just before serving. Coffee- or espresso-flavored chocolate bits (sometimes found in the shape of coffee beans) are available in gourmet and candy stores.

FOR THE CRUST AND FILLING

One Chocolate Crumb Crust, baked and cooled according to the recipe on page 279

1½ pints (3 cups) premium coffee ice cream

1 cup coffee-flavored or espresso-flavored chocolate bits

FOR THE WHIPPED CREAM

⅓ cup Kahlúa or other coffee-flavored liqueur

1 tablespoon instant espresso powder or granules

3 tablespoons granulated sugar

1 pint (2 cups) heavy cream, chilled

1. To make the filling, soften the ice cream by leaving the carton at room temperature for about 20 minutes or by microwaving the carton for 20 to 30 seconds on high. Scoop the ice cream into a large metal mixing bowl and add the chocolate bits with a mixing spoon or a rigid plastic spatula. Scrape the filling into the chocolate crust and freeze the pie, uncovered, until the surface is solid, then cover it with plastic wrap and a layer of aluminum foil. When you put the pie in the freezer, place a large metal mixing bowl and the beaters of the mixer in the freezer as well.

2. To make the whipped cream, heat the Kahlúa in the saucepan set over medium heat until it is barely simmering. Remove the saucepan from the heat and stir in the espresso powder and sugar. Continue to stir until both are dissolved, then transfer the mixture to a small metal mixing bowl or measuring cup. Place the container in the freezer to chill for 15 minutes.

3. Pour the chilled cream into the large chilled metal mixing bowl. With the mixer on high speed, using the chilled beaters, whip the cream until it holds soft peaks. Reduce the mixer speed to low and beat in the chilled Kahlúa mixture, then beat the cream for 1 more minute on high speed. Spread the whipped cream over the top of the frozen pie.

4. You may serve the pie immediately, or you may return it to the freezer for up to 1 week before serving. If you return the pie to the freezer, leave it uncovered until the whipped cream has hardened, then cover the surface with plastic wrap.

Classic Apple Pie

Makes: one 9-inch double-crust pie

What you'll need:

citrus zester

citrus reamer

fine-mesh sieve for straining lemon juice

sharp, heavy knife

paring knife

9-inch deep-dish pie plate, 2 inches deep

pastry brush

scissors

aluminum foil–lined baking sheet large enough to hold the pie plate

aluminum foil

Baking time: 50 to 60 minutes

The true key to success for great apple pie is to forget about making a pie that looks like something you'd buy in a bakery. My mother's pies are untidy creations that she throws together in a matter of minutes. Once I stopped being so fussy about the way mine looked, they improved immensely. A scoop of ice cream will make the messiest slice of pie irresistible.

The kind of apple you use is important. You want very flavorful, firm, tart apples, such as Baldwin, Macoun, or Fuji. I suggest placing the pie plate on an aluminum foil– or Silpat-lined baking sheet when you bake the pie, in case of overflow.

One Basic Piecrust recipe for a double crust, page 274, both portions of dough rolled out in plastic bags and refrigerated

4 pounds (about 8 medium) tart apples

Finely grated zest of 1 large lemon

3 tablespoons fresh, strained lemon juice

3 tablespoons Minute® brand (see page 49) tapioca

½ cup granulated sugar plus 1 tablespoon for sprinkling on top crust

½ teaspoon ground cinnamon

¼ teaspoon ground nutmeg

⅛ teaspoon ground cloves

¼ cup milk

1. Make sure that each portion of piecrust dough is rolled into a circle that is at least 13 inches in diameter, because the crust needs to hold a tall pile of apple slices. Following the recipe on page 274, place one portion of rolled dough in the pie plate. Leave the second portion rolled out in the plastic bag. Refrigerate the pastry-lined pie plate and the second crust until you are ready to fill and bake the pie.

2. Preheat the oven to 425°F with a rack in the center of the oven.

3. Peel the apples. Use a chef's knife to quarter them, then use a paring knife to remove the core and seeds and any tough parts of the center. Cut apple quarters into ¼-inch-thick slices, or cut across the quarters to form 1 by ½-inch chunks. Place the apple pieces in a large mixing bowl, then sprinkle them with the lemon zest, juice, and tapioca. Make sure that the apples are well coated with the juice; this will prevent them from turning brown. Combine ½ cup sugar, cinnamon, nutmeg, and cloves in a small mixing bowl, then sprinkle over the apples and toss to coat the pieces well. The easiest way to do this is with your hands.

4. Pile the apples in the pastry-lined pie plate, mounding them in the center several inches higher than the pie shell level. It will look as if you have a lot of apples. Pour any accumulated apple juice from the bowl over the apples. Use a pastry brush to moisten the exposed pastry rim with some of the milk.

5. Remove the second portion of rolled dough from the refrigerator and use scissors to cut off the top half of the plastic bag; discard the top piece of plastic. Place your hand flat under the bottom piece of plastic and then flip the crust over onto the top of the apples so that the center of the pastry rests on top of the center of the apples. Remove and discard the plastic. Flour your fingers and gently pinch the top and bottom crust together at the rim of the pie plate. You can make small, regular, decorative indentations with your thumb, or you can use the tines of a fork to seal the crust closed. This is called "crimping." Trim off the excess dough with a small, sharp knife. Use the knife to cut several 1-inch slits in the top crust to act as vents to let steam escape during the baking process. This will help to keep the crust from getting soggy as it bakes.

6. Brush the top and edges of the crust with milk (but don't leave puddles on the pastry!) and sprinkle the top of the pie with the additional 1 tablespoon sugar. Place the pie on the baking sheet to catch any juices that spill over from the pie as it bakes. Place the baking sheet with the pie on it in the preheated oven and bake for 20 minutes. At this point, tent the pie loosely with aluminum foil to prevent the crust from browning too much, and reduce the oven temperature to 375°F. Continue to bake until the crust has browned nicely and the apples are bubbling, 30 to 40 minutes more. After 40 minutes of total baking time, remove the aluminum foil tent. Check the pie after 50 minutes total baking time.

7. When the pie has baked, turn off the oven, open the oven door, and let the pie cool. If it is a really hot day and you don't want to heat up your kitchen, remove both the pie and the baking sheet from the oven and allow the pie to cool on a wire rack on the counter.

8. The pie is best served warm, or at room temperature. Once it is baked, it is not advisable to refrigerate or freeze this pie, as the crust will get soggy.

9. If you are going to freeze apple pie, it is best to do it before it is baked. Prepare the pie as described, but do not brush the pastry with milk or sprinkle it with the sugar. Place it in the freezer for about 3 hours until it is completely frozen, then wrap it, plate and all, securely in plastic wrap. Place it in a freezer-strength recloseable jumbo-size plastic storage bag, label it with a waterproof marker, and return it to the freezer. The pie may be kept frozen for up to 3 months. When you are ready to bake the pie, let it stay at room temperature, wrapped, for 1 hour, then remove the wrapping and brush the pastry with milk and sprinkle it with sugar as described in the recipe. Place it in a preheated 425°F oven and bake as directed.

LORA SAYS: Some apples are naturally sweeter than others, and some people like their apple pies on the tart side. You can adjust the sweetness or tartness by adding 2 to 3 tablespoons additional sugar or the equivalent amount of maple syrup or honey to sweeten the filling, or you can add 3 tablespoons less sweetener plus the finely grated zest and strained juice of one additional lemon to the filling.

Cherry Pie with Streusel Topping

Makes: one 9-inch pie;
8 servings

What you'll need:

baking sheet for toasting almonds

sharp, heavy knife for chopping almonds

small, sharp knife for cutting up butter

small saucepan

mixing spoon

fork

baking sheet large enough to hold the pie plate

aluminum foil

wire rack

Baking time: 25 minutes

This pie is a county fair blue ribbon winner. It's beautiful to look at, amazing to taste, and really, really simple to make. You can use a traditional crust or a graham cracker crumb crust.

FOR THE PIE

1 Basic Piecrust for a single crust (page 270), partially baked in a 9-inch pie plate, 1¼ inches deep, according to the directions in the recipe, or one recipe Graham Cracker Crumb Crust (page 277), baked and cooled

½ cup orange juice

1 cup dried sweet or sour cherries (see page 47)

One 21-ounce can cherry pie filling

FOR THE STREUSEL TOPPING

⅔ cup all-purpose flour

¾ cup packed dark brown sugar

1 cup slivered blanched almonds, toasted and roughly chopped (see pages 18–19)

6 tablespoons (3 ounces) unsalted butter, cut into chunks and softened

1 teaspoon ground cinnamon

1. Preheat the oven to 375°F with a rack in the center of the oven.

2. Place the orange juice and dried cherries in a small saucepan. Bring the mixture to a simmer over medium heat, then remove the pan from the heat and set it aside to cool slightly, about 15 minutes. Pour off and discard all but 1 tablespoon of orange juice from the rehydrated cherries. Place the drained cherries with their reserved tablespoon of juice in a medium mixing bowl. Stir in the cherry pie filling and mix well. Pour the cherry mixture into the partially baked pastry crust and set aside.

3. Make the streusel by combining the flour, dark brown sugar, nuts, butter, and cinnamon in a bowl. Mash with a fork until it forms a crumbly paste and you can no longer see the flour. Use your fingers to distribute the streusel topping evenly over the cherries. It makes a rather thick layer, but that's okay.

4. Place the pie plate on the baking sheet with a piece of aluminum foil under the pie plate. Bake in the preheated oven for 15 minutes. Reduce the oven heat to 350°F and continue baking for about 10 minutes more, or until the crust has browned and the streusel is a deep golden brown. If the crust becomes too brown as the pie bakes, pull the aluminum foil up around the rim of the crust. Remove the pie from the oven on its baking sheet. Transfer the pie to a wire rack to cool.

5. The baked pie can be stored at room temperature, wrapped loosely in aluminum foil, for up to 36 hours. Placing it in the refrigerator will make the crust and topping soggy. The pie cannot be frozen either before or after baking.

Strawberry-Rhubarb Pie with Almond Crumble Topping

Makes: one 9-inch pie;
8 servings

What you'll need:

9-inch pie plate, 2 inches deep

small, sharp knife

colander for cleaning
strawberries

citrus reamer

fine-mesh sieve for straining
lemon juice

fork

mixing spoon

food processor or sharp, heavy
knife and 2 table knives or
pastry blender

aluminum foil–lined baking
sheet large enough to hold the
pie plate

Baking time: 50 minutes

Spring is the time for fresh rhubarb. Frozen rhubarb is certainly an acceptable substitute if you can't wait until spring. Using tender stalks makes for a less stringy result. The easiest way to peel the stalks is with a sharp paring knife. Be sure to use flavorful strawberries for the ultimate in great taste.

FOR THE CUSTARD AND FILLING

One Basic Piecrust for a single crust (page 270), rolled and fitted into the pie plate

8 ounces rhubarb (fresh or frozen), peeled and cut into 1-inch slices (about 2 cups)

1 quart (4 cups) fresh strawberries, rinsed, hulled, and halved

4 tablespoons Minute® tapioca (see page 49)

1 cup granulated sugar

⅓ cup strained fresh lemon juice

FOR THE TOPPING AND GARNISH

½ cup slivered blanched almonds

½ cup packed light brown sugar

½ cup oats, old-fashioned or quick-cooking (see page 46)

¾ stick (6 tablespoons) unsalted butter, chilled and cut into 10 pieces

Vanilla ice cream (optional)

1. Preheat the oven to 350°F with a rack in the center of the oven.

2. Use a fork to prick the bottom of the piecrust, then place it in the freezer while the oven preheats and while you prepare the fruit and topping.

3. To make the filling, place the rhubarb and strawberries in a large mixing bowl. Sprinkle with the tapioca, sugar, and lemon juice. Use a large spoon to stir the ingredients together well. Set the fruit aside for 10 minutes while you prepare the topping.

4. To make the topping, place the almonds, light brown sugar, oats, and butter in the work bowl of a food processor fitted with the metal blade. Pulse several times until the mixture is just combined and the almonds are half their original size. You may also mix the topping by hand: Chop the almonds with a chef's knife (see page 19), then place them in a medium mixing bowl with the brown sugar and oats. Scatter the butter on top and use two table knives in a crisscross motion, or a pastry blender, to cut the butter into the other ingredients. Set aside.

5. Remove the piecrust from the freezer and place it on the baking sheet to catch any spills from the pie during baking. Pour and scrape the fruit mixture into the prepared pastry crust, distributing the fruit evenly. Scatter the topping over the fruit, and pat it down lightly with your fingers. Place the filled pie plate on its baking sheet in the oven and bake for 50 minutes, or until the topping is nicely browned and the filling is bubbling.

6. When it has baked, remove the pie from the oven and cool it on the baking sheet for at least 20 minutes before serving. Serve the pie with a scoop of vanilla ice cream, if desired.

7. The baked pie can be stored at room temperature, wrapped loosely in aluminum foil, for up to 36 hours. Placing it in the refrigerator will make the crust and topping soggy. The pie cannot be frozen either before or after baking.

LORA SAYS: Use both a spoon and a pie cutter to serve this pie.

Three Berry Cobbler

Makes: 8 servings

What you'll need:

9 × 13-inch baking dish

citrus zester

citrus reamer

fine-mesh sieve for straining lemon juice

small, sharp knife

mesh sieve

2 table knives or pastry blender

fork

heavy rolling pin

2-inch or 2½-inch round cookie cutter

aluminum foil–lined baking sheet

wire rack

Baking time: 25 to 30 minutes

At the height of fresh berry season, you can make this homey dessert with blueberries, raspberries, blackberries, and strawberries. If the urge to have berry cobbler overcomes you in the winter, frozen unsweetened berries are fine; there is no need to defrost them first.

FOR PREPARING THE PAN

1 tablespoon unsalted butter, softened

FOR THE FRUIT

2 cups (1 pint) fresh strawberries, rinsed and gently patted

2 cups (1 pint) fresh red raspberries, picked over, rinsed only if necessary

2 cups (1 pint) fresh blackberries

1 cup granulated sugar

3 tablespoons Minute® tapioca (see page 49)

Finely grated zest of 1 large lemon

⅓ cup fresh, strained lemon juice

FOR THE BISCUIT TOPPING

2 cups all-purpose flour

½ cup granulated sugar

1 teaspoon baking powder

½ teaspoon salt

1 tablespoon Lora Brody's Dough Relaxer (optional)

¾ stick (6 tablespoons) unsalted butter, chilled and cut into small pieces

1 cup milk

1½ teaspoons pure almond extract

3 to 4 teaspoons sugar for sprinkling on the cobbler (optional)

1. Preheat the oven to 375°F with a rack in the center of the oven. Use the butter to coat the baking dish. Set aside.

2. To prepare the fruit, stem and core the strawberries, then slice them into a medium mixing bowl. Add the raspberries and blackberries. Sprinkle the sugar, tapioca, and lemon zest and juice over the berries, then toss them together gently with a rubber spatula. Scrape the fruit into the prepared pan and set it aside while you prepare the biscuit topping.

3. Place a mesh sieve over a medium mixing bowl and add the flour, sugar, baking powder, salt, and optional Relaxer. Shake the contents into the bowl, then scatter the butter pieces over the flour. Use two table knives in a crisscross motion, or a pastry blender, to cut the butter into the flour until it resembles fine meal. If you use a pastry blender, clean between the wires with a table knife from time to time. Combine the milk and the almond extract in a measuring cup with a spout or small mixing bowl and pour it over the flour and butter mixture. Stir with a fork until the dough just comes together, then turn it out onto a lightly floured work surface. Flour your hands, then knead the dough together briefly, and pat it into a rough circle. Use the rolling pin to roll the dough to a ½-inch thickness. Use the cookie cutter to cut out 12 circles and place them on the fruit, leaving ½ inch between pieces. Reroll the dough scraps, if necessary. Cut a few circles in half if need be, to cover the surface of the fruit evenly with pieces of dough. The biscuits will spread as they bake. Sprinkle the tops of the biscuits with the sugar, if desired. Place the baking dish on an aluminum foil–lined baking sheet.

4. Bake for 25 to 30 minutes, or until the tops of the biscuits are golden and the berries are bubbling. Transfer the baking dish to a wire rack to cool. Serve the cobbler hot, warm, or at room temperature.

The baked cobbler can be stored at room temperature, covered with aluminum foil, for up to 12 hours, although it is best eaten soon after baking. Leftovers can be refrigerated, covered, for 24 hours, although the crust will gradually absorb the fruit cooking juices and become soggy. It cannot be frozen.

Reverse Fruit Un-Buckle

Makes: 6 to 8 servings

What you'll need:

baking dish 2 inches deep, with a 6-cup capacity

microwave or small saucepan for melting butter

large, heavy saucepan

citrus zester

citrus reamer

fine-mesh sieve for straining lemon juice

hand-held electric mixer

mesh sieve

mixing spoon

wire rack

Baking time: 45 minutes

arole Bloom, in her excellent book *The International Dictionary of Desserts, Pastries, and Confections,* says: "A buckle, which is an old-fashioned American dessert, consists of a layer of rich cake batter, which is spread over the bottom of a deep round or square baking pan, and sweetened sliced fruit is spread on top. As the buckle bakes, the cake bubbles up between the fruit slices, and the cake batter combines with the fruit juices to form a sweet, crisp crust."

Since I like lots of crust I turned this buckle upside down (hence the name "Un-Buckle") so that the fruit is on the bottom and the cake part is on the top and it becomes (I'm not kidding here) a "grunt." You can, of course, make it the other way around, if you wish. This buckle is slightly untraditional in that it calls for dried fruit instead of fresh, which makes it more of a winter dish. See the variation for making this dish with fresh fruit.

FOR THE FRUIT

4 cups (about 2 pounds) mixed dried fruit, such as apples, pitted prunes, apricots, peaches, pears, cherries, and cranberries

1 large lemon

2 cups orange juice

FOR THE BATTER

3 extra-large eggs

¾ cup granulated sugar

2 teaspoons pure vanilla extract

1 stick (8 tablespoons) unsalted butter, melted and cooled

1 cup all-purpose flour

1 teaspoon baking powder

½ teaspoon salt

Ice cream, optional

1. Preheat the oven to 350°F with a rack in the center of the oven.

2. Place the dried fruit in the saucepan. Zest the lemon and set the zest aside for the cake batter. Squeeze the juice from the lemon, strain it, and add it to the fruit along with the orange juice. Bring the fruit to a simmer, cover, and cook gently, covered, for 3 minutes, or until the fruit has softened. Turn off the heat, leave the saucepan covered, and let the fruit cool while you prepare the cake batter.

3. Break the eggs into a medium mixing bowl. Add the sugar and vanilla. Beat with the mixer on high speed until the mixture is light and foamy and slightly thickened, about 3 minutes. Move the beaters around the bowl and scrape down the sides of the bowl with a rubber spatula several times while mixing. Add the cooled butter and the reserved lemon zest; mix on low speed until the butter is just incorporated. Place a mesh sieve over the bowl, and put the flour, baking powder, and salt in the sieve. Sift the dry ingredients directly onto the batter. Use a rubber spatula to fold in the flour mixture, scraping down the sides of the bowl as you work. Mix just until you can no longer see signs of flour; the batter will appear slightly lumpy.

4. Spoon the fruit into the baking dish, making sure to include all the juices. Drop the batter by spoonfuls over the top of the fruit, and use a rubber spatula to spread it gently over the fruit. Ideally the batter will be ½ inch below the top of the pan. Bake for 45 minutes, or until the cake is slightly puffed and golden brown. Remove the cake to a wire rack to cool. Serve warm or at room temperature, along with a scoop of ice cream.

5. The baked buckle can be stored at room temperature, covered with aluminum foil, for up to 12 hours, although it is best eaten soon after baking. Leftovers can be refrigerated, covered, for 24 hours, although the crust will gradually absorb the fruit cooking juices and become soggy. It cannot be frozen.

VARIATION: To make a fresh fruit buckle, substitute 4 cups fresh sliced peaches, apricots, nectarines, or plums for the dried fruit. Sprinkle the sliced fruit with ⅓ cup granulated sugar, 3 tablespoons Minute® tapioca, and the finely grated zest and strained juice of 1 lemon, then mix together gently. Pour the fruit mixture into the baking dish and let it sit while you prepare the batter. Prepare the same batter as for the mixed fruit buckle, and drop the batter on the fruit. Bake as directed.

Coco Loco Bananas Foster Crumble

Makes: 6 servings

What you'll need:

heavy, 10-inch ovenproof skillet

small, sharp knife

citrus zester

fork

wooden mixing spoon

Baking time: 45 to 50 minutes

If you've ever been to New Orleans and had Bananas Foster, had Bananas Foster anywhere else, or never, but like the idea of a dessert that involves many of the ingredients of a banana daiquiri, then you've come to the right place. Serve this hot from the skillet, along with a cup of strong coffee, and you'll hear Dixie Land jazz wafting in from just outside your window.

FOR THE TOPPING

¾ stick (6 tablespoons) unsalted butter, cut into pieces and softened

¾ cup oats, old-fashioned or quick-cooking (see page 46)

¾ cup packed light brown sugar

1 cup unsweetened shredded coconut (see page 48)

FOR THE BANANAS

3 large bananas, firm but not green

3 tablespoons unsalted butter

½ cup packed light brown sugar

Generous ¼ cup rum or orange juice

⅓ cup coconut milk (see page 48)

Finely grated zest of 1 lemon

1. Preheat the oven to 375°F with a rack in the center of the oven.

2. To make the topping, place the butter in a medium mixing bowl. Add the oats, light brown sugar, and shredded coconut. Stir all the ingredients together with a fork or, even better, use your fingertips to rub the ingredients together to coat the dry ingredients thoroughly with butter. The mixture will be in uneven lumps, but that's okay. Set aside.

3. Peel and slice the bananas into ¼-inch slices. Place the butter and light brown sugar in the skillet over medium heat. Stir constantly with a wooden spoon until the butter melts and bubbles, about 1 minute. With the skillet still over the heat, add the rum (or orange juice) and the coconut milk. Continue to cook and stir with the spoon until the mixture bubbles again. Carefully stir in the bananas and lemon zest. Remove the skillet from the heat and gently stir to coat the bananas with the syrup, being careful not to mash them. The mixture will be quite soupy.

4. Distribute the reserved topping mixture evenly over the banana mixture in the skillet. Bake for 45 to 50 minutes, or until the mixture no longer jiggles when you shake the pan. Do not be tempted to touch the contents of the skillet with your fingers; boiling sugar is dangerous and will burn you badly. Remove the skillet from the oven and allow to cool for 10 to 15 minutes.

5. This is best served right away, when hot, with a scoop of vanilla ice cream, but can be served warm or at room temperature, preferably no longer than 2 hours after it was baked. Store leftovers, covered with plastic wrap, at room temperature for up to 2 days. It cannot be frozen.

LORA SAYS: Don't use soft, brown, overripe bananas or hard green ones in this recipe; nice, firm, yellow ones work the best.

Pumpkin Pie

Makes: one 9-inch pie; 8 servings

What you'll need:

9-inch pie plate, 2 inches deep

hand-held electric mixer

baking sheet large enough to hold the pie plate

Baking time: 50 minutes

All these years, Grandma, Mom, or Aunt Betty has brought dessert to Thanksgiving and Christmas dinners. How about dazzling and amazing them with the fact that you can create a pumpkin pie from scratch? You can make this one the day before and store it at room temperature until it is ready to serve. Be sure to buy canned pumpkin puree—not pumpkin pie filling—as you will be adding your own spices.

One Basic Piecrust for a single crust (page 270), partially baked according to the directions in the recipe, fitted into the pie plate

½ teaspoon ground cinnamon

½ teaspoon ground ginger

½ teaspoon ground nutmeg

¼ teaspoon ground cloves

¼ teaspoon ground allspice

½ teaspoon salt

2½ cups (20 ounces) canned pumpkin puree (see page 49)

3 extra-large eggs

¾ cup pure maple syrup or ¾ cup packed dark brown sugar

1¼ cups heavy cream

Lightly sweetened whipped cream, optional (see page 21)

1. Preheat the oven to 350°F with a rack in the center of the oven.

2. To prepare the filling, put the cinnamon, ginger, nutmeg, cloves, allspice, and salt in a small mixing bowl and mix them together well with a fork: There's nothing quite as jolting as getting a lump of spice in a bite of pie. Set aside.

3. In a large mixing bowl, combine the pumpkin puree, eggs, maple syrup or dark brown sugar, heavy cream, and the spice mixture. With the mixer on low speed, mix the ingredients only until they are thoroughly combined. Move the beaters around the bowl and scrape down the sides of the bowl with a rubber spatula several times while mixing. If you beat this mixture too long, you will aerate it. (If you aerate it, it will rise up in the oven, and then it will crack as it cools. It may crack anyway, but that's okay. It's added proof that the pie is homemade.) Pour and scrape the filling into the partially baked pastry shell. Place the pie plate on a baking sheet (so that the pie can be easily removed from the oven) and bake for 50 minutes, or until the top is slightly firm when touched. Remove the pie from the oven and cool it completely on a rack before serving. Serve with lightly sweetened whipped cream, if desired.

4. The pie can be stored at room temperature for up to 6 hours or refrigerated up to 24 hours. Store leftovers, covered with plastic wrap, in the refrigerator. This pie cannot be frozen.

LORA SAYS: Ground spices lose their potency and flavor within a few months after opening the jar or can. You can maximize their shelf life by storing them in tinted jars with lids tightly closed, in a cool, dry place—not in clear jars on top of your stove.

Key Lime Pie with Graham Cracker Crumb Crust

Makes: one 9-inch pie; 10 servings

What you'll need:

9-inch pie plate, 1¼ inches deep

citrus zester

citrus reamer

fine-mesh sieve for straining lime juice

whisk

small, sharp knife for testing to make sure the pie is done

plastic wrap

nonstick vegetable spray

chilled medium metal bowl and chilled beaters of hand-held electric mixer

hand-held electric mixer

Baking time: 40 minutes

Lots of restaurants have something on the menu called Key Lime Pie. Don't be fooled into thinking this is the real thing unless it's made with real Key limes. Fresh Key limes pack more personality and flavor than their larger cousins, and are a rare find in all but the fanciest greengrocers or in Florida during the season. You can, however, buy real Key lime juice in gourmet stores such as Williams-Sonoma and some supermarkets too. If you ever do find fresh Key limes, buy a whole bag, squeeze them, and freeze the juice in ¾-cup amounts; it will keep, frozen, for a year. Having said all that, you can still make a decent lime pie with regular limes, so don't deny yourself the pleasure of a good dessert for lack of genuine Key limes.

FOR THE CRUST AND FILLING

3 extra-large egg yolks

Two 14-ounce cans sweetened condensed milk

Finely grated zest of 2 medium regular limes (see Lora Says)

¾ cup strained Key lime juice or ¾ cup freshly squeezed and strained regular lime juice (about 4 medium regular limes)

1 Graham Cracker Crumb Crust, baked and cooled (page 277)

1½ cups heavy cream

2 tablespoons granulated sugar

2 teaspoons pure vanilla extract

10 very thin slices of lime

1. Preheat the oven to 325°F with a rack in the center of the oven.

2. Place the egg yolks, sweetened condensed milk, and the lime zest and juice in a large mixing bowl. Whisk them together until the ingredients are completely incorporated. Scrape the filling into the prepared crust and bake for 40 minutes, or until the filling no longer moves when you tilt the pie and a knife inserted into the filling halfway from the crust to the center comes out clean.

3. Remove the pie from the oven and cool it on a wire rack for 30 minutes. Lightly spray a piece of plastic wrap with nonstick vegetable spray, then place the plastic wrap, sprayed side down, on the filling. Refrigerate the pie until it is completely cold, at least 2 hours. Place a medium metal mixing bowl and the beaters of the mixer in the refrigerator at the same time, so that they are chilled when it is time to whip the cream for the topping.

4. When you are ready to serve the pie, place the heavy cream in the chilled bowl. Beat it on high speed until it holds soft peaks, then beat in the sugar and vanilla. Place a generous dollop of whipped cream on each slice of pie as it is served. Garnish each serving with a slice of lime.

5. This pie is best served within 24 hours of baking, but it may be refrigerated, covered with plastic wrap as directed, for up to 4 days. The pie cannot be frozen.

LORA SAYS: If you are lucky enough to find real Key limes for the juice for this pie, you will not be able to use their zest because their skins are too thin. You will need to use the zest from 2 regular limes.

Coffee Toffee Pie

Makes: one 9-inch pie;
10 servings

What you'll need:

one 9-inch pie plate, 1¼ inches deep

baking sheet for toasting pecans

sharp, heavy knife for chopping pecans and chocolate

fork

microwave or small metal bowl of simmering water for melting chocolate

hand-held electric mixer or food processor

chilled medium metal bowl and chilled beaters of hand-held electric mixer

Baking time: 12 minutes (crust)

This fabulous dessert has a crunchy crust and a silky-smooth coffee-chocolate filling and a lighter-than-air whipped-cream topping. It was inspired by a recipe in my favorite dessert cookbook: *Maida Heatter's Book of Great Desserts* (Knopf, 1974). If you are looking for something really special to wow the dessert lovers in your life, look no further. This is *very* rich, so cut small pieces.

FOR PREPARING THE PIE PLATE

1 tablespoon unsalted butter, softened

FOR THE CRUST

1¼ cups packaged piecrust mix, such as Flako® or Jiffy® (about half a 9-ounce package)

2 tablespoons best-quality unsweetened cocoa powder, regular or Dutch-processed

¾ cup (3 ounces) pecans, toasted and coarsely chopped (see pages 18–19)

¼ cup packed dark brown sugar

1 tablespoon pure vanilla extract, mixed with 2 teaspoons water in a small measuring cup

2 ounces (2 squares) unsweetened chocolate, chopped

1¼ sticks (10 tablespoons) unsalted butter, softened

4 ounces cream cheese, at room temperature

1 cup packed light brown sugar

¼ cup espresso, freshly brewed, or 1 tablespoon espresso powder or granules dissolved in ¼ cup boiling water

1½ cups heavy cream, well chilled

1 tablespoon pure vanilla extract

¼ cup confectioners' sugar (if sugar is lumpy, sift first, then measure)

1. Preheat the oven to 375°F with a rack in the center of the oven. Use the butter to coat the inside of the pie plate. Set aside.

2. To make the crust, combine the piecrust mix, cocoa, pecans, and dark brown sugar in a medium mixing bowl. Toss the ingredients together with a fork, and gradually drizzle in the vanilla mixture. The mixture will be crumbly and dry. Scrape it into the prepared pie plate. Shake the pan to distribute the crumbs over the bottom of the plate, then use your fingers to push the mixture up the sides. Try not to make the bottom too thick. Bake the crust in the preheated oven for 12 minutes, until it has slightly hardened. Do not allow it to burn. Remove it from the oven to cool while you make the filling.

3. Melt the chocolate either in the microwave or in a small metal mixing bowl set over a pan of gently simmering water. Remove it from the heat and let it cool completely.

4. Meanwhile, place the butter and cream cheese in a medium bowl and use a hand-held mixer on high speed to cream the butter until it is light and fluffy, about 2 minutes. Add the brown sugar and beat the mixture on high speed for 3 minutes. Reduce the mixer speed to low and mix in the cooled melted chocolate and the espresso or dissolved espresso powder. Move the beaters around the bowl and scrape down the sides of the bowl with a rubber scraper several times during the mixing. Alternatively, the filling can be made in the food processor. Place the butter and cream cheese in the food processor, process until blended and smooth—about 30 seconds. Scrape down the sides of the work bowl and add the brown sugar and process until incorporated. Add the chocolate and coffee and process until smooth.

5. Pour and scrape the filling into the prepared crust and smooth the top with a rubber scraper. Refrigerate the pie until it is firm, at least 6 hours, or overnight.

6. Thirty minutes before you are ready to serve the pie, place a medium metal mixing bowl and the beaters of a hand-held electric mixer in the freezer to chill. Place the heavy cream and the vanilla in the chilled bowl and whip them with the chilled beaters on high speed until the cream is slightly thickened. Sprinkle in the confectioners' sugar and continue beating until firm peaks form. Take care not to overbeat or you'll be serving your pie with butter and buttermilk. Use a rubber scraper to spread the whipped cream over the top of the pie. Serve immediately.

7. The pie can be refrigerated, without the whipped cream topping, for up to 3 days. Once the whipped cream is put on, it should be served immediately. Leftovers can be covered and refrigerated, but they will not be as good as when first assembled. The pie can be frozen without the whipped cream topping. Wrap it securely, in the pie plate, in plastic wrap, then place it in a freezer-strength recloseable jumbo-size plastic bag. Label it with a waterproof marker, and freeze for up to 3 months. Defrost the pie in its wrappings, at room temperature.

LORA SAYS: You can whip cream up to 3 hours ahead of time and "hold" it in the following way: Whip as described above. Place a fine mesh sieve over a mixing bowl. Place the whipped cream in a sieve and refrigerate the sieve and bowl. The whipped cream will lose some liquid, but it will be fine to serve on the dessert.

LORA SAYS: Try sprinkling some crumbled Heath Bars on top of the whipped cream.

Brownie Pie

Makes: one 9-inch pie;
8 to 10 servings

What you'll need:

9-inch pie plate, 2 inches deep

scale for weighing chocolate
(optional)

sharp, heavy knife for breaking
up chocolate and chopping
pecans

cutting board

microwave or 2 small metal
bowls and pan of simmering
water for melting chocolate with
butter

mixing spoon

mesh sieve

hand-held electric mixer

whisk

wire rack

medium saucepan

Baking time: 30 minutes

Here, a brownie batter forms the crust of an ice cream–filled pie that is topped with hot fudge sauce just before serving. You can make the crust ahead, fill it, and freeze the pie until ready to serve. Make sure to cut it with a sharp, serrated knife. I like this pie best filled with peppermint stick or mint chocolate chip ice cream, but you can opt for your favorite flavor, of course.

FOR PREPARING THE PIE PLATE

1 tablespoon unsalted butter, softened

FOR THE PIE

12 ounces semisweet chocolate, broken in small pieces

3 tablespoons unsalted butter

½ cup all-purpose flour

¼ teaspoon baking powder

3 extra-large eggs

1 cup granulated sugar

1 teaspoon pure vanilla extract

1½ cups (6 ounces) pecans, coarsely chopped (see page 19)

6 ounces semisweet chocolate chips

6 ounces bittersweet chocolate, chopped (see page 16)

3 tablespoons unsalted butter

1¼ cups milk

½ cup granulated sugar

2 tablespoons light corn syrup

1 teaspoon pure vanilla extract

Best-quality ice cream of your choice

1. Preheat the oven to 350°F with a rack in the center of the oven. Use the butter to coat the bottom and sides of the pie plate. Set aside.

2. Melt the chocolate with the butter either in the microwave or in a small metal mixing bowl set over, but not touching, a pan of gently simmering water. Stir occasionally until the mixture is smooth. Remove from the heat to cool slightly and set aside.

3. Place a mesh sieve over a small mixing bowl and add the flour and baking powder. Shake the contents into the bowl and set aside.

4. Break the eggs into a large mixing bowl, then add the sugar. With the mixer on high speed, beat the eggs with the sugar until the mixture is light and thickened, 3 to 4 minutes. Reduce the mixer speed to low and beat in the vanilla. With the mixer on lowest speed, mix in the melted chocolate mixture. Use a rubber spatula to fold in the flour mixture; mix only until the flour disappears. Fold in the pecans and the chocolate chips.

5. Scrape the mixture into the prepared pie plate and smooth it with a rubber spatula. The mixture will almost fill the pie plate, but it will not spill over into your oven as it bakes. Bake for 30 minutes, or until the crust is shiny and the edges are slightly dry and begin to pull away from the top of the plate. Do not overbake. The center will be somewhat soft, even though the edges are firm. Remove the pie from the oven to a wire rack to cool, but do not refrigerate it.

6. Make the hot fudge sauce. Melt the bittersweet chocolate and butter either in the microwave or in a small metal mixing bowl set over, but not touching, a pan of gently simmering water. Stir until the mixture is melted and smooth. Stir the milk and the sugar together in the saucepan. Place the saucepan over medium heat and cook, stirring with a wire whisk, until the milk begins to simmer and the sugar dissolves completely. Reduce the heat to low and scrape in the melted chocolate mixture, then add the corn syrup. Continue to cook over low heat, whisking constantly, until the mixture is smooth and slightly thickened. Remove the pan from the heat and stir in the vanilla. Allow the sauce to cool slightly.

7. The sauce should be served very warm. You can make the sauce just before serving, or you can make it ahead and refrigerate it in a covered container for up to 1 month. Reheat it over medium heat, stirring occasionally, until very warm.

8. To serve, cut the pie into wedges and place a scoop of your favorite ice cream on top. Drizzle with some of the hot fudge sauce.

9. The baked pie can be stored, wrapped with plastic wrap, at room temperature for up to 3 days. It can also be frozen in the pan. Wrap it securely in plastic wrap and place in a freezer-strength recloseable jumbo-size plastic bag. Label with a waterproof marker and freeze for up to 3 months. Defrost, wrapped, at room temperature.

LORA SAYS: My favorite way to serve this is with a scoop of mint chocolate chip ice cream and the fudge sauce above, with 1 teaspoon mint extract added to the sauce recipe.

White Chocolate and Cherry Bread Pudding

Makes: 12 to 14 servings

What you'll need:

baking dish with 12-cup capacity, about 2 inches deep

scale for weighing chocolate (optional)

sharp, heavy knife for chopping chocolate

whisk

ladle

roasting pan or baking sheet

baking sheet for weighting pudding

plastic wrap

heavy-duty aluminum foil

mesh strainer

wire rack

Baking time: 60 minutes

Need to feed a crowd a fabulous, but easy-to-make dessert? Want to really knock their socks off? Put aside caloric concerns and step right up to the world of bread pudding; think mega-French! The basic recipe calls for slices of slightly stale bread, eggs, cream, and sugar. You can make it plain, or doll it up all you want with sexy ingredients, such as chocolate and fruit, and with liquor like rum or brandy. This is an incredibly rich dessert so don't be tempted to cut overly generous servings; it would be a crime to see it left on the plate! This dessert uses up lots of stale bread. If you don't have any on hand, please see Lora Says on page 313.

This dish cooks in a water bath, which keeps it nice and moist. Make sure to check that your baking pan fits comfortably inside either a roasting pan or a baking sheet before you start.

FOR PREPARING THE PAN

2 tablespoons unsalted butter, softened (see Lora Says)

2 tablespoons granulated sugar

5 extra-large eggs

5 extra-large egg yolks (save the whites to make meringues, page 128, or freeze them for a later use)

2 cups whole milk

2 cups heavy cream

1 cup packed light brown sugar

1 tablespoon pure vanilla extract or ⅓ cup light or dark rum

18 to 20 slices slightly stale, rich white bread such as challah, or good-quality, firm, sliced white bread such as Pepperidge Farm or Arnold

12 ounces best-quality white chocolate, such as Lindt or Tobler, broken into 1-inch pieces (see page 16)

1¾ cups (9 ounces) dried sweet cherries, such as Bing or Rainier

3 tablespoons unsalted butter, softened, for dotting the pudding before baking

½ to ¾ cup confectioners' sugar, for glazing the pudding after baking (if sugar is lumpy, sift first, then measure)

1. Butter the bottom and sides of the baking dish lavishly with the butter. Sprinkle the sugar on the bottom of the buttered pan; this will caramelize during baking and lend a caramel taste to the pudding.

2. Place the whole eggs, egg yolks, milk, cream, light brown sugar, and vanilla (or rum) in a large mixing bowl. Whisk them together thoroughly.

3. Line the bottom of the prepared pan with slices of bread, breaking them into pieces as necessary to completely cover the bottom. Use a ladle to pour about one-third of the egg mixture over the bread layer. Stir the egg mixture with the ladle occasionally so that the sugar does not sink to the bottom. Sprinkle half the chocolate and half the cherries over the bread. Add another layer of bread, then ladle on half the remaining egg mixture. Sprinkle with the remaining chocolate and cherries, then top with a final layer of bread. Ladle on the remaining egg mixture, pouring slowly and carefully, so that top bread layer absorbs some of the egg mixture. The dish will be very full.

4. Place the pudding pan in a roasting pan or a rimmed baking sheet, to catch any spill-over. Cover the top of the pudding with plastic wrap, then place a baking sheet over the pan. Weight the baking sheet with a heavy pan so that it pushes the bread pieces level with the top of the baking pan. Let the pudding sit at room temperature for 30 minutes, or in the refrigerator overnight.

5. When you are ready to bake the pudding, preheat the oven to 375°F with a rack in the center of the oven. Remove the weight, the top baking sheet, and the plastic wrap. Leave the pudding in the roasting pan or baking sheet, and dot the top of the pudding with the butter, cut into 6 pieces. Cover the pudding loosely with heavy-duty aluminum foil. Fill a measuring cup with a spout with very hot tap water. Place the pudding in the larger pan in the oven, then carefully pour about 1½ inches of hot water into the larger pan. Bake the pudding for 1 hour. Remove the aluminum foil after the first half hour so that the top will brown. Check the water level halfway through the baking time and add more, if necessary, to keep the water in the larger pan about 1½ inches deep.

6. At the end of the baking time, the pudding will have a crisp golden brown crust and it will still jiggle slightly when the dish is moved. Remove the pudding from the water bath. Place the confectioners' sugar in a mesh strainer and shake it generously over the top of the pudding. Preheat a broiler with an oven rack in the top third position so that the heat source is 3 to 4 inches from the top of the pudding. Place the pudding under the broiler. Leave the oven door ajar and watch carefully; this process goes from golden brown to burned in a twinkling. Carefully rotate the pudding under the broiler so that the whole surface gets browned. It won't color evenly. The top will bubble and turn caramel-colored in places. Be careful—it is hot! Remove the pudding to a wire rack to cool for at least 15 minutes. Cut in squares and serve hot, warm, or at room temperature.

7. The baked pudding can be refrigerated, covered with plastic wrap, for up to 4 days. Reheat before serving, covered loosely with aluminum foil, in a 350°F oven. One of the best features about bread pudding, besides the amazing taste and texture, is that it freezes beautifully after baking, so the dessert can be made ahead of time and defrosted in the refrigerator overnight, then reheated in a 350°F oven, covered loosely with aluminum foil. To freeze, make sure that the pudding is completely cooled, then wrap it in several layers of plastic wrap and then in aluminum foil. Don't forget to mark the package so you'll know what you're defrosting when the time comes!

LORA SAYS: When removing a water bath from the oven, remove the baking pan first. If possible, leave the larger pan with the hot water in the turned-off oven until it is cool, to avoid danger of scalding. In this recipe, where you have to put the pudding under the broiler, you can't leave the water bath pan in the oven to cool unless you have a second oven. *Be careful!*

LORA SAYS: For this recipe you will need a pan with a 12-cup capacity, with sides about 2 inches deep. A 9 by 13-inch Pyrex baking pan will work, but the shape can be oval, rectangular, or round. It is important that the pudding fill the pan right up to the top when assembled. Use a freezer-to-oven pan if you want to freeze the bread pudding after baking and cooling. Also, Corning Ware makes good cookware that goes from oven to freezer to oven to table.

LORA SAYS: This recipe calls for slightly stale bread. To harden bread to a stale-like condition, place the slices of bread in one layer on oven racks. Turn on the oven to 300°F and check the bread after 10 minutes. The slices should be lightly toasted and slightly hard. Remove the slices to wire racks to cool, to prevent them from becoming soggy as they cool, and let them cool completely before proceeding with the recipe.

LORA SAYS: Although you may use nonstick vegetable spray to coat the pan, butter will make this rich dessert taste even better.

Where are the pictures?

They're on my website—at least a baker's dozen of them. Come and visit *www.lorabrody.com* to get a full-color sneak preview along with a shopping list, lots of baking tips, plus information about how to purchase or where to find the ingredients and equipment mentioned in my book. You can also leave me a message or ask me a question. I love to hear from my readers. Rise and shine!

Baking Resources

INTERNET: *www.lorabrody.com*: for questions, products, and cookbooks
www.kingarthurflour.com: for equipment and ingredients
www.tavolo.com: for equipment and ingredients
www.cooking.com: for equipment and ingredients
www.fantes.com: for equipment and ingredients
www.armchair:com: for equipment and ingredients

RETAIL STORES THAT SELL EQUIPMENT AND INGREDIENTS: Fante's Gourmet & Kitchen Wares Shop
1006 S. Ninth Street
Philadelphia, PA 19147-4798
Phone: 215-922-5557
(800) 44-FANTES

Sur La Table
84 Pine Street
Seattle, WA 98101
Phone: (206) 448-2244
For other locations call: (800) 243-0852

Williams-Sonoma: call (800) 541-1262 or (800) 541-2233
for store locations

Cardullos
6 Brattle Street
Cambridge, MA 02138
Phone: (617) 491-8888
Internet: *www.cardullos.com*

La Cuisine—The Cook's Resource
323 Cameron Street
Alexandria, VA 22314-3219 USA
E-mail: *lacuisine@worldnet.att.net*
Phone: (800) 521-1176

Dairy Fresh Candies
57 Salem Street
Boston, MA 02113
Phone: (617) 742-2639
(800) 336-5536
Internet: *www.dairyfreshcandies.com*
A wide variety of premium imported and domestic chocolate in bulk and retail size, as well as extracts, flavorings, nuts and ground nuts

Boyajian Boston
349 Lenox Street
Norwood, MA 02062
Phone: (800) 419-4677
Internet: *boyajian@tiac.net*
Citrus oils and essences

King Arthur Flour Baker's Catalogue
P.O. Box 876
Norwich, VT 05055-0876
Phone: (800) 827-6836
Internet: *www.kingarthurflour.com*

Lora's Bookshelf

Here's a list of some of my favorite dessert baking books. When you look at the bookshelf in my kitchen, it's easy to see by their chocolate- and butter-stained pages that these are the ones I use most often. Before you move on to big, fancy chef-written books with full-page color photographs, use these first.

Baking with Jim Dodge, by Jim Dodge with Elaine Ratner (Simon & Schuster, 1991).

Great Cakes, by Carole Walter (Ballantine Books, 1991).

Great Pies and Tarts, by Carole Walter (Random House, 1998).

King Arthur Flour 200th Anniversary Cookbook, by Brinna Sands (Norton, 1992).

Maida Heatter's Book of Great Chocolate Desserts, by Maida Heatter (Random House, 1995).

Maida Heatter's Book of Great Cookies, by Maida Heatter (Knopf, 1977).

Maida Heatter's Book of Great Desserts, by Maida Heatter (Random House, 1991).

The Family Baker, by Susan Purdy (Broadway Books, 1999).

The Simple Art of Perfect Baking, by Flo Braker (Chapters Books, 1997).

Index

chocolate, bittersweet:
  in chocolate cheesecake, 173–74
  in chocolate fudge sauce,
    307–9
  in creamy chocolate frosting,
    177
  in flourless chocolate cake,
    156–57
  in layered marbled cheesecake
    brownies, 81–83
  in world's richest fudge frosting,
    155
chocolate, semisweet:
  in brownie pie, 307–9
  in chocolate-cherry muffins,
    225–26
  in creamy chocolate frosting,
    177
  in homemade chocolate
    pudding for pie filling, 283
  in world's richest fudge frosting,
    155
chocolate, unsweetened:
  in birthday cake brownies,
    61–62
  in chocolate miracle cake,
    135–37
  in chocolate pound cake,
    163–64
  in coffee toffee pie, 304–6
  in fantasy brownies, 59–60
  in flourless chocolate cake,
    156–57
  in homemade chocolate
    pudding for pie filling, 283
  in Sam's mint squares, 74–76
chocolate, white:
  and cherry bread pudding,
    310–13
  in chocolate chip cookies, 104–5
  chunk cookies, macadamia nut–,
    108–9
  cream, 158
  in macadamia nut–topped three-
    chocolate wedges, 88–90

chocolate bits, coffee-flavored, in
  double espresso ice cream pie
  with chocolate espresso
  whipped cream, 284–85
chocolate chip cookies, 104–5
  peanut butter–, truly
    exceptional, 114–15
chocolate chips, bittersweet, in
  chocolate chip cookies,
    104–5
chocolate chips, coffee-flavored, in
  cappuccino bars, 77–78
chocolate chips, milk:
  in chocolate chip cookies, 104–5
  in macadamia nut–topped three-
    chocolate wedges, 88–90
chocolate chips, mint, in Sam's
  mint squares, 74–76
chocolate chips, semisweet:
  in brownie pie, 307–9
  in chocolate chip cookies, 104–5
  in chocolate crunch cupcakes,
    178–80
  in double chocolate meringues,
    130–31
  in heavenly oatmeal bars, 84–85
  in macadamia nut–topped three-
    chocolate wedges, 88–90
  in triple peanut butter cookies,
    111–13
  in truly exceptional peanut
    butter–chocolate chip
    cookies, 114–15
chocolate chips, white, in
  chocolate chip cookies,
    104–5
chocolate chip scones, 201–3
chocolate frostings:
  creamy, 177
  milk chocolate, 145–46
  world's richest fudge frosting,
    155
chocolate pudding:
  in chocolate cream pie, 281–82
  homemade, for pie filling, 283

cinnamon streusel coffee cake,
  230–32
clafouti, pear and honey,
  265–66
classic apple pie, 286–88
classic pound cake, 160–62
classic scones, 201–3
cobbler, three berry, 293–94
cocoa powder, unsweetened:
  in chocolate crunch cupcakes,
    178–80
  in chocolate miracle cake,
    135–37
  in coffee toffee pie, 304–6
  in devil's food layer cake with
    fudge frosting, 152–55
  in double chocolate meringue,
    130–31
  in swirled sour cream coffee
    cake, 236–38
coco loco bananas Foster crumble,
  298–99
coconut:
  in coco loco bananas Foster
    crumble, 298–99
  frosting, 150–51
  toasting of, 20
coconut milk:
  in coco loco bananas Foster
    crumble, 298–99
  in pumpkin muffins with cream
    cheese filling, 214–16
coffee:
  in devil's food layer cake with
    fudge frosting, 152–55
  in honey cake, 251–53
  in milk chocolate frosting,
    145–46
  toffee pie, 304–6
  see also espresso
coffee cakes, 227–66
  cinnamon streusel, 230–32
  cranberry-cherry, 233–35
  swirled sour cream, 236–38
  see also quick breads; tea loaves

coffee-flavored chocolate bits, in
    double espresso ice cream pie
    with chocolate espresso
    whipped cream, 284–85
coffee-flavored chocolate chips, in
    cappuccino bars, 77–78
coffee-flavored liqueur, in double
    espresso ice cream pie with
    chocolate espresso whipped
    cream, 284–85
cookies, 93–131
    almond biscotti, 118–20
    almond ice box sugar, 97–98
    camp, 116–17
    chocolate chip, 104–5
    David's butterscotch, 106–7
    double chocolate meringues,
        130–31
    ginger, 126–27
    holiday sugar, 99–101
    homemade slice-and-bake,
        95–96
    macadamia nut–white chocolate
        chunk, 108–9
    meringue clouds, 128–29
    oatmeal raisin, 102–3
    rugelach, 121–23
    shortbread, 110
    snow balls, 124–25
    triple peanut butter, 111–13
    truly exceptional peanut
        butter–chocolate chip, 114–15
cooking, safety tips for, 8–9
cooking terms, 50–53
cooling, 35
cranberry(ies):
    -almond-orange muffins,
        220–22
    -cherry coffee cake, 233–35
    granola bars, 72–73
    orange bread, 255–56
    scones, 201–3
cranberries, dried:
    in cranberry-almond-orange
        muffins, 220–22

in cranberry-cherry coffee cake,
    233–35
in cranberry granola bars,
    72–73
in mixed fruit compote, 254
in reverse fruit un-buckle,
    295–97
cream, whipping of, 21
cream cheese:
    in big boy cheesecake, 168–70
    in butter rum frosting, 186–87
    in chocolate cheese cake, 173
    in cinnamon streusel coffee
        cake, 230–32
    in coffee toffee pie, 304–6
    filling, pumpkin muffins with,
        214–16
    frosting, 141
    in layered marbled cheesecake
        brownies, 81–83
    in little guy cheesecake,
        165–67
    in pumpkin cheesecake,
        171–72
    in rugelach, 121–23
    in strawberry-filled muffins,
        211–13
creamy chocolate frosting, 177
crumb cake, 246–48
crumble, coco loco bananas Foster,
    298–99
cupcakes, 175–76
    chocolate crunch, 178–80

date nut cake, song-of-the-South,
    with butter rum frosting,
    183–85
David's butterscotch cookies,
    106–7
defrosting, of baked goods, 24
devil's food layer cake with fudge
    frosting, 152–55
doneness, testing for, 11
double chocolate meringues,
    130–31

double espresso ice cream pie with
    chocolate espresso whipped
    cream, 284–85

eggs, 29–30
    separating of, 12
egg whites, whipping of, 12–13
equipment, 36–43
espresso:
    in coffee toffee pie, 304–6
    double, ice cream pie, with
        chocolate espresso whipped
        cream, 284–85
    see also coffee
extracts, 32

fantasy brownies, 59–60
fats, 26–28
figs, dried, in mixed fruit compote,
    254
flavorings, 32
flour, 29
flourless chocolate cake, 156–57
folding, 14
food chemistry, 25–36
freezing, of baked goods, 23–24,
    35–36
frostings:
    butter rum, 186–87
    coconut, 150–51
    cream cheese, 141
    creamy chocolate, 177
    of layer cakes, 22
    milk chocolate, 145–46
    for Sam's mint squares, 74–76
    world's richest fudge, 155
fruit, dried:
    in mixed fruit compote, 254
    in reverse fruit un-buckle,
        295–97
fruit compote, mixed, 254
fudge:
    frosting, world's richest, 155
    sauce, chocolate, for brownie
        pie, 307–9

ginger:
    candied, in three wishes
        gingerbread, 249–50
    cookies, 126–27
    scones, 201–3
gingerbread, three wishes,
    249–50
graham cracker crumb(s):
    crust, 277–78
    in lemon squares, 67–68
granola, cranberry bars, 72–73
granulated sugar, colored, in
    holiday sugar cookies,
    99–101

heavenly oatmeal bars, 84–85
hermits, 91–92
    see also bars; squares
holiday sugar cookies, 99–101
honey and pear clafouti,
    265–66
honey cake, 251–53

ice cream pie, double espresso,
    with chocolate espresso
    whipped cream, 284–85
ingredients:
    essential, 44–48
    nonessential, 48–50
    omitting of, 22
    order of, 34
    quality of, 44
    sifting of, 11–12
    substituting of, 33
    temperature of, 33–34

jam muffins, 217–19

Kahlúa, in double espresso ice
    cream pie with chocolate
    espresso whipped cream,
    284–85
Key lime pie, with graham cracker
    crumb crust, 302–3
kuchen, peach, 262–64

layer cakes:
    classic yellow, with milk
        chocolate frosting, 142–44
    devil's food, with fudge frosting,
        152–54
    frosting of, 22
    snow white, with coconut
        frosting, 147–49
layered marble cheesecake
    brownies, 81–83
leavening agents, 31
lemon:
    anise tea cake, 259–61
    poppy seed muffins, 209–10
    squares, 67–68
Linzer torte, American, 189–92
little guy cheesecake, 165–67

macadamia nut(s):
    in chocolate crunch cupcakes,
        178–80
    -topped three-chocolate
        wedges, 88–90
    -white chocolate chunk cookies,
        108–9
maple syrup:
    in peanut brittle bars, 86–87
    in pumpkin muffins with cream
        cheese filling, 214–16
    in pumpkin pie, 300–301
maraschino cherries, in pineapple
    upside-down cake, 181–82
marzipan, in almond ice box sugar
    cookies, 97–98
measurements, 9–10
meringue(s), 30–31
    clouds, 128–29
    double chocolate, 130–31
milk chocolate frosting, 145–46
mini pies:
    pecan, 79–80
    see also bars; squares
mixed fruit compote, 254
mixing, 13
muffins, 193–226

banana walnut muffins,
    223–24
chocolate-cherry, 225–26
cranberry-almond-orange,
    220–22
Emmy's blue ribbon blueberry,
    206–8
jam, 217–19
lemon poppy seed, 209–10
pumpkin, with cream cheese
    filling, 214–16
strawberry-filled, 211–13
see also biscuits; scones

nut(s):
    -apricot bars, 69–71
    chopping of, 19
    toasting of, 18–19
    see also specific nuts

oatmeal:
    apricot scones, 204–5
    bars, heavenly, 84–85
    raisin cookies, 102–3
oats:
    in American Linzer torte,
        189–92
    in camp cookies, 116–17
    in coco loco bananas Foster
        crumble, 298–99
    in cranberry granola bars, 72–73
    in peanut brittle bars, 86–87
    in strawberry-rhubarb pie with
        almond crumble topping,
        291–92
orange:
    -cranberry almond muffins,
        220–22
    cranberry bread, 255–56
orange chips, caramelized, 188
oven:
    preheating of, 5
    preventing overflows in, 11
oven racks, positioning of, 7
overbrowning, preventing of, 11

pantry, 43–50

see also ingredients

peaches, dried:

in mixed fruit compote, 254

in reverse fruit un-buckle,
295–97

peach kuchen, 262–64

peach preserves, in jam muffins,
217–19

peanut brittle bars, 86–87

peanut butter:

in camp cookies, 116–17

–chocolate chip cookies, truly
exceptional, 114–15

cookies, triple, 111–13

in heavenly oatmeal bars, 84–85

peanut butter chips, in triple
peanut butter cookies,
111–13

peanuts, dry roasted:

in camp cookies, 116–17

in peanut brittle bars, 86–87

in triple peanut butter cookies,
111–13

pear and honey clafouti, 265–66

pears, dried:

in mixed fruit compote, 254

in reverse fruit un-buckle, 295–97

pecans(s):

in banana walnut bread, 257–58

in blondies, 63–64

in chocolate chip cookies, 104–5

in cinnamon streusel coffee
cake, 230–32

in coffee toffee pie, 304–6

in cranberry orange bread,
255–56

in David's butterscotch cookies,
106–7

mini pies, 79–80

in pumpkin muffins with cream
cheese filling, 214–16

in snow balls, 124–25

in sticky hands caramel bars,
65–66

pie crust(s):

basic double, 274–76

basic single, 270–73

chocolate crumb, 279–80

graham cracker crumb, 277–78

pies, 267–313

brownie, 307–9

cherry, with streusel topping,
289–90

chocolate cream, 281–82

classic apple, 286–88

coffee toffee, 304–6

double espresso ice cream, with
chocolate espresso whipped
cream, 284–85

Key lime, with graham cracker
crumb crust, 302–3

pumpkin, 300–301

strawberry rhubarb, with
almond crumble topping,
291–92

pineapple upside-down cake,
181–82

poppy seed lemon muffins, 209–10

pound cakes:

chocolate, 163–64

classic, 160–62

presentation, of baked goods,
24–25

prunes, in mixed fruit compote,
254

pudding, bread, white chocolate
and cherry, 310–13

pudding, chocolate:

in chocolate cream pie,
281–82

homemade, for pie filling, 283

pumpkin:

cheesecake, 171–72

muffins, with cream cheese
filling, 214–16

pie, 300–301

quick breads, 227–66

banana walnut, 257–58

cranberry orange, 255–56

see also coffee cakes; tea loaves

raisins:

in camp cookies, 116–17

in carrot cake with cream cheese
frosting, 138–41

in hermits, 91–92

in honey cake, 251–53

in mixed fruit compote, 254

oatmeal cookies, 102–3

in rugelach, 121–23

raspberry(ies):

in big boy cheesecake, 168–70

in little guy cheesecake, 165–67

sauce, 159

in three berry cobbler, 293–94

raspberry-flavored liqueur, in
raspberry sauce, 159

raspberry preserves:

in American Linzer torte,
189–92

in jam muffins, 217–19

recipes:

choosing of, 4

doubling and halving of, 22–23

following of, 3–4

reverse fruit un-buckle, 295–97

rhubarb-strawberry pie with
almond crumble topping,
291–92

rugelach, 121–23

rum, dark, in butter rum frosting,
186–87

rum, in coco loco bananas Foster
crumble, 298–99

salt, 28–29

Sam's mint squares, 74–76

sauces:

berry, strawberry shortcake
with, 198–200

chocolate fudge, for brownie
pie, 307–9

raspberry, 159